Liew Chin Tong's *Second Takeoff* brilliantly captures Malaysia's unique opportunity for transformative growth. His profound insights are crucial to the much-needed public discourse on vital issues shaping our nation. This book inspires us to shed cynicism and renew our commitment to progress. An essential read for anyone aspiring for a better Malaysia.

Anthony Loke
Democratic Action Party Secretary-General and Minister of Transport, Malaysia

Chin Tong's 25-year public service experience at both federal and state levels, voracious reading and deep social democratic leanings provide a rich concoction of well-informed thoughts, ideas and ruminations on building an economic framework that is not just sustainable, but also equitable to all. The development of such deep intellect is evident from the collection of essays and speeches in *Second Takeoff: Strategies for Malaysia's Economic Resurgence*. Vision, intellect, and passion for service – the embodiment of these qualities in Chin Tong – have come across clearly through this book which could be regarded as a potential blueprint of what is necessary for our nation to build on past 'hits', and right past 'misses'. In short, this book should be a must-read for every earnest policymaker.

Tengku Zafrul Aziz
Minister of Investment, Trade and Industry, Malaysia

Chin Tong's *Second Takeoff* builds on a workable, relevant industrialisation policy – which is effective in rejuvenating the labour market. However, much rests in Malaysia's ability to fully utilise ideas to rejuvenate the economy across the policy spectrum – away from the usual market-based approach which has proved problematic during the pandemic.

Kudos to a fellow reformist, who remains unflinching in his advocacy of ideas for a better, more dynamic Malaysia.

Nurul Izzah Anwar
Vice President, People's Justice Party, Malaysia

Chin Tong's commentaries on Malaysia's future show a remarkable ability to weave together politics, economics, and other trends to give a perceptive assessment. As a political leader, he has a read on developments, which few others have. The reader will be well rewarded with rich insights.

Manu Bhaskaran
Regional economist and long-time commentator on Asia

SECOND TAKEOFF

Strategies for Malaysia's Economic Resurgence

LIEW CHIN TONG

Ministry of Investment, Trade and Industry, Malaysia

World Scientific

NEW JERSEY • LONDON • SINGAPORE • BEIJING • SHANGHAI • HONG KONG • TAIPEI • CHENNAI • TOKYO

Published by

World Scientific Publishing Co. Pte. Ltd.
5 Toh Tuck Link, Singapore 596224
USA office: 27 Warren Street, Suite 401-402, Hackensack, NJ 07601
UK office: 57 Shelton Street, Covent Garden, London WC2H 9HE

Library of Congress Cataloging-in-Publication Data
Names: Liew, Chin Tong, author.
Title: Second takeoff : strategies for Malaysia's economic resurgence / Liew Chin Tong.
Description: New Jersey : World Scientific, [2025] | Includes bibliographical references and index.
Identifiers: LCCN 2024025405 | ISBN 9789811290558 (hardcover) |
ISBN 9789811291609 (paperback) | ISBN 9789811290565 (ebook) |
ISBN 9789811290572 (ebook other)
Subjects: LCSH: Economic development--Malaysia. | Economics--Malaysia--Sociological aspects.
Classification: LCC HC445.5 .L44 2025 | DDC 338.9595--dc23/eng/20240716
LC record available at https://lccn.loc.gov/2024025405

British Library Cataloguing-in-Publication Data
A catalogue record for this book is available from the British Library.

For any available supplementary material, please visit
https://www.worldscientific.com/worldscibooks/10.1142/13769#t=suppl

Desk Editor: Jiang Yulin
Design and layout: Loo Chuan Ming

For My Parents

Contents

Abbreviations and Acronyms

1MDB	1Malaysia Development Berhad
3D	Dangerous, dirty and demeaning jobs
ASEAN	Association of Southeast Asian Nations
B40	Bottom 40% of the income distribution
BN	Barisan Nasional
BNM	Bank Negara Malaysia
CCUS	Carbon capture, utilisation and storage
DAP	Democratic Action Party
DDI	Domestic direct investment
DMU	Delivery Management Unit
DOSM	Department of Statistics Malaysia
DWP	Defence White Paper
DYMM	Duli Yang Maha Mulia (His Majesty)
E&E	Electrical and electronics sector
EEZ	Exclusive economic zone
EMS	Electronics manufacturing services
EPF	Employees' Provident Fund
ESG	Environmental, social and governance
ETP	Economic Transformation Programme
EU	European Union
EV	Electric vehicle
FDI	Foreign direct investment
FTZ	Free Trade Zone
GDP	Gross Domestic Product
GHG	Greenhouse gases
GKL	Greater Kuala Lumpur
GLC	Government-linked company

GLIC	Government-linked investment company
GST	Goods and Services Tax
G-to-G	Government-to-government
HM	His Majesty
HSST	Harmonised Sales and Service Tax
IC	Integrated circuit
ICE	Internal combustion engine
i-ESG	National Industry ESG framework
ILO	International Labour Organization
IMF	International Monetary Fund
IPPU	Industrial processes and product uses
IR4.0	Industrial Revolution 4.0
IRDA	Iskandar Region Development Authority
KL	Kuala Lumpur
LCTF	Low Carbon Transition Facility
LLC	Large local company
LRT	Light Rail Transit
M40	Middle 40% of the income distribution
MAF	Malaysian Armed Forces
MCA	Malaysian Chinese Association
MDB	Multilateral development bank
MIDA	Malaysian Investment Development Authority
MISIF	Malaysian Iron and Steel Industry Federation
MITI	Ministry of Investment, Trade and Industry
MNC	Multinational corporation
MP	Member of Parliament
MRT	Mass Rapid Transit
MSA	Malaysian Steel Association
MSI	Malaysia Steel Institute
NEM	New Economic Model

NETR	National Energy Transition Roadmap
NEVSC	National EV Steering Committee
NIA	National Investment Aspirations
NIMP 2030	New Industrial Master Plan 2030
NIP	New Investment Policy
PAS	Malaysian Islamic Party
PDRM	Royal Malaysian Police
PH	Pakatan Harapan
PKPJ	Johor Housing Development Corporation
PN	Perikatan Nasional
PPP	Purchasing power parity
PTPTN	National Higher Education Fund
R&D	Research and development
RTS	Johor Bahru-Singapore Rapid Transit System Link
Sdn. Bhd.	Sendirian Berhad (private limited company)
SEAISI	South East Asia Iron and Steel Institute
SME	Small and medium enterprises
SPV	Special purpose vehicle
SST	Sales and Service Tax
STEM	Science, technology, engineering and mathematics
T20	Top 20% of the income distribution
TFP	Total factor productivity
TVET	Technical and vocational education and training
UMNO	United Malays National Organisation
UK	United Kingdom
US	United States
WTO	World Trade Organization
xEV	Electric vehicles and their extended variants

Foreword

Second Takeoff: Strategies for Malaysia's Economic Resurgence is a compendium of articles written by Liew Chin Tong over the past two decades. They cluster around several key themes such as transport, social mobility, housing, defence, international relations, as well as industrial and technology policy.

Brought together, updated, and wonderfully curated, these essays are the product of many hours of reflection. Yet, while these essays have been produced at different points in time, they are consistent in their perspective and, collectively, paint a coherent vision for the country going forward. This coherence is due to the specific attributes of the author, Liew Chin Tong.

Chin Tong has been active in politics for some twenty-five years. A long-time member of the Democratic Action Party, he is a three-time member of parliament, and has held federal and state-level positions in party politics as well as in government, notably in the Departments of Defence as well as International Trade and Industry.

While many decision-makers revel in the public dimension of politics, Chin Tong has a keen interest in policy making. This permeates both his writings as well as how he has engaged in the duties of public administration. Whether it be introducing free bus transport in Penang, promoting the wide-ranging and highly technical work of producing a White Paper for the Ministry of Defence, or even promoting measures to increase the efficiency of parliamentary debates – the focus is on implementable, practical initiatives.

Yet, this focus on praxis is informed by countless hours of reading and reflection. This collection is infused with the works of Alfred Marshall, Jane Jacobs, Max Weber and Mariana Mazzucato, who inform discussions on productivity, urban planning, governance, and industrial policy. Countless other works on Malaysian history and politics underpin the deep contextual discussions on the development of the Malaysian state as well as key institutions such as the armed forces and police. Wide-ranging intellectual interests also enable an awareness of approaches adopted elsewhere. These are brought in to illustrate points and provide examples, ranging from constitutional design in India to transport policy in Colombia, as well as technology and upgrading drives in East Asia.

Chin Tong is one of the few Malaysian policymakers who has served in more than one federal constituency and at both the parliamentary and state levels. This has given him a deep appreciation of the benefits and challenges offered by the country's multi-levelled governance system. This is brought to bear in his treatment of topics such as local government elections, autonomy for state governments, and geographically based initiatives such as growth corridors.

These collective experiences also underlie Chin Tong's keen understanding of Malaysia and its political dynamics. He is one of the few people to have foreseen the events of May 2018 and the political reconfiguration it entailed for Malaysia. In April 2017, in a public seminar at the ISEAS-Yusof Ishak Institute entitled *Black Swans in Malaysian Politics*, he argued that the sentiment among Malay voters towards the Najib Razak administration was beyond repair, and – one year out from the election – correctly identified the key electoral change that would tip the balance against the ruling coalition, Barisan Nasional. This same perceptiveness informs the articles in this work.

Second Takeoff: Strategies for Malaysia's Economic Resurgence successfully blends the craft of policy making, practical methods of implementation, and passion for change.

Francis E. Hutchinson
Senior Fellow and Coordinator of the Malaysia Studies Programme
ISEAS-Yusof Ishak Institute

Preface

Few countries get a second chance. Fewer still get a potential massive upswing thanks to the confluence of very major generational global shifts. The purpose of this book, *Second Takeoff: Strategies for Malaysia's Economic Resurgence*, is to demonstrate that if Malaysia gets its strategies and policies right this time, and builds a new broad-based economic, social, and political consensus that has eluded the nation, Malaysia's resurgence as an economic powerhouse and an important middle power will no longer be a far-fetched idea.

Since the term "middle income trap" was invented nearly two decades ago by economists at the World Bank, Malaysia has been the chief candidate for such a description outside Latin America. We have been a nation drifting purposelessly. Our elites indulged in self-aggrandisement and enrichment to unprecedented levels, as evidenced by the 1MDB scandal, while inequality and precarity have become increasingly serious.

Malaysia can get a second chance in the form of a second economic takeoff largely due to once-in-a-generation global shifts – decoupling, de-risking, the world not putting all its manufacturing eggs in the China basket – and made possible by the advent of Prime Minister Datuk Seri Anwar Ibrahim's Unity Government, which provided a sense of purpose and stability, not available in the last decades.

During Malaysia's first takeoff between 1988 and 1997, Malaysia was confident, broadly coherent, outward looking, ambitious and hopeful. The first takeoff had its origins in global shifts as well. In 1985, Japan was forced by the United States to appreciate the yen, resulting in the exodus of Japanese firms, and their South Korean and Taiwanese supply chains, to Southeast Asia in search of cheaper production sites. Malaysia experienced a self-imposed recession in 1985 due to an austerity overdose. The government quickly pivoted in the next year to open its arms to foreign investments in manufacturing, thus the Promotion of Investment Act bears the date of 1986, setting the scene for prosperity until 1997.

The Asian Financial Crisis in 1997 bruised the self-esteem of the nation, and resulted in an inward-looking approach, with a make-do attitude towards policy making. In 1998, the supposed transition from an older generation authoritarian leader (Tun Dr Mahathir Mohamad, then 73 years old) to a much younger and more open-minded deputy (Datuk Seri Anwar Ibrahim, then 51 years old) not only did not happen but tragedy struck. Both battled and Anwar was sacked, beaten up physically, and languished in jail. Politically, there has not been elite cohesion or unity of purpose ever since. In 2001, China joined the World Trade Organization (WTO) and became the factory of the world, trapping economies such as Malaysia – which was not sophisticated enough to own its technologies – in a neither-here-nor-there situation.

During the first takeoff, among Asian developing countries, Malaysia was a distant third in terms of manufacturing technology to South Korea and Taiwan, and in terms of services a near-peer to Singapore. Those should still be Malaysia's comparisons in the second takeoff. Of course, China is so much bigger as an economy and so much more sophisticated as a technology powerhouse now. But rather than paralysing Malaysia, we stand to benefit from China's might in this day and age: China is a potential source of new technologies and investment, apart from being a sizable market.

In the second takeoff, Malaysia needs to be strategic. In simplest terms, it means choosing what to do and what not to do, and at the right time. Malaysia should position itself in three "middles": an indispensable middle in the global supply chain; a middle power and middle ground in geopolitical terms; and an aspiring middle-class society.

During the hyper-globalisation years, the world's factory was in China and "just-in-time" was the motto: everything was moved through containers in sea freight without taking into consideration the potential risks from pandemics, wars, financial crises, and the climate. Now the world operates with "just-in-case" as the dominant assumption, or, in other words, "de-risking". Major multinational corporations are keeping Chinese operations for China's large middle-class markets. At the same time, guided by their governments, companies are looking for opportunities for home-shoring (to set up manufacturing in the United States, Germany, France, Japan, etc.); or near-shoring (in Mexico, Poland, Ireland or other parts of Eastern Europe); or friend-shoring in a US ally like India.

And then there is Southeast Asia. When one looks at Southeast Asia very seriously, Malaysia clearly occupies an indispensable middle position – the economy is admittedly not as sophisticated as Singapore's but not too far off from it while costs are much lower. Malaysia has similar logistical strengths as Singapore: both are situated next to the Malacca Straits. Malaysia also has a large English-educated workforce and a common law framework. In fact, many of the more than a million Malaysians working in Singapore are ready to return to Malaysia for a pay equivalent to two-thirds of Singapore's pay. Yet Malaysia and Singapore are not exactly in competition. In this new time when supply chain resilience is top on the minds of manufacturers, Singapore needs a hinterland whereas there was no such need in the past 20 years when the world economy was highly financialised while China was its main factory.

In terms of technologies, Malaysia's semiconductor cluster, along with the precision engineering sector and other supporting industries, certainly occupies an indispensable middle in regional and global supply chains. When factory operations in Malaysia were hit by subsequent waves of COVID-19 infections, for instance, the automotive industries in Germany and the US had to scale back production, too. We just have to keep pushing the technological frontier to see Malaysia closing the gaps with South Korea and Taiwan in the years to come.

The second middle where Malaysia as a middle power aspirant with a non-aligned foreign policy tradition is an important economic asset in this new time of global upheavals and realignment. The US hegemony, prevalent between the fall of Berlin Wall in 1989 and until very recent years, is challenged by China and Russia, as well as defied by some other countries, while many others exercise agencies of their own to chart a path not exactly as demanded by the US. The world is likely to be a more multipolar place with the US still the largest power-that-be but with many others competing for influence.

Our non-aligned tradition means that Malaysia is friendly to trade with all sides, and, with its various endowments such as a multilingual workforce and strategic location, may potentially serve as the Asian or ASEAN hubs for Chinese and Middle Eastern firms, apart from American and European firms. Malaysia should envisage enhancing and developing a comprehensive service sector to be the near-peer of Singapore in all sorts of services, such as legal, architecture, engineering, finance, and the like.

The third middle is the "middle class". When it joined the WTO in 2001, China had arguably fewer than 100 million citizens who were considered middle class. Two decades later, the Chinese middle-class numbers at least 400 million people. The second takeoff should envisage Malaysia and our Southeast Asian neighbours becoming middle-class societies in a decade or two to come. We should not sell ourselves cheap. As Malaysia aims higher and aspires to be technologically more advanced, we no longer have to see ourselves as being in competition with Indonesia, Vietnam, Thailand or the Philippines. Instead, Malaysia complements these more populous countries that have demographic dividends. Malaysia should envisage building stronger vertical integration with these neighbours, thereby not racing to the bottom in terms of wages but lifting all societies in Southeast Asia into some form of a middle-class society.

A Southeast Asian middle-class society will be a sizable market for intra-regional trade as well as a market for global businesses. A strong middle class in Southeast Asia will also be a strong stabilising factor for regional peace. And a peaceful and coherent Southeast Asia is a great balancing force in a troubled world.

All these are achievable if Malaysia is strategic in what we do with this rare and precious second chance moment that is now at hand.

Liew Chin Tong
January 2024

About This Book

Over the years, Chin Tong has worn many hats, from activist to think tanker to politician, and everything in between. It is therefore no surprise that his policy interests run the gamut from the potential for automation in manufacturing to the modernisation of defence procurement.

Ideologically, however, he has been remarkably consistent. Many of the ideas expressed throughout this book have their roots in pieces he wrote in the 2000s and 2010s. For instance, he first called for a state government for Kuala Lumpur in 2004, started pushing for a Defence White Paper in 2008, and emphasised the centrality of good jobs as early as 2013.

Accordingly, this book is a compilation of Chin Tong's writings in the last two decades across a range of critical subjects, including jobs, industrial policy, climate change, housing, transport, the parliamentary system, federalism, security, and foreign policy among others. It is the product of poring over 130 of Chin Tong's op-eds, press statements and speech transcripts over the years, and consolidating, rewriting, updating, fact checking and structuring them to arrive at the final figure of 33 chapters.

While some of these ideas may be familiar to his long-time followers, they have been expanded considerably with scholarship, statistics, and most importantly, context. In essence, they are all tied together by Chin Tong's most recent brainchild – the overarching narrative that Malaysia is at the cusp of its second economic takeoff *if* we play our cards right.

This book explores how to turn that "if" into a "when" by providing policy suggestions to catapult Malaysia's development to the league of high-income nations amid ongoing geopolitical trends. As Chin Tong puts it in the pages that follow, the Malaysian economy is currently at a crossroads, being in a prime position to benefit from the renewed appetite for investment into Southeast Asia on the back of tensions elsewhere. The last time we capitalised on such an opportunity for rapid growth was in the 1980s and 1990s when Malaysia embarked on wide-scale industrialisation with substantial capital investment from East Asia.

As his Special Officer at the Ministry of Investment, Trade and Industry (MITI) in 2023, I can attest to the fact that these are exciting times, having accompanied Chin Tong to dozens of courtesy calls from interested investors the world over, alongside meetings with countless embassy partners, chambers of commerce, and other industry players, all keen to get a slice of the pie.

While this is all well and good, Chin Tong never ceases to stress that headline GDP and FDI figures are only one small part of the picture. Macroeconomic success must be accompanied by clear improvements in people's standard of living and quality of life, which have been elusive so far. Central to his thesis in this book is the need for Malaysia to create a middle-class society, in which the economic structure supports the creation of dignified jobs with decent pay for all Malaysians.

With this in mind, the book is divided into three Sections:

- *Building a Middle-Class Society*, which explains the low pay problem at the root of Malaysia's economic challenges and the ways to address it through labour market reforms, industrial policy, and fiscal policy;
- *Changing the Way We Measure Success*, which explores the renewed role of the state in the age of the environmental, social and governance (ESG) agenda, along with urbanisation policies to promote a good life for all;

- *Think System*, which emphasises the importance of addressing longstanding calls for reforms in Malaysia's model of federal-state relations, the parliamentary system, the security and defence sectors, and foreign policy.

Put simply, these are the crucial missing ingredients in the pursuit of Malaysia's next economic miracle. Just as a plane needs to generate enough thrust and lift in its engines and wings to get off the runway, Malaysia's second takeoff cannot happen without careful consideration of these three engines of prosperity.

Of course, history matters in this process. We trust an aircraft with a strong flight record and crew with extensive flight hours. At the same time, as we embark on policies to build a better Malaysia, we need to examine what we got right and where we went wrong in our economic and institutional histories. That is precisely what this book does. Drawing from his own memories as a bookish child in a working-class family through to his 15-odd years in public life, Chin Tong imbues the often clinical discussion of policy with heart and humanity.

In the spirit of consistency, allow me to reiterate Chin Tong's message at the launch of his previous book *The Great Reset* in August 2020: "We need a new model that pays ordinary Malaysians better, that allows Malaysia to climb the technological ladder, and that builds capacities for the next phase of prosperity, one where wealth is shared by all Malaysians, and not by just a small group of people." May this book, in some small way, serve as a blueprint of the very model that he spoke about nearly four years ago.

Jaideep Singh
Editor

Acknowledgements

I owe the passion and aspiration for a resurgent Malaysia to many friends, colleagues, and supporters. It is their undefeatable spirit that keeps me going. We believe that Malaysia deserves better. I thank everyone who has contributed to and supported me with the publication of this book although there are too many to mention here. Regardless, from the bottom of my heart, I thank you all.

I am immensely grateful to this book's editor and my former research staff Jaideep Singh for taking the initiative to bring together my past articles and presenting them in a coherent and systematic fashion.

As a full-time politician with government duties, my time is often punctuated and truncated by many travels and meetings, making the task of writing a book a luxury which eluded me many times. I could only resort to writing short opinion pieces to influence public discourse. This book provides an overview of the ideas that I have laboured on over the years and stitches them together to show why I continue to be an optimist about Malaysia's future.

I thank Wan Hamidi Hamid and Ng Wei Ling for editing most of the pieces before their first-ever publication. Frederik Paulus spent many hours giving valuable comments on many earlier versions, and Tan E Hun and Lim Li Lian read the proofs, which I am grateful for. Nik Rashid Nik Zurin, Ng Sze Fung, and Soo Shi Yang provided much appreciated research inputs for the pieces on defence and security, parliament, and electric vehicles, respectively. Thank you to Lydia Chan Shi Song for the cover design.

The generous endorsements by Anthony Loke, Tengku Zafrul Aziz, Nurul Izzah Anwar, Francis Hutchinson and Manu Bhaskaran are greatly appreciated.

We originally planned to publish this book through the think tank I chair, Research for Social Advancement (REFSA). In November 2023, as Jaideep was almost done with the compilation of the book, a chance introduction to Chua Hong Koon of World Scientific Publishing Company lifted the book from a Malaysian production to reach a much wider audience.

Finally, I would like to thank my parents – Liew Sooi Yong and Choo Mee Lan – and my sister Chin Wei for the constant support they have given me throughout my quest for a better Malaysia.

Introduction

If we get it right and at the same time get our acts together, when we look back 10 years down the road, 2023 may be remembered as the beginning of Malaysia's second takeoff.

If we fail, our country will continue to stagnate as has been the case for the past quarter century. The last time a vast majority of Malaysians felt that the next generation would be far better-off than the current one was before the Asian Financial Crisis hit in 1997.

First takeoff

Malaysia experienced its first takeoff with the transformative and massive growth averaging 9% annually between 1988 and 1997 (see Table 1).

Table 1: Malaysia's average annual GDP growth rate by period

Period	GDP growth rate (%)
1978-1987	5.6
1988-1997	9.3
1998-2007	4.3
2008-2017	4.8
2018-2022	3.1

Source: World Bank (2023).

Up until 1969, Malaysia's economic structure had been essentially commodity-based, its fortunes tied to Britain's needs, with a half-hearted import-substitution strategy that did not produce many jobs for the baby boomers who were coming of age in the 1960s.[1] The 1969 General Election saw protest votes by youth of all ethnicities and a post-election ethnic riot, known as the May 13 Incident. The regime crisis paved the way for a new leadership – under Prime Minister Tun Abdul Razak Hussein – which adopted a more interventionist economic stance and an export-oriented industrialisation strategy, catching the first wave of outsourcing from American and later European firms.

Under the premiership of Tun Dr Mahathir Mohamad, who came into office in 1981, Malaysia launched the Look East Policy in 1982 to pivot away from British influence. Accelerating Malaysia's industrialisation, the policy focused on strengthening trade and investment with Japan and East Asia as well as learning from their industrial experience more broadly.[2] At that time, Japan, South Korea and, to a lesser extent, Taiwan, had become well-entrenched in Western manufacturing supply chains, serving as major exporters to North America and Europe. By the early 1980s, these East Asian nations were leaders in manufacturing in Asia, and they had a growing appetite for foreign investment into Southeast Asia.

The crucial turning point in the journey towards Malaysia's first takeoff happened in 1986. The US had forced the Japanese yen to appreciate a year earlier through the Plaza Accord. The yen's rapid climb led to an influx of Japanese investment into Southeast Asia, including Malaysia, amid a search for cheaper production bases. The Malaysian Government moved to liberalise and open further to foreign investment to try to resuscitate the economy after a recession in 1985, which had been caused by austerity and falling commodity prices. This move was well-timed, allowing Malaysia to receive a tremendous boost from Japanese, South Korean and Taiwanese FDI.

Malaysia benefitted from the greater global situation. As the rest of the world shied away from China following the Tiananmen incident in 1989, a Taiwan-educated Kluang civil engineer, Mr Ong Kim Wah, who was at that time working in China for a Taiwanese firm, was retrenched as Taiwanese firms folded operations in China. Soon, he made his first fortune in just three years by building factories for Taiwanese firms in none other than Johor, his home state.

Regularly we heard about how teachers opted for early retirement to go into business or work for private companies as the private sector paid so much better than the public sector. Meanwhile, some relatives who had emigrated or worked illegally as migrant workers in Japan and Taiwan in the 1970s and 1980s returned home to find decent jobs with decent pay in Kuala Lumpur.

I was a teenager then and I recall vividly the mood of the time. Confidence, optimism, and a sense of national unity and purpose defined that golden era. The country was looking outward, not inward. Malaysia was sufficiently confident to see herself as an active leader for the Global South and the Third World; as a global investor, going as far as investing in Africa; and playing a peacekeeping role during the Balkan wars.

Like most people during that time, we were not exempted from the influence of the powerful ideas of Vision 2020 and Bangsa Malaysia.[3] In my valedictorian speech on behalf of the class of 1995, I was praising the seemingly perfect timing of my generation, which I thought would mean decades of prosperity and well-being for Malaysia and the region.

Asian Financial Crisis

The 1997 Asian Financial Crisis shattered those dreams. The massive optimism generated by the first takeoff had turned into exuberance that seeded Malaysia's worst economic crisis before the turn of the century.

On July 2, 1997, the Thai baht was attacked by speculators. Everything in Malaysia and Asia changed after that day. My life, along with that of my entire generation, changed, too.

I was 20 and could not comprehend what the crisis meant. Back then, I was a student at a private college in Klang, Selangor pursuing an American degree transfer programme in the hope of furthering my education in the United States. The year started with the ringgit at 2.5 to a dollar, falling to a record low of 4.885 in January 1998.[4]

By August 1997, when the currency attacks spread from Thailand to Malaysia, Indonesia and South Korea, college mates who were leaving for the US for the fall intake in September were scrambling to exchange their ringgit to dollars before the currency value slid any further.

One September morning, a course mate who was reasonably well-off suddenly cried non-stop during a class presentation. He told the class his father had lost the family's fortune just the previous week. Until then he had never experienced poverty. I have not seen him since.

Fortunes built from decades of hard work and proceeds from currency speculation in the 1990s were wiped out within months, if not days, in the first major contagious regional crisis in recent memory, before the far greater global crisis in 2008.

Looking back a quarter of a century today, I realise the Asian Financial Crisis was one of the most important ruptures in our history. The region-wide economic crisis soon led to political crises in Southeast Asian states, which saw the fall of Indonesia's dictator Suharto in May

1998 and the sacking and persecution of Datuk Seri Anwar Ibrahim in Malaysia on September 2, 1998.

A lost generation

Our generation was not supposed to start off adulthood this way.

The economic and financial crises, coupled with China's entry into the WTO in 2001 as a competitor for cheap manufacturing, resulted in two decades of lacklustre economic performance in Malaysia and the region.

Malaysia remains stuck in an old model of low-wage, low quality growth based on unskilled labour. Malaysia no longer sees herself as an aspiring middle power. Malaysia lost the ambitions she had in the 1990s. We had become myopic, inward-looking, transactional, and to a certain extent, we lost hope.

The new era: from polycrisis to opportunity

The world of today is experiencing a perfect storm of simultaneous crises across many fronts – a "polycrisis" – that have changed the regional dynamics altogether.

- After three years, the COVID-19 pandemic's disruptive effects have not left us entirely while the emergence of other pandemics can never be ruled out;
- The climate crisis is only going to accelerate while collective actions of the world's governments are difficult to come by;
- With supply chain disruptions, debt accumulation, inflation, massive interest rate hikes by the Federal Reserve, and various other forms of financial upheaval, the global economy faces the most serious stress since the 1970s; and

- Great power rivalries, geopolitical challenges and wars that involve at least one of the superpowers are no longer far-fetched but probable. The US is now stretched dealing with the wars in Ukraine, Israeli aggression in Gaza and beyond, and various permutations in the Middle East and Asia, on top of a US-China rivalry that will colour many things in the years to come.

This age of polycrisis is also marked by an evolution in the global politico-economic order. From the end of World War II in 1945 until 2022, the world experienced three successive orders:

- The first was the tense early stages of the Cold War period from 1945 to the late 1960s, covering the chaos of the Korean War, the formation of NATO and the Warsaw Pact, the Cuban Missile Crisis, and the construction of the Berlin Wall among others;
- The second period from the late 1960s till 1989 saw the Vietnam War that diminished American prestige, the dismantling of the Bretton Woods system and the death of the Gold Standard, the Nixon-Kissinger opening to China, the oil crisis in 1973, the Iranian revolution in 1979, Deng Xiaoping's opening up of China from 1978, and the emergence of Reagan-Thatcher neoliberal economic ideas;
- The fall of the Berlin Wall in 1989 and the collapse of the Soviet Union in 1991 heralded the post-Cold War "age of innocence", a relatively peaceful period that was already unravelling by the time COVID-19 arrived in 2020, and officially ended when Russia invaded Ukraine on February 24, 2022.

We have now entered a new and difficult era of multipolarity and geopolitical tensions, which may last for another decade or two. American dominance is fraying while China's role as a "peer competitor" is rising, and at the same time, middle powers the world over – Australia, the European states, India, Indonesia, Iran, Japan, North and South Korea, Russia, and Turkey among others – are constantly waxing and waning in influence. Understanding this will allow us to see the world differently. If the US and China could find some forms of "G2" cohabitation and coexistence, there may be less friction and conflicts. But this is still a big "if".

The polycrisis has brought with it a new host of opportunities and a chance to reset the economic order, especially for our region. Western firms are looking to home-shoring (bringing manufacturing back to the US with President Joe Biden's subsidies, or to return to Germany), near-shoring (to set up operations in Mexico or Ireland or Poland or other parts of Eastern Europe), friend-shoring (chief among which is India), and Southeast Asia.

Southeast Asia has come under the global spotlight. American and European firms are looking to diversify their operations beyond China ("China Plus One"), whether in addition to existing Chinese activity (such as an "Asia minus China" hub), or even an exit from China into Southeast Asian states altogether.[5] Chinese firms are also coming to the region to set up shop, especially if they have to export to the US and Europe.

Effectively we can no longer talk about trade without talking about geopolitics and geoeconomics. The world has moved from a search for "just-in-time" economic efficiency to one for "just-in-case" economic security. The polycrisis has resulted in a resurgence in the recognition of the crucial role that governments play in safeguarding the economy. This does not just include the necessity of boosting aggregate demand in times of disaster, such as during the pandemic, but also the return of industrial policy, by virtue of geo-economic legislation like the CHIPS and Science Act.

If we play our cards right, the stage is set for Malaysia's chance at a second takeoff, moving on from the low wage, low skill economic model to become a high-income nation with a vibrant and dynamic economy. To "play our cards right", we need to position Malaysia strategically.

The ideas presented in the National Investment Aspirations and the New Industrial Master Plan 2030 (see pages 57-64) – creating high value jobs, building strong linkages to the domestic industry, developing strong industry clusters, creating an economy that produces complex products and services, improving inclusivity, with ESG as an overarching theme – should guide us on what to do next.

Malaysia occupies a unique value proposition among the Southeast Asian countries. We should not be competing with Vietnam, Indonesia, Thailand, or the Philippines. Each of these countries has a population of close to or more than 100 million, and they are generally quite young. They have demographic dividends – where a large increase in the working-age population in proportion to the non-working population (both young and old) produces higher economic productivity – which have eluded Malaysia for over 20 years.

Yet Malaysia has many other dividends, such as being located in the middle of the world's busiest trade routes, an existing industrial base, quality infrastructure, a multilingual workforce, high level of educational attainment, and a reasonably sound legal system.

Whenever I have discussions with Malaysian employers, the issue of shortage of talent would be raised. I always explain that it is not a question of talent, but the issue of pay. It is just that many of our skilled workers have taken up better paying jobs in Singapore.

If Malaysia can position herself as a two-third alternative to Singapore, where the local pay is two-thirds of what Malaysians can get in Singapore, many of our talents across the causeway would be ready to come back (see pages 25-30).

Building a middle-class society, changing the way we measure success and think system

During Malaysia's second takeoff era, our ultimate mission is to build a middle-class society. A middle-class society looks diamond-shaped when it comes to income and wealth: this is a society with a strong, huge, and prosperous middle class, where the economic security of its citizens is at the centre (see pages 2-9).

Currently, Malaysia's economic structure is of a pyramid shape where the top is small and the bottom is huge, and in effect very few people earn enough to pay income tax. Precarity and insecurity affect thousands of Malaysian workers, and many are forced to take up multiple jobs or choose to vote with their feet to Australia, Singapore, the UK, and other developed countries to make ends meet.

Only a diamond-shaped society can ensure a high collection of taxes based on higher wages and higher incomes, thereby maintaining the stability of our socio-economic fabric and propelling Malaysia to new heights as a high-income nation in the years to come. I hope those who campaign for the revival of the Goods and Services Tax (GST) understand this point. There is no point in saying that most of the poor do not pay tax and so we should tax them for their consumption to expand the tax base.

A strong middle class can only be created if there are efforts to grow wages, skills, technology, and productivity at once. The government clearly has a major role to play in formulating industrial policy that places emphasis on attracting high-quality investment, promoting the upskilling and reskilling of our talent, and strengthening automation to reduce our dependence on low-skilled foreign workers.

But at the same time, all of society has to be involved in the creation of a middle-class society for Malaysia's second takeoff. For one, businesses need to pay their workers better in line with their level of skills and education.

Our entire economic and social structure needs to change as well. A healthy middle class needs not only good jobs but also a "good life" – a sustainable urban environment to live in, with affordable housing, a strong public transportation network and climate-resilient infrastructure. All regions of our country, beyond just the Klang Valley, deserve attention based on their economic strengths and needs in line with our Federal structure (see Section II).

For Malaysia's second takeoff, success should not be measured solely in terms of GDP growth or inward FDI figures, but also the increase in median wage, the disaggregated socio-economic outcomes by region and the impact of our activities on the climate among others.[6]

For maximum impact, decision-making and governance would also need to be modernised. With the end of hegemonic one-party rule in our electoral system, long-standing talks of reforms to our Federal-state relationship, a stronger parliamentary system, an effective civil service and a resilient security sector must be addressed once and for all (see Section III).

Finally, we must be outward-looking again. Malaysia should see herself as an aspiring middle power. The key is to be strategic and proactive in Malaysia's conduct of foreign policy and diplomacy. We must realise that Malaysia's economic fate and our people's well-being require a robust yet balanced foreign policy.

This is what Prime Minister Datuk Seri Anwar Ibrahim's Malaysia Madani is all about. Ultimately, a middle-class society is the material basis for Malaysia's second takeoff. We need to change the way we measure success, redefine the role of government and find a suitable place for Malaysia in the world.

It is my hope that in a decade's time when we look back, Malaysians would be able to identify the upward mobility in their lives and the improvement of livelihoods with Prime Minister Anwar and the Kerajaan Perpaduan. But we have to start now to see the fruits in 2033.

SECTION I

BUILDING A MIDDLE-CLASS SOCIETY

Low pay and precarity at a glance

Malaysia's most crucial problem is low pay. Here are some statistics to explain the real current situation:

1. The median wage

The median wage as of 2022 is RM2,424. In simple terms, it means half of the 9.95 million wage earners in Malaysia are earning less than RM2,424 per month, according to the Department of Statistics Malaysia (DOSM).[1]

In the formal sector specifically, the median wage as of August 2023 is RM2,600, with the bottom 10% of wage earners (first decile or D1) making less than RM1,482 a month while 70% of them (seventh decile or D7) earn under RM4,000 monthly, barely qualifying to pay income tax (see Table 2).

Table 2: Median wage among formal sector workers by decile (first decile to ninth decile), August 2023

Decile	Median wage (RM)
D1	1482
D2	1564
D3	1800
D4	2145
D5	2600
D6	3200
D7	4000
D8	5500
D9	9100

Source: DOSM (2023).

2. The underpaid, underemployed well-educated workers

It used to be that a higher education equalled a good salary and a decent life. The current chronic low pay however has left higher educated people with low wages. According to DOSM, skill-related underemployment (defined as the share of tertiary-educated workers in semi-skilled and low-skilled jobs that do not require tertiary education) has risen since the pandemic, clocking in at 37.3% in the third quarter of 2023 compared to 34.8% in the last quarter of 2019.[2]

A late 2019 study by the National Higher Education Fund (PTPTN) meanwhile found that 87.7% of the fund borrowers – university and college-educated adults – are earning less than RM4,000 per month after graduation.[3]

3. The large contingent of gig workers

While the true size of the gig economy is difficult to ascertain due to its informal nature, DOSM estimated that there were almost three million potential gig workers in 2018, making up over 19% of total employed workers in Malaysia.[4] More recent figures are not available, but the share of gig workers is expected to have risen since the late 2010s owing to the growth of the digital economy, the pandemic-induced normalisation of remote work, and the realisation that tertiary education does not guarantee a fairly and decently paid job.

Further, a 2020 survey by Zurich Insurance Group found that 38% of Malaysian respondents in full-time employment were looking to switch to gig work within a year, well above the global average of 20%.[5]

Gig work may sometimes bring higher income but with no certainty, limited social protection and poor upward social mobility.

4. The rise of the economically insecure 'precariat'

'Precariat' is a combination of the words 'precarity' and 'proletariat', and they have grown as an economic segment in Malaysia. Economic insecurity is part and parcel of their daily lives.

Some examples of Malaysians living as precariats today are p-hailing drivers and food delivery riders. Anecdotally, these gig workers, whom I have spoken to personally, have told me that they often work 14 hours or more each day just to make ends meet, and they are trying to earn at least RM4,000 a month.

Further, according to a 2022 World Bank survey, 20% of the country's poorest households (with a monthly income below RM2,000) said they were running out of food.[6] Five years earlier, a Gallup poll found that 23% of Malaysians did not have sufficient money for shelter.[7]

While most Malaysians describe the current economic woes as a "cost of living" problem, it is a not-too-hidden crisis that over 70% of Malaysians are experiencing economic insecurity through a number of factors, the most important among which are low wages, the cost of housing and the cost of transport.

These statistics suggest that Malaysia has a pyramid-shaped economic structure where the top is small and the bottom is huge, as Figure 1 illustrates. As a general rule, the lower the wage bracket, the larger the share of individuals in that category, with a disproportionate share in the three lowest wage brackets (RM1999 and below, RM2,000-2,999 and RM3,000-3,999). More than 55% of all employees in the formal sector earn less than RM3,000 a month, meaning over half the working age population is effectively ineligible to pay income tax from the get-go.[8]

Figure 1: Share of individuals employed in the formal sector by wage bracket, August 2023

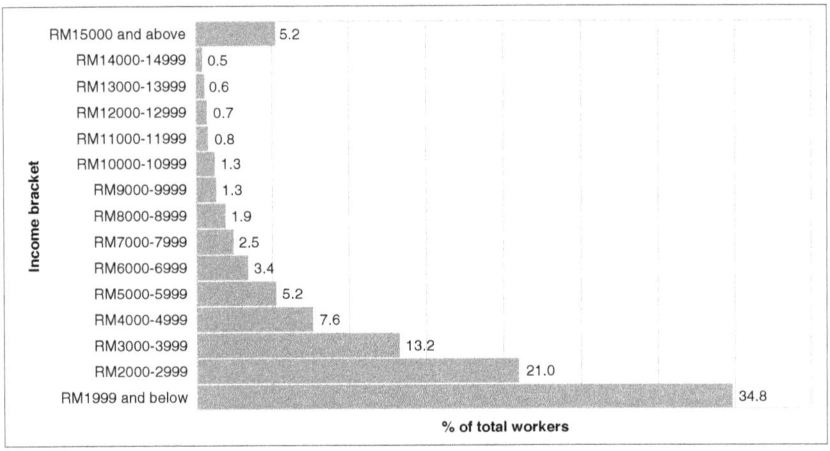

Source: DOSM (2023).

The B40 (bottom 40%) and M40 (middle 40%) labels are therefore of little meaning.[9] Essentially, most Malaysians do not live well and do not live with a decent quality of life. As the subsequent chapters highlight, this is a consequence of the low-wage structure model of the 1980s and 1990s that Malaysia has not fully graduated from. A stylised fact that characterises the situation is that to sustain the low-wage structure, Malaysia imports a huge number of unskilled workers from Bangladesh and Indonesia while low-end workers from Malaysia work in Singapore.

The low earning power of the average worker in Malaysia is symptomatic of virtually every major socio-economic issue in the country, including low labour productivity, brain drain, inadequate social protection, inequality, and job dissatisfaction. Low pay also creates the sort of insecurity that fuels far-right populism. This scenario will have to change to ensure the survival of our society.[10]

If we do not face up to this deep long-term economic challenge, measures taken by us risk amounting to a mere reshuffling of chairs on the deck of the Titanic. What this implies is that distribution should not be done only through welfare and handouts. The main effort of distribution has to come through jobs and wages, and provision of good public services for all. In other words, addressing low pay means rethinking the entire economic model.

From a pyramid-shaped to a diamond-shaped society

Ultimately, we should aim to build a middle-class society in which the middle-income group – the middle 60% – is the foundation of the economy. We should envisage that 60% of Malaysians earn enough to qualify to pay income taxes. Then our society is a diamond-shaped structure where the middle is huge. We may want to envisage that in five years, 50-60% of Malaysians will be earning more than RM4,000 per month (two-thirds of Singapore's pay for low end workers).

Figures 2(i) and (ii) provide a simple illustration of what it would mean to move from a pyramid-shaped society to a diamond-shaped society in terms of income distribution. Currently, over two-thirds of Malaysian wage earners make less than RM4,000 a month, making them either disadvantaged or largely precarious. While there is no universally agreed upon definition of the 'middle-class', Figure 2(i) shows that the individuals in the middle-income brackets, i.e. RM4,000-

RM9,999, who may be assumed to have middle-class aspirations, make up about a fifth of the share of formal wage earners. Finally, those at the very top of the wage distribution ladder, who make more than RM10,000 a month, comprise about 9% of all workers in the formal sector.

Figure 2(ii) represents an idealised diamond-shaped society, in which the 'aspirational' group in the middle make up the largest share of wage earners while the share of the population earning near or below the minimum taxable income threshold should at least halve to about a third of those employed.

Figures 2(i) and (ii): Moving from a pyramid-shaped society (left) to a diamond-shaped society (right), with the current income share held by each stratum of society and the goal under a middle-class, diamond-shaped income distribution

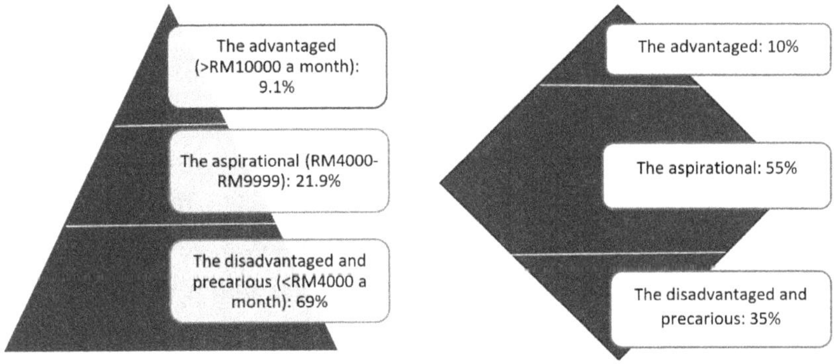

Note: This illustration is meant to be a generalisation, which does not take variables like location, sex, age and education into account due to data constraints. The numbers in Figure 2(i), as in Figure 1, come from the dashboard of Formal Sector Wages by DOSM (2023), meaning it does not consider wage earners outside the formal sector, which may affect the percentages above but would not be expected to change the overall shape of the income distribution. What it means to be 'aspirational' or '(dis)advantaged' may also change in line with inflation, but the general point holds.

Engines of growth and lessons to be learnt

To reach there, we need to rethink jobs, skills development, and investment policies. In today's geo-economic climate, I can see at least three major engines of growth that we should take advantage of for the country:

- ***Automation, innovation, technology adoption and digitalisation.*** Also known as "Tech Up" in the government's latest policy documents, the push for more automation, innovation, technology adoption, and digitalisation will increase the productivity of Malaysia's manufacturing sector whilst reducing reliance on unskilled foreign labour. Such a move, which necessitates the upskilling and reskilling of local employees, will involve building stronger linkages between multinational companies (MNCs) operating in Malaysia and our small and medium enterprises (SMEs) as well as our large local companies (see pages 79-87).
- ***Reindustrialisation.*** China's entry into the WTO in 2001 represented a "giant sucking sound" of FDI away from Southeast Asia. Malaysia languished in a state of premature deindustrialisation for about two decades thereafter. But de-risking strategies on the back of geopolitical trends are happening right now. The total investment into Malaysia for the first eight months of 2023 was larger than in any previous one-year period.[11] There are major shifts into the region, and we must seize this opportunity to facilitate supply chain reorganisation and to upgrade our economy in a big way (see pages 89-97).
- ***Green transition.*** ESG is no longer a niche concept. Rather than a burden, ESG is an opportunity to create green jobs, green businesses, and green industries on the back of the growing global interest in and need for sustainable practices. To give a simple example, we

should leverage our strengths in solar panel production and the electronics sector to develop our capabilities in renewable energy and electric vehicles or EVs (see pages 99-115).

Across these three trends, and in our economic debate more broadly, good and decent jobs for Malaysians should be at the centre. If we follow the economic debates in the US and most other economies, jobs are front and centre in every discussion.

We need a strong, dynamic, and competent state to set conditions for industrial policy to work, for education to work, for ensuring that workers have enough income to feed their families and raise their children to be a more educated generation for the next generation's industries.

For Malaysia to have a clear path ahead, we need a strong state with integrity, and with a just and fair regulatory framework that would allow good industries to grow through productivity gains. We must regulate businesses so that they pay workers decent wages. We must also facilitate world-class education to serve as a catalyst for science and technological research, which is often costly and not easy to fund privately, and safeguard our environment not to be destroyed.

A strong, dynamic, and competent state with a just regulatory framework and a decent wage-decent-work model is good for the private sector and for workers alike. It would in fact be in the interest of the richest to see a strong middle-class society with a strong state, as such a state would be more economically, socially, and politically stable.

With a concerted state-coordinated effort to move wages, skills, technology, and productivity to increase at once, Malaysia may reach a stage of a diamond-shape society within a reasonable timeframe, say a decade.

PART I

RESTRUCTURING THE LABOUR MARKET

The foundation of any society is its workers, and as we have seen, Malaysia does not pay its average worker enough for them to enjoy the fruits of economic growth. A consequence is the growth of the precariats as a sizeable socio-economic class.

Therefore, the first step in catalysing Malaysia's next takeoff – and more importantly to make sure it leads to a sustainable increase in income, especially among the lower and middle classes – is to acknowledge the need to address economic insecurity.

More than just basic welfare, Malaysians, especially those in the bottom 70% of the income distribution earning less than RM4,000 a month, need better jobs, better pay, better business opportunities and better upward mobility for their children.

What this means for policymakers is that we need to empower a large segment of the population if the country is not to deteriorate, with a majority of our people living with a deep sense of precarity. Empowerment comes first and foremost through the restructuring of the labour market.

Unsustainable labour market structure

The fundamental issue at hand is that Malaysia's labour market structure is not sustainable. The growth of real median wages in Malaysia has averaged only about 2.2% annually since 2010. While wage growth generally outstrips inflation, real income remains low: the median wage in 2022 is still below the pre-pandemic wage level (see Figure 3). Coupled with rising cost of living, this contributes to the sense of economic insecurity many Malaysians feel.[1]

Figure 3: Overall median wage (left) and median wage growth and inflation (right), 2010-2022

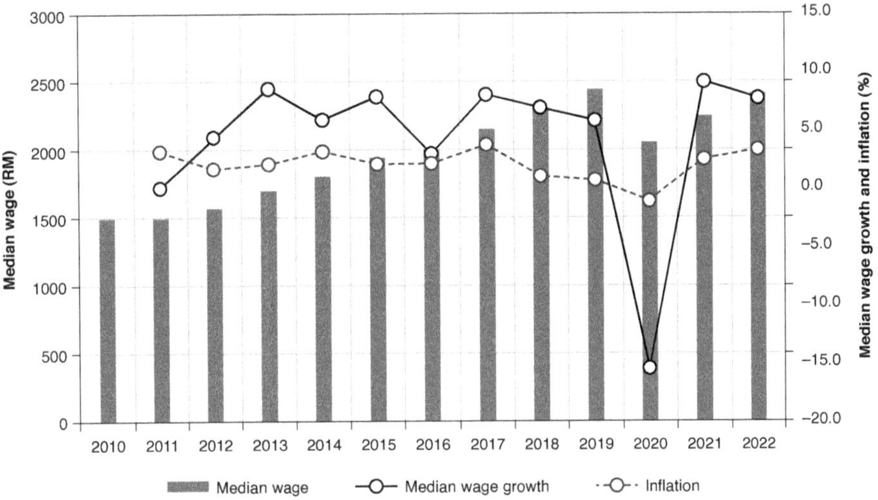

Source: DOSM (2023).

What is particularly worrying today is the presence of a huge "educated underclass" in our midst. Malaysia has a relatively well-educated population: 63% of the adult population has completed upper secondary education (comparable to Hong Kong and better than Italy) while nearly a quarter has some type of post-secondary qualification (on par with Portugal).[2] At the same time, many Malaysian graduates are overqualified for the jobs offered in the economy. According to Figure 4, the average annual growth in the number of new graduates between 2017 and 2022 is more than double that of the number of high-skilled jobs created (proxied by the growth in the number of skilled workers in the country).

Figure 4: Growth rate in the numbers of skilled workers and tertiary-educated graduates (%), 2017-2022

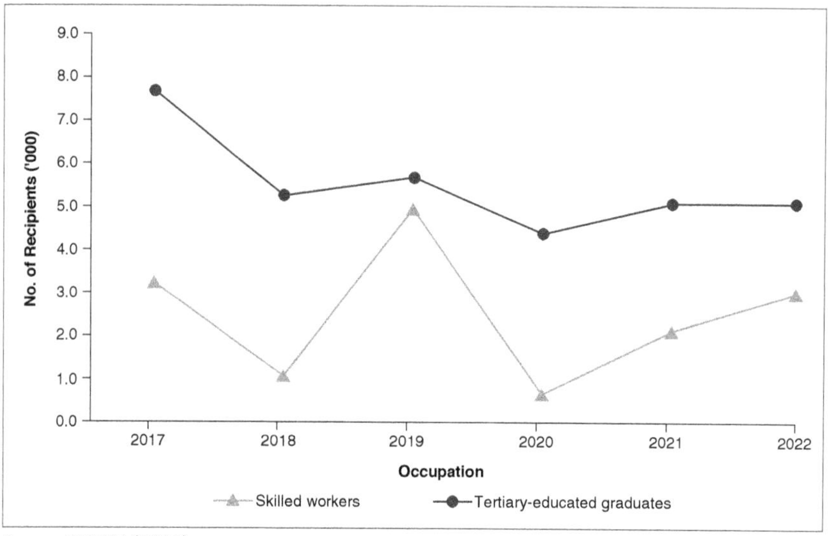

Source: DOSM (2023).

Clearly, there is a contradiction between the population's high educational attainment and the lack of sophistication of Malaysia's industries and businesses. Fresh graduates are arguably among the most vulnerable in this regard, particularly since the start of the pandemic. DOSM found that their median salary fell by a quarter from just over RM2,000 in 2019 to a paltry RM1,624 in 2022.[3]

Popular belief in Malaysia is that graduates are not of good quality or that they demand too high a salary, and hence cannot find a job. But the real issue is that our economy does not create enough jobs that require their tertiary education skills.

Low pay has caused many Malaysians to vote with their feet to work in Singapore, Australia, South Korea and so on, some of whom are there illegally.[4] Many work abroad in jobs below their qualifications. For example, many graduates from Malaysia work as 3D (dangerous, dirty and demeaning) workers in Singapore, such as security guards, cleaners, mechanics and factory workers (see pages 25-30).[5]

Low pay and the inadequate supply of viable jobs in the formal sector also cause many Malaysians to work multiple jobs or seek employment in the gig economy, which tends to be precarious as well as lacking access to social protection.

A paradigm shift is needed

Precarity is the result of decades of lopsided economic policies that failed to lift the wages of ordinary Malaysians. Harming the long-term well-being of many a Malaysian, both in employment and in retirement, precarity can be explained by our economic structure, which is stuck in a vicious cycle of low wage, low productivity and low technology adoption.

Chapter 1 explains how we arrived at the present situation due to Malaysia's outdated model of low-cost, labour-intensive economic activities, coupled with our reliance on foreign workers. Long story short, Malaysia's labour market features millions of both documented and undocumented foreign labourers, whose presence in the market drives wages down and removes incentives for employers to upgrade their equipment and processes, upskill their workers and climb the technological ladder.

The consequence of having a huge unskilled migrant labour force within our midst is that our own citizens in turn become cheap labourers in Singapore – they are two sides of the same coin. Chapter 2 proceeds to explore the Singapore factor in Malaysia's labour market, namely the fact that over a million Malaysians have found employment in Singapore. Once again, low pay is at the heart of the matter: our country suffers from a pay problem first and foremost rather than a talent issue.

The situation will not change overnight. Chapter 3 articulates important mindset shifts and policy suggestions needed to end the low pay problem, starting with recognising precarity and acknowledging that jobs and pay are front and centre in the minds of Malaysian voters.

The role of the government comes into play here. To deal with precarity, which is both an immediate political economic problem and a potential long-term threat to social cohesion, the government should step in to facilitate the restructuring of the economy.

Successive Malaysian governments have somehow accepted the idea that the government must act as the HR Department for private investors, especially global capital. Over three decades ago, the Ministry of Labour was renamed the Ministry of Human Resources.

Instead, the state should use a combination of carrots and sticks – by disincentivising the hiring of low-skilled foreign workers and incentivising the move towards innovation and skills development – to create economic activities that would generate sufficient formal employment with decent pay for Malaysian workers.

But the government should not shoulder all the responsibility for creating an empowered workforce with decent pay. According to Bank Negara Malaysia (BNM), many industries in Malaysia compensate workers less than in other benchmark economies, even after adjusting for productivity.[6] Therefore, at the end of the day, resolving the wage problem is a whole-of-nation effort, and the work must start as soon as possible.

CHAPTER 1

The Centrality of Decently Paid Jobs

Malaysia's last two general elections revealed what I have always known to be true: the foremost concern of Malaysians is not one's racial identity, but one's rice bowl.

Racial and religious rhetoric and divisions have not disappeared. But these divisions only matter when those in power fail to generate equitable economic growth. Under economic hardship, our fears and anxieties are easily taken advantage of and channelled into distracting conversations about racial and religious differences.

Ensuring Malaysians have decent jobs and decent pay is economically and socially necessary. Our democracy will be secured if an equitable economy can provide the basis for a strong nation with fewer divisions, keeping unrest and the rise of right-wing populism at bay. Moreover, a job also has non-economic benefits. It is integral to a person's identity, self-esteem and his or her overall well-being.

That is why no other economic concern is more important than the question of jobs. We should place the agenda of job creation front and centre. And the government should be the catalyst to drive this agenda, not necessarily by paying for all the new jobs created but by using all the policy tools at its disposal to create the conditions for better jobs and better pay.

Jobs, jobs, jobs: A tale as old as time

During the Cold War, capitalist societies were most concerned and most prepared to intervene to ensure that ordinary citizens were getting a good deal from the economy to prevent them from being attracted to Communism.

In the 1960s and 1970s, South Koreans called their universities "cow bone" towers ("우골탑" or "ugoltap") – a twist on "ivory tower". Their parents sold one cow per semester to finance their children's education. The thing was, the peasants had accumulated wealth in the form of cows, thanks to post-war agrarian reforms, a measure advised by the Americans to battle Communism.[1] In essence, Koreans invested massively into education, which not only saw the literacy rate quadruple within a generation from 22% at the end of World War II to 87.6% by 1970, but also gave rise to social mobility as the country embarked on wide-scale industrialisation.[2]

Agrarian reform in Taiwan had the same origins and the same logic. Whoever you leave behind in your economic development becomes the person who will seek your downfall.

To a certain extent, preoccupation with the imperative of providing jobs and preventing youth unemployment in Malaysia in the 1960s and 1970s was driven by the same source of concern. The FDI that entered Malaysia in the 1970s was facilitated by the Malaysian federal and state governments (especially Penang) with a very clear policy objective – to provide better-paying jobs for Malaysians than what the domestic sector could provide.

More recently, that job objective and imperative was blurred. Often FDI would be attracted in service of some form of a numbers game, which may add nicely to GDP figures, but offer little scope for thorough, balanced human capital development.

Stuck in the 1980s model

There are some who argue that pay must not rise too fast as it would cause inflation. One of those who staunchly held on to such a view is former Prime Minister Tun Dr Mahathir Mohamad.

I requested a one-to-one meeting with Dr Mahathir in February 2019, when he was the Prime Minister and I was the Deputy Defence Minister. Apart from a brief discussion on the then upcoming Defence White Paper, I devoted almost the entire hour trying to explain to him that the current wage structure and the prevalent presence of the educated underclass were politically destabilising and dangerous.

I argued that creating jobs that pay RM4,000 per month should be placed at the centre of all economic considerations of the government. A caveat must be made here that this is not about a legal minimum wage but the creation of jobs at such levels through policy interventions.

A few months later, Syed Saddiq Syed Abdul Rahman informed me that Dr Mahathir told the Cabinet that we were mad to talk about creating jobs that pay RM4,000. I could only conclude that Dr Mahathir was stuck in the FDI-driven industrialisation mindset of the 1980s, when cheap labour was a competitive edge that propelled the economy to thrive. Understanding the context is important.

In the 1970s-1980s, Malaysia became a key beneficiary of the "flying geese" model, which presupposed that the US (and Europe to a lesser extent) was the final export destination for Asian industrial output. Japan had joined the ranks of the industrialised nations of the Western world while the Four Asian Tigers – Taiwan, Hong Kong, Singapore and South Korea – followed closely behind. Malaysia was part of the third stage of the flying geese model, alongside Indonesia and Thailand.

As the post-war baby boomers entered adulthood and began seeking employment in the late 1960s through to the 1970s, there were not simply enough jobs to go around. By the time the country's first FDI-driven industrialisation move started in Penang in 1971, the state's unemployment rate had surpassed 14%[3] while the national unemployment rate stood at 7.4%.[4] The Malaysian economy had plenty of spare capacity when Western and Japanese investors came knocking.

The new jobs created in the country's earliest Free Trade Zones (FTZs) in Bayan Lepas, Petaling Jaya and Shah Alam in the 1970s and 1980s were low-paying when compared with wages in advanced nations. However, the men and women (the latter forming the majority)[5] in the electrical and electronics (E&E) sector in the 1970s and 1980s were comparatively very well paid domestically.

Compared to what? For a Chinese youth living in George Town's inner city, compared to unemployment,[6] a job in the nascent Bayan Lepas Industrial Park was extremely uplifting. For young Malay women from rural Selangor and Negeri Sembilan, a factory job in one of the FTZs in Shah Alam or Sungai Way was socially transformative. There were plenty of social gains and upward mobility to be had.

Many swiftly left their villages or small towns to come to the cities to work at these factories, landing jobs that often paid double those offered in other domestic sectors, or, at the very least offered superior benefits, such as free hospitalisation, maternity and retirement benefits, recreational facilities, and hostel accommodation.[7]

But then came the fourth stage of the flying geese model in the 1990s-2000s, during which China and Vietnam opened up. China's huge productive capacity flooded the US market since China joined the WTO in 2001, further quickening outsourcing from the US. Malaysia was in an awkward position where it could not compete with China's emergence as the factory of the world and its low prices, but at the same time it had not industrialised quickly enough to serve the more advanced segments of the value chain like Japan and the Asian Tigers.

The 2008 Global Financial Crisis, and the health and economic crises of the early 2020s, brought about the demise of the flying geese model. The low-wage structure that Malaysia and other Asian economies pursued to export to the developed world had come to the end of its shelf life. In other words, the model that made Malaysia grow fast in the 1980s and 1990s was no longer working.

Previously, suppressing wages helped make exports cheaper and more competitive. Now consumers in the West are finding it hard to consume so many Asian products due to their own low wage and inequality struggles: the American middle class only hold 42% of total US household income as of 2020 compared to 62% in 1970.[8]

In the end, what we are left with is low pay, the problem that confronts us now.

Low pay: A 25-year problem

When I was 14 years old in 1991, I worked as a waiter in Subang Parade, Selangor to help make ends meet for my struggling family. The initial pay was RM2.50 per hour. A lot more skilled a year later, I was paid RM4.50 per hour.

Thirty years on, in 2023, the average fast-food restaurant still pays its staff less than RM10 per hour.[9] In the last three decades, wages in the industry have barely doubled while the average fast-food meal has more than tripled in price.[10]

In the boom years of the early 1990s, when unemployment was below 3%, Malaysia struggled with labour shortages, which explained why as a 14-year-old, I landed a waitering job. Petrol stations, for instance, were told by the government to implement "self-service" at the pumps while drive-through car wash machines were introduced in the cities to much fanfare. Today, as unskilled labour is abundant, often there will be petrol station attendants offering services such as cleaning the windscreen, even though the filling of petrol is generally done through self-service.

What changed between the early 1990s and the present day? The simple answer is that in response to the labour crunch, the government liberalised the process of hiring foreign workers, allowing them to work in more sectors, including manufacturing and certain services, to complement their long-standing presence in agriculture and construction. This was meant to be a temporary measure to address the tightness of the domestic labour market.[11]

What ended up happening was that Malaysia received a huge influx of unskilled foreign labour, particularly from Indonesia, Bangladesh and Nepal, who continue to make up about a fifth of total employment in manufacturing and construction based on the latest estimations in 2016.[12] It did not help that along the way, successive home ministers, human resources ministers and senior civil servants at the home ministry found that there was so much illegal money to be made by making foreign unskilled labour ubiquitously available at all times.[13]

As Figure 5 highlights, the share of registered foreign workers climbed from just over 4% of the workforce in 1990 to 11% today. While legal migrant workers make up a smaller share of Malaysia's labour force today than in the 2000s or 2010s, particularly following the pandemic, this data is likely to be an underestimate, as it excludes illegal, irregular and unregistered foreign workers, who are believed to be over a million in number.[14] A 2018 paper by the ISEAS-Yusof Ishak Institute estimates the total number of migrant workers in Malaysia to be at least 3.85 million, or over a fifth of the total workforce.[15]

Effectively, dependence on unskilled foreign labour has been the defining feature of Malaysia's economy for three decades. Reversing

Figure 5: Foreign workers as a share of the labour force (left) and the number of registered foreign workers (right)

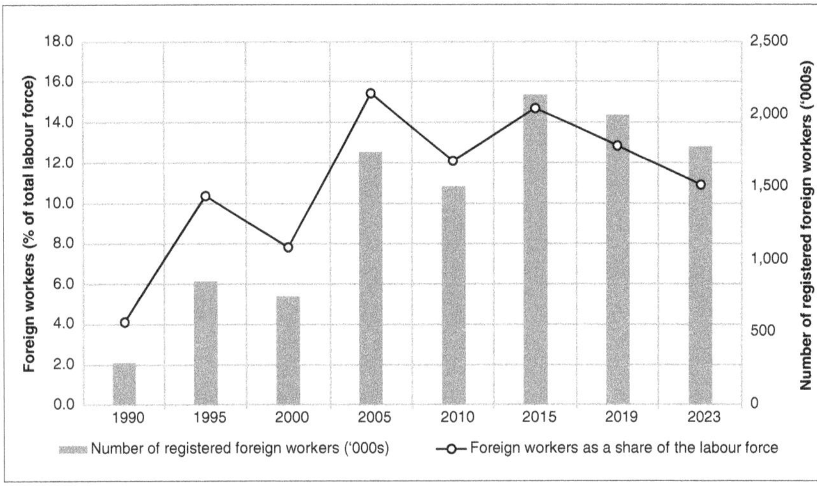

Source: Author's tabulations based on the Government of Malaysia's various Malaysia Plans and the Ministry of Finance's annual budget documents. Note that the figure for 2019 is used instead of 2020 to minimise the immediate distortions brought about by the pandemic (and associated lockdowns) on short-term hiring practices. Note further that the figure for 2023 is up to August.

this would require political will, societal consensus and a gradual but planned exit that reduces disruption.

Consequences

Policymakers must understand that low pay and the heavy dependence on unskilled foreign labour are slowing productivity gains and innovation as there is no need for businesses to automate or do things differently. Of course, it is important that Malaysia does not descend into xenophobia against foreigners. But it is also important to note that hiring millions of unskilled foreign workers in our economy is no longer viable.

Low pay has other societal consequences. Apart from the exodus of Malaysians for greener pastures elsewhere, persistent low pay since 1997 has resulted in a generation with no savings for retirement. According to the Employees' Provident Fund (EPF), a government statutory body that manages a mandatory savings and retirement scheme for Malaysian workers, over half of the 13.1 million account holders have less than RM10,000 in savings.[16]

Chronic low pay is detrimental to the economy as domestic consumption is not going to be high, and since many do not earn enough, they resort to consumption funded by various forms of debt, such as hire purchase and personal loans.

Low pay also results in the perpetually low number of tax-paying citizens, with less than 17% of the workforce paying income tax according to the latest available data as of late 2017.[17] This narrow tax base has prompted some to champion the reintroduction of the GST, which would worsen the situation: low-income households who are on the edge would be taxed for the first time, causing even lower disposable income and a lot of anger, creating a political tinderbox (see pages 133-138).

Rather than further burdening the poor with regressive indirect taxes, what is needed is to raise household incomes and create sustained real wage growth so that everyone earns at least a living wage and can live in dignity.

CHAPTER 2

The Singapore Factor in the Malaysian Labour Market

The second takeoff for Malaysia requires us to understand this reality: that the Malaysian and Singapore labour markets are intertwined, in some cases operating as one single entity.

According to the former Minister for Human Resources, V. Sivakumar, there are 1.13 million Malaysians residing in Singapore.[1] The number of Malaysians working in Singapore – whether in skilled or unskilled jobs, documented or otherwise – is likely to be even larger.

Every day, over 300,000 people and 145,000 vehicles make the trek across the Johor-Singapore Causeway and the Second Link crossings, many of whom are our citizens who commute to the city-state for work to earn a higher income amid the weakening ringgit.[2]

From competition to cooperation

When I was assisting the Penang Government nearly a decade ago, I was surprised to learn that Penang had to compete tooth and nail with Singapore for investments. I thought that Singapore would be in the realm of industries very much ahead of Malaysia.

The strange thing is, Singapore was able to compete with Malaysia at the relatively low-end because they imported cheap labour from

Malaysia. Singapore could have its cake (having very admirably high-tech sectors) and eat it (continue to compete at the low-end) thanks to the imported labour from Malaysia.

But will we always be in competition with Singapore? Not exactly. In the new geopolitical situation, Malaysia and Singapore are not rivals. We are partners that complement each other to face a complex and troubling world.

Rental and other costs in Singapore have risen very significantly over the past three years as a significant number of Western firms have been relocating their regional headquarters from Hong Kong to Singapore. In December 2022, rents for condominiums and public housing flats in Singapore rose by 34.4% and 28.5% respectively in year-on-year terms.[3] Many rich Chinese nationals have also moved their wealth to Singapore.

Relocating industries and services to Malaysia, as well as paying a wage closer to Singapore's, is a mutually beneficial exercise for both our countries.

Two-thirds of Singapore

A good rule of thumb is for Malaysia to position herself as a two-third alternative of Singapore, at least at first. Admittedly, Singapore's economy is more dynamic and more sophisticated than Malaysia's, but this also comes with a higher price tag.

If an investor is prepared to pay two-thirds of Singapore's pay and tolerate that Malaysia is less efficient by a third compared to Singapore, they would find Malaysia a perfect destination of investment.

Once there are jobs that pay two-thirds of Singapore's wages, there will be no shortage of highly skilled Malaysians who are migrant workers in Singapore now. Each day from 4am onwards, about 50,000

Malaysians leave for Singapore from my federal constituency of Iskandar Puteri and my state constituency of Perling on motorbikes to work for SGD2,000 (around RM6,500-7,000) per month as labourers in the manufacturing and services sectors.

Indeed, 44% of Malaysian workers in Singapore are considered low- and semi-skilled and work as cheap labour.[4] They work as cleaners, security guards, bus drivers, hotel and F&B workers, factory workers and machine operators.

Why are Malaysians not staying in Malaysia to do the dirty jobs? Obviously, the jobs themselves do not deter them. After all, they are prepared to work in 3D jobs in Singapore as well as in Australia or South Korea. If Malaysian workers are paid too low, they would most likely move someplace geographically convenient and culturally similar, with a higher wage. It makes sense that Singapore would be their first choice.

It all boils down to the pay rate as they are paid better in those countries. They are simply not interested in jobs that pay RM1,500-2,000 per month.

When I ask them – the older ones with ageing parents or those with young children – many are ready to come back if the pay is roughly two-thirds of what they get in Singapore. For those who are earning SGD2,000 and below, for example, RM4,000-4,500 would be sufficient to entice many to return.

Yet, now they can only get one-third of Singapore's pay. Herein lies the challenge of mismatched wage expectations.

A pay problem, not a talent problem

Each time a Malaysian employer comes to the Ministry of Investment, Trade and Industry (MITI) to tell me that Malaysia does not have enough talent, I will simply say, "I beg to differ." Malaysia has most of the talents needed by our industries.

The problem is, they are mostly working in Singapore. Malaysian engineers, technicians or chefs, or even unskilled workers, would take up jobs the moment there is an opening in Singapore.

There is little point complaining that too many Malaysian engineers leave for Singapore after working in Penang for two or three years. It is not as if Malaysia does not have a sufficient supply of young engineers. It is the inability or unwillingness on the part of corporations to pay these people adequately to make it worth their while to stay.

The corporations often retort that the dire situation is the result of currency differentiation. While it is true that the exchange rate differential has pushed more Malaysians, especially Johoreans, to find better paid jobs in Singapore, it is worth noting that the real problem lies in the overall economic structure more generally. If employers in Malaysia are prepared and able to pay just two-thirds of what Singapore pays to attract Malaysian workers, they would be able to turn things around and retain more employees.

We also know that many qualified technicians avoid formal employment and a relatively low industrial sector wage and prefer, instead, to enter the gig economy as an e-hailing driver or food delivery rider. Again, it is a pay question whose roots are structural.

Way forward

The previous governments approached the subject of Malaysians working in Singapore (and other countries) as "brain drain": to regain the so-called "brains", expensive incentives were targeted towards highly qualified and skilled individuals with high income so that they would return to Malaysia. TalentCorp was formed for this purpose: its

Returning Experts Programme managed to bring back over 6,000 Malaysians in 2022.[5]

However, 6,000 is only a small fraction of the number of Malaysians living and working abroad. At the end of the day, those highly qualified professionals, usually holders of one or more university degrees, are unlikely to be persuaded if the economy does not offer the same breadth and depth of opportunities as abroad. Less than a third of the Malaysian workforce is in highly-skilled professions.[6] Hence, there is a mismatch between new jobs created in the economy and educational attainments of Malaysians.

Accepting the fact that pay in Malaysia is psychologically benchmarked to Singapore's is a good start for a paradigm shift. To pay more to retain good engineers and to stop good technicians from becoming food-delivery riders, Malaysia must work towards building a high wage, high productivity, highly skilled and technologically advanced economy.

These Malaysian workers, mostly semi-skilled, are looking for jobs that pay RM4,000 and not RM1,500. Again, they do not necessarily need RM6,500-7,000 to nominally match the SGD2,000 they receive in Singapore, especially if they lose their job in a downturn. The pay they give up is easily compensated by the better quality of life and lower cost of living back home.

Creating jobs that pay RM4,000, and not RM1,500, for semi-skilled positions is really about restructuring the economy in order to reduce the number of and need for unskilled foreign labourers in Malaysia, in addition to moving from labour-intensive to capital-intensive activities. We need to start automating in a massive way so that jobs that now require 10 foreign labourers can be handled by one Malaysian worker who has "graduated" from working in Singapore.

This is not only the responsibility of the government of the day. We need buy-in from both the private sector and society at large. For the Malaysian economy to move forward, there is a need to recognise that the huge number of unskilled foreign labourers is causing Malaysian workers to become cheap foreign labourers in Singapore. There needs to be a societal consensus that our economy must value and pay for skills in line with their contribution to higher productivity, as well as the need to prioritise the well-being and economic need of Malaysians. Revaluing skilled labour in this way will not lead to inflation or loss of competitiveness; on the contrary, it is essential to ensure our economy's vitality.

CHAPTER 3

Ending Low Pay

The Malaysian economy is at a crossroads. Indeed, Malaysia as a nation is at a crossroads, and the decisions we make today could change the course of our history, for better or for worse.

With the 15th General Election in November 2022 and the subsequent state elections in August 2023 well out of the way, the democratically legitimised Unity Government has the opportunity to reverse the precarity caused by decades of economic policies that failed the ordinary folks.

If we take a reformist stance to create general prosperity from the bottom up, we stand to herald a new political and economic order that will last beyond election cycles. More importantly, with policies focused on restructuring the economy to create general prosperity and end low pay, Malaysia will be able to hold its social fabric coherent.

Conversely, if we default to the old way of doing things, not only will the nation's voters put the government of the day out of business, but also the country itself runs the risk of becoming the "sick man" of Southeast Asia, unable to deal with growing inequality, relative poverty and an increasingly disgruntled populace.

Restructuring the economy

I would like to offer three ways we can use the levers of state power and the tools of policy making at our disposal to restructure our economy, so that all Malaysians can have access to meaningful employment with decent wages to rebuild an inclusive economy.

First, the tough change begins by upgrading wages and jobs at the bottom. We must invest in our most valuable assets – our people. We want to create a virtuous cycle of higher pay, higher skills and higher productivity, leaving no one behind.

Our economy must not only do "body counts" through huge numbers of low-skilled or unskilled foreign workers but must value skilled workers and, increasingly, care workers.

Finally, as an overarching player in the national economy, the state will have to take on an active entrepreneurial role, set clear directions for the private sector to develop, and grow our economy to be regionally dynamic and globally competitive.

(i) Upgrading of jobs begins at the bottom

If one goes by the International Labour Organization's (ILO) categorisation of jobs, many of Malaysia's jobs are semi-skilled, making up 58% of total employment in 2022.[1] However, if one looks at the median pay, the majority of Malaysian workers are paid less than RM2,500 per month. In other words, our wage structure is bottom heavy.

Is this the best that we can offer them? Can we not upgrade the wages of local jobs, especially in the 3D sectors, to allow them to earn a comfortable wage at home?

We can, for example, pay a garbage collector RM3-4,000 per month. You must be thinking that I am joking. How can one fathom the possibility of a garbage collector being paid RM3-4,000 per month in the current job market?

But it is possible if we reorganise our economy. The practice of authorities handing lucrative garbage collection contracts to cronies has resulted in many layers of subcontractors. Often, they are middlemen or rent-seekers who profit from the contract obtained through political connections.

By the time it reaches the real subcontractor, the job may not be lucrative any more. The subcontractor, ever worried about cutting costs, would pay a minimal amount to unskilled foreign workers.

It is imperative that we raise the pay level of these jobs by taking out the unnecessary middlemen. The Seberang Perai Municipal Council, under the Penang Government, did exactly that by using the first five years from 2008 to remove over a hundred garbage collection contractors, replacing them with 2,500 Malaysian workers with a take-home salary of RM1,900 (equivalent to about RM2,500 in 2023).[2] Instead of paying a crony contractor, contract workers were hired directly. Each recruitment exercise saw 10 times more applicants than positions offered, a strong signal that Malaysians are prepared to work in the 3D sector at that wage level.

Wage growth through restructuring will not only benefit those at the bottom. If garbage collectors are paid more, it would stimulate everyone else's income to rise. As wages at the bottom of the distribution rise, job vacancies in similar low-skilled fields will become more competitive. Should other employers not raise salary levels, they would find it difficult to get anyone to work for them, since most, if not all, fresh graduates would choose to become garbage collectors instead.

Only when those at the bottom are paid much better can a rising tide of higher productivity and higher wages be generated. When low-skilled workers earn more, they have higher purchasing power and can afford to spend more. Their collective spending adds to the income of businesses, who will be able to pay their own workers better. There is greater demand for, and spending on goods and services all around. When the working class is better off, the entire economy is better off: this is the essence of "bottom-up" growth in the circular flow of income economic model.

Even Alfred Marshall, the father of neoclassical economics, theorised way back in 1890 that paying workers better could improve productivity and enhance welfare in the economy as a whole:

> *"... [A]ny change in the distribution of wealth which gives more to the wage receivers and less to the capitalists is likely, other things being equal, to hasten the increase of material production [...] ... if ... it provided better opportunities for the great mass of the people, increased their efficiency, and developed in them such habits of self-respect as to result in the growth of a much more efficient race of producers in the next generation. For then it might do more in the long-run to promote the growth of even material wealth than great additions to our stock of factories and steam-engines."*[3]

Empirically, the Peterson Institute for International Economics reviewed the economic and econometric literature on the benefits of paying low-skilled workers higher wages and found that better pay (i) increased employees' motivation to work harder; (ii) improved firms' ability to attract and retain better talent; (iii) reduced turnover and hiring costs; and (iv) enhanced workers' concentration and cognitive performance due to reduced economic insecurity.[4]

One might argue that even if higher pay has the potential to create a virtuous cycle of growth, paying workers more would burden employers, especially at the start. So how should businesses pay for the initial wage increase? How do we get some employers to move past the short-sighted approach of squeezing their workers for every *sen* to keep costs low?

There is arguably no quick fix, as it requires us to reinvigorate the role of the state and restructure the entire economic system to focus on harnessing the engines of development, such as re-industrialisation and automation, as the subsequent chapters explain.

But there are ways to be strategic in specific industries, with appropriate state-sanctioned incentives where necessary to nudge behaviour, as the following non-exhaustive examples highlight:

- Going back to the garbage collection case, instead of hiring five to six foreign garbage collectors, why not employ one Malaysian driver capable of operating an automated garbage collection truck and pay him or her the combined wages of those foreign workers?
- In the glove industry, instead of condoning sweatshop-like conditions with operations almost amounting to slave labour,[5] why not introduce an automation and Malaysianisation programme with a carrot to incentivise the glove sector to automate and with a stick to punish poor labour practices?
- Among security guards, instead of hiring unskilled foreign workers who often cannot make a police report or explain a crime scene due to language barriers, why not transform the sector through the introduction of better security technology and a certification scheme to professionalise these jobs, turning them into positions that pay RM3,500 or more (see pages 84-85)?

Of course, government action is just one part of the picture. Businesses must also shoulder part of the responsibility. Our society should frown at companies that could afford to pay more but choose not to do so.[6] I do hope there will be a new generation of businesses that understand the need for economic security for Malaysians. I hope these businesses will start wearing on their sleeve badges messages such as "we pay a living wage" to change the wage debate altogether.

(ii) A paradigm shift from the low-cost manufacturing export growth model

As indicated, Malaysia's reliance on foreign labour has been key to sustaining the export model. In sizable segments of our industry, foreign workers are hired to assemble imported parts with minimal value-adding, insufficient local content and low multiplier effects.[7]

Foreign labour competes with local workers by downgrading wage levels. This ultimately harms the local economy because the potential that domestic consumption holds cannot be unlocked when the *rakyat* has little spending power.

Our domestic market will grow if industries make a sustained effort to create new middle-class skilled jobs. The challenge here is to grow the market by growing income levels, not by relying on unsustainable debt-driven consumption.

What can replace cheap foreign labour in our manufacturing industries to achieve similar cost efficiencies? Clearly, it is automation. The automation of our manufacturing industry, in line with NIMP 2030 and Tech Up must be accelerated in the next five years.

Reducing our reliance on foreign workers is not an act of xenophobia. Oftentimes, unethical employment agencies attract foreign workers into low-wage jobs with minimal protection. In these dangerous lines of work, they are subjected to abuse, lax protection and health hazards.

Moreover, foreign workers repatriate a large share of their income, which limits the spillover effect on the domestic economy.

Instead of hiring thousands of cheap foreign workers to work in factories assembling goods, we should instead pump resources into automation research and development. We must create better-paying jobs for a smaller pool of locally-hired skilled technicians, software developers and equipment managers who each contribute an important skill set to ensure that the production line runs smoothly.

Broadly speaking, the economy needs to push for robust productivity gains through the creation of sustainable high-skilled jobs, which requires a greater focus on R&D, innovation, capacity building and high-quality FDI, coupled with the adoption of technology (IR4.0), automation and the improvements of processes.

It is high time that we get rid of Malaysia's reputation as a low-skilled, low-cost exporter. This is a model that can no longer work in a less trade-oriented global economy. In its place, we should re-skill Malaysians to prepare them for middle and high-skilled jobs, as well as care work, because the demand for such work will rise with a growing middle class. Part III addresses this point in more detail.

Low pay is ultimately a systemic issue. We cannot ignore the role that the government should play in providing policy help to businesses and industries to transition into a model that reduces the use of unskilled labour and heavily emphasises technological upgrade and automation. It is often a mind block that has to be dismantled.

(iii) The importance of the state in managing this transition

There are those who argue that wages should be "left to the market", guided by the notion that labour supply and demand will equilibrate and produce an efficient, optimal outcome. But this only makes sense in a perfect market where workers and employers face no friction in job search and matching, firms do not have some market or bargaining power, and wages reflect productivity.

In reality, the market is in disequilibrium with mismatches between labour supply and demand, which is why there is involuntary unemployment, coupled with frictions in the hiring process, and some degree of bargaining power on the part of the employers. In Malaysia, as I have mentioned, wages are often further suppressed due to the prevalence of low-skilled foreign workers, the lack of high-skilled job creation, and the weak or non-existent power of labour unions.

Another argument frequently made in the same vein is that Malaysian workers are unproductive, which is why they are not paid well. While there is certainly scope for greater productivity gains through technology as the previous point makes clear, a 2018 BNM study found that the ratio of wages to GDP per worker (as a proxy for productivity) was 0.34, below the corresponding average of 0.51 in the US, UK, Australia, Germany and Singapore. In other words, Malaysian workers are paid less than they deserve, even after taking productivity into account.[8]

At this point, it is time to move on from the idea that the state has no role to play in the creation of good, fair jobs. The market is already distorted and highly imperfect even without any involvement of the state. The government should not only step in to address these failures, but also set clear directions for industries and the private sector to develop in a nationally coherent manner.

This is the essence of an "entrepreneurial state", a term coined by London-based Italian-born economist Mariana Mazzucato. The economy cannot grow sustainably when the state abides by a free-market doctrine. The state has to be an active player through funding investment into innovation and technology, and setting policies to regulate industries and incentivise private sector growth, especially in having a clear road map on how to evolve the labour market into the next phase.

Growth is a whole-of-society endeavour, and the state will have to play its role as the central coordinator of different stakeholders in the economy. For example, government-linked companies (GLCs) are dominant players in many industries in Malaysia. Yet, it is often not clear whether their mandate is simply profit-maximising or to be key drivers of national economic development. Without sacrificing the need to be profitable, GLCs can carry more weight in our national aspiration to become a high-tech, high-skilled economy (see pages 157-168).

This is what I mean by an active entrepreneurial state. It is a state that actively sets strategic goals for industries through its various financial, business and investment arms, as Part II describes in more detail.

Growth and distribution are like two propellers on an aircraft. Growth without distribution would spell trouble for the aircraft because demand would not be broad-based and may not be sufficient to sustain long-term growth. Failure to distribute adequately may also spell non-economic troubles that may threaten the prospect of growth.

But the most important tool for distribution is not welfare. It is jobs – decently paid jobs. These jobs will hopefully allow Malaysians to afford more than just basic necessities and to enjoy a good quality of life.

PART II

REDEFINING THE ROLE OF GOVERNMENT

In the years to come, unprecedented uncertainties will be the norms, not exceptions. Nations will have to grapple with inequality, health crises, climate and environmental challenges, and geopolitical rivalries and wars.

To move forward in turbulent times, Malaysia needs to end silos and band-aid, piecemeal solutions in our reform efforts. We have to get our act together as one unified voice with a common purpose.

How we have done things: Policy making on autopilot

For the longest time, Malaysia seemed unprepared for any of these systemic challenges. Being a lucky country well-endowed with natural resources and strategically located in globally critical waterways, Malaysia muddled through many past problems without fundamental reforms for an extended period, arguably at least since the last crisis in 1997.

After Malaysia's first takeoff, policy making seemed to have been left on autopilot – basing on just back-of-the-envelope calculations. Often, the thinking would be outsourced to consultants or business lobbying to make ad hoc decisions implementable

Compounding the situation is the prevalence of silos within the government and across society: agencies within a particular ministry do not coordinate with each other, let alone across ministries and with GLCs, private businesses and non-profit organisations.

Hence, there has never been a proper political or civic tradition of asking tough strategic questions at the systemic level. It has always been a piecemeal solution for each calamity that would later re-emerge as a new problem.

Granted, there were attempts to resurrect the economy. When Tun Abdullah Ahmad Badawi assumed office as the 5th Prime Minister in

2003, he tried to rein in vested interest groups but found the economic beast too big to control.

The subsequent Prime Minister Dato' Sri Najib Razak launched the New Economic Model (NEM) in March 2010, a year after he took office, in the hope of taking the economy to the next level by focusing more on improved human capital and innovation, rather than putting more investments and labour into the economy, which would not push the envelope.

The mildly radical NEM was shelved quickly. In its place came a nice sounding marketing ploy named the "Economic Transformation Programme" (ETP), which slowly went back to the Mahathir-era public investments into big infrastructure projects and FDI.

After the election in May 2013, the only preoccupation of the government seemed to be the opinion of the rating agencies. In the name of "fiscal stability", new taxes were imposed and budgets were slashed. At the heart of the matter, "Najibnomics" had no empathy for the small guy and no holistic understanding of economic insecurity of a large part of the population that required broad-based and massive reforms to solve. The symptom of fiscal risks – high deficits and debts – was addressed superficially without taking into consideration macroeconomic risks faced by the nation.

In 2018, Malaysia witnessed its first real change of government with the victory of Pakatan Harapan (PH) at the ballot boxes under Tun Dr Mahathir Mohamad's second premiership. Apart from attempting to reverse the excesses of previous cabinets, the PH administration brought in a few policy changes precipitated on a whole-of-government approach, such as the Defence White Paper (see pages 266-268 and 279-281) and Industry4WRD (see pages 82-83), the country's first policy on Industry 4.0.

However, after just 22 months in power, the PH government collapsed in February 2020 due to a parliamentary coup through a wave of defections. PH's short stint in government was not enough to undo all the country's systemic problems, especially given that the rug had been pulled unexpectedly from under our feet.

The subsequent Perikatan Nasional governments in 2020-22 under Tan Sri Muhyiddin Yassin for 17 months and then Dato' Sri Ismail Sabri Yaakob for 15 months did not push the envelope in any significant way, focusing more on short-term, populist measures amid the pandemic.

Now with Datuk Seri Anwar Ibrahim in the seat of power since November 2022, the Unity Government has the opportunity to learn from the previous administrations' mistakes and right the wrongs in our economic structure.

Accordingly, Chapter 4 in this Part II touches on these existing wrongs by highlighting the contradictions that underlie Malaysia's economic structure as well as the new ethos that should guide policy making.

How we should do things: Mission economy

The previous chapter alluded to the role of the entrepreneurial state in facilitating job creation. Beyond just the labour market, however, there needs to be a fundamental shift of mindset across all economic sectors in this new era of uncertainty. This is where the "mission economy" enters the picture. In simple language, Malaysia must get its act together as a nation.

Political leadership is required to build societal-wide consensus on overarching common purposes or "missions" in the manner that Mariana Mazzucato advocates.[1] Her core idea is that the public sector is not just the last resort rescuer in the case of a market failure. Instead, private investments should be steered towards some forms of public purpose, which would in turn generate society-wide benefits.

In other words, it is alright to make money, but profits should be made on innovation that would solve common societal problems, and not just rent-seeking or profit maximisation without benefiting society.

The economy is therefore not growing for its own sake. We grow the economy to achieve socially desirable outcomes that we cherish, and the market needs policy orientation from the government. We need a "mission economy", with the government as the coordinating body (see the next page for a fact sheet on mission-oriented strategies prepared by REFSA, the think tank of which I am chair).[2]

The government must coordinate actions across the board and act as one, not the left hand fighting the right hand or blaming each other. Those who own capital must take into consideration the interests of all stakeholders, including workers, consumers, and the environment, beyond quarterly profits.

There is no running away from the government creating *some* jobs through its payroll. As long as the spending does not go to waste or corruption but goes into creating jobs and investing into the future, the positive impact on the economy will be many times greater than the original investment.

In today's age, the ultimate mission at hand is to ensure that Malaysians have good jobs to put food on the table, while in this process we also strive to build back better. Chapter 5 in this Part II outlines some of the steps the Unity Government is currently taking to push the envelope and make this a reality.

Fact sheet on mission-oriented policy making

Innovation and public value

Innovation is a key driver of economic growth. Private companies competing in a free market is the most conducive setting for a high rate of innovation, but left to their own devices, markets often deliver more of the same, and head into a sub-optimal direction.

Society today is confronted with grand **challenges**, which the UN has summed up under the Sustainable Development Goals: for example, reducing poverty, providing quality education to everyone, reducing inequality, producing clean energy and taking action on climate change.

To make it possible to achieve these goals, they need to be broken down into smaller, achievable chunks: these are **missions**. They are meant to act as a trigger for innovation and produce solutions with spillover effects for the economy overall. In short, **missions provide a direction to innovation**.

Missions do not specify how to achieve success, because the right answers are not known in advance. They do not seek to pick winners and losers or set a top-down direction, but aim to stimulate the development of many different solutions.

Mission-oriented strategies, then, are a portfolio of missions, which require collaboration across sectors, to solve a challenge society faces.

The classic example of a mission-oriented strategy is the Apollo moonshot, an achievement that was first posited as a challenge, then translated into hundreds of missions across many sectors, and which ended up yielding many spillovers, some laying the foundation for new industries.

What makes a good mission

Missions, by design, are decentralised and look to involve the largest number of stakeholders. They aim for both radical and incremental innovation, with the largest possible number of firms participating. As a result, they are also cross-sectoral, intending to spark innovation across sectors and disciplines.

A well-designed mission meets **five criteria**:

1. It is bold and inspirational, with wide relevance to society
2. It sets a clear direction, measurable outcome (even just whether it was achieved or not) and within a given timeframe
3. It is ambitious but realistic
4. It encourages cross-sectoral and cross-disciplinary cooperation
5. It involves multiple, bottom-up solutions, using a range of technologies

How to manage missions

Today's social challenges are more difficult and complex than the space race. These problems require more attention to the **relationships** between all stakeholders, particularly the way in which social structures and problems interact with political and technological issues.

Care must also be given to behavioural changes, smart regulation and a well-functioning critical feedback loop. In other words, social missions must involve the widest range of stakeholders, both in defining and executing the mission.

By nature, innovation is uncertain, with long lead times. Traditional private-sector based financing approaches are not a good fit for this kind of activity, so missions require **patient, strategic committed finance**, a need which the government can fulfil, for example, through state investment banks.

Why missions now

The current age of polycrisis – marked by the COVID-19 pandemic and its aftermath, global geopolitical tensions, climate disruptions and supply chain vulnerabilities – has shown how fragile our economy can be, and how quickly lives and livelihoods can be affected. These threats are not going to go away any time soon, and future manifestations of these crises are likely to have an even bigger impact. Hence, we need to come up with drastic solutions, and at the same time make our economy more resilient.

Through their focus on public value, innovation and the creation of spillovers for the wider economy, missions are the ideal tool. Armed with a clear goal, committed stakeholders and patient finance, missions could not only bring us closer to solving the grand challenges we face, but also lay the foundation for a more dynamic, prosperous and inclusive economy.

CHAPTER 4

Critical Shifts Needed in Malaysia's Economic Thinking

Our economic contradictions

Since the Asian Financial Crisis, the Malaysian economy has faced several contradictions.

First, ever since the first Free Trade Zone opened in Bayan Lepas, Penang in 1971, Malaysia is essentially still an export-oriented economy with a substantial manufacturing sector. Manufacturing remains the principal driver of Malaysia's trade and investment, making up 84% of total exports and 66% of net inflows of FDI as of 2022.

However, the median wage in the sector is just RM2,205, well below the national median wage of RM2,424 as of the latest 2022 data, despite the technical skills, experience and education that manufacturing work should require.[1] At the same time, the contribution of manufacturing to the Malaysian economy declined precipitously from the 2000s onwards without a marked increase in productivity or workers' compensation, suggestive of premature deindustrialisation (see pages 73-75).

Second, FDI is often seen as the be-all and end-all, with tax breaks and associated incentives given to boost the figures. Every March, the Malaysian Investment Development Authority (MIDA) – an agency within MITI responsible for investment promotion and related policies – releases a well-publicised annual investment report, which has as its headline figure the value of approved investment the country managed to bring in the year before.

Meanwhile, the qualitative and quantitative benefits to the domestic economy, including the creation of high-skilled Malaysian jobs; the potential linkages built between foreign MNCs and domestic SMEs; and the extent of the transfer of knowledge and technology between investors and their supposed local beneficiaries, are much less prominent.

Third, Malaysia's dependence on foreign unskilled labour is notable given the relatively small size of our economy. On the other hand, brain drain among skilled labour and the professional class is massive.

The two are linked. The ubiquitous availability of foreign unskilled labour not only results in a race to the bottom in terms of wage for domestic unskilled labour, but also more importantly makes skill upgrade and technological advancement relatively costly (compared to just hiring labour) and therefore undesirable. As a consequence, those who have skills and those who could help technological upgrade are not rewarded sufficiently for them to stay at home.

These three contradictions were united by a common belief in trickle-down economics – the idea that macroeconomic growth through investment and big projects would be good for job creation and household income.

Instead, what happened was that Malaysia became a two-speed economy. By the mid-2010s, those in the export sectors, including foreign investors who enjoyed huge tax holidays and other incentives, had seen growth. These sectors often relied on foreign workers to assemble and re-export imported parts. At the same time, domestic sectors cut off from exporting opportunities suffered from the combined effects of austerity, the depreciation of the ringgit and fluctuating commodity prices. Our big headline numbers like GDP and FDI figures grew, but the benefits did not automatically accrue to the average Malaysian.

Changing how we measure success

Malaysian employers and policymakers need a paradigm shift to invest in productivity and to be willing to pay for skills, particularly given that Malaysia has not had a demographic dividend for over two decades. Such thinking will require governments at all levels to explore all the available tools in their policy toolbox, including looking at industrial policy with job creation (thereby ensuring the economic security of its citizens) as a primary objective.

The role of the government is not to find foreign workers to fill foreign-owned factories but to play a balancing role to ensure that growth is equitably distributed between Malaysian capital owners and Malaysian workers. The state can help build a strong Malaysian industry base through a robust and disciplined industrial policy that helps local industries, provided they generate decently paid jobs or provide services needed by society.

The state needs to help Malaysian businesses and capital owners because they pay taxes, generate employment for Malaysians and hopefully, build up Malaysia's industrial capacity. The state should not need to go out of its way to assist foreign capital owners unless they generate jobs or provide needed services that Malaysian businesses and capital owners could not provide even with the support of industrial policy.

We need to think about the sort of investments and industries we wish to attract into the Malaysian economy. High approved investment figures do not guarantee anything if they do not lead to decent paying jobs for Malaysians.

These days, in my capacity as Deputy MITI Minister, when I meet industry players, I often remind them that Malaysia can afford to be – and should be – selective in picking high-quality investments. In the 1980s and 1990s, MITI was guided by the ethos that beggars could not afford to be choosers, accepting whatever investment we could get. But in today's multipolar world, we have bargaining power, and we need to think about what is best for our country and people.

As I said on my website back in 2017:

> *"What Malaysia needs are investments that transfer technology and skills which Malaysians need to acquire. Where foreign investments of any kind are concerned, the government is obliged to ensure that local workers are offered better employment and that local industries gain from an expanded market and from technological upgrades, and by learning from their foreign partners.*
>
> *We must reject investments that do not utilise local materials. It makes no economic sense to allow full importation of foreign materials for huge projects as this will just worsen the balance of payment, and side-line local enterprises.*
>
> *Foreign investments must also stimulate local employment. It is worrying that some projects generate almost zero domestic employment, and are therefore of hardly any benefit to Malaysians."*

Put simply, we need to change the way we measure the impact of investments. This is where Mazzucato's mission economy comes into play.

CHAPTER 5

Planning the Future of Industrialisation

Malaysia is not short of plans, frameworks, visions and other fancy-sounding policy documents, from the five-year Malaysia Plans to sector-specific action plans. But for the longest time, good ideas seemed to be in short supply, particularly in the bygone era of the ETP where consultant-driven projects were the norm.

Of course, execution is important, and plans are toothless without proper implementation. However, to begin with, we need to have solid plans formulated on a mission-oriented, whole-of-society basis. After all, plans are important for indicative purposes, and what the plan commits and omits would have consequences on the well-being of ordinary joes.

With the mission economy in mind, the government in the last year has announced a few policy documents and initiatives that redefine the parameters of success, serving as a new dashboard for tracking the state of our economy and industrial development.

The three most important economic documents in current times, with a direct impact on industrial policy, are the Madani Economy, the National Investment Aspirations and the New Industrial Master Plan 2030, as described below.

Madani Economy: Empowering the People

On July 27, 2023, Prime Minister Datuk Seri Anwar Ibrahim launched the "Madani Economy: Empowering the People" initiative. As a high-level framework, it is a clear indication that the government is ready to chart a new future to take Malaysia to the next level as an economic powerhouse in Asia, starting with a targeted average annual GDP growth rate of 5.5-6%.[1]

Sustainable economic growth at 6% per year, about 1.5% points higher than what we have been able to achieve in the last decade, will help increase the size of the pie and strengthen our fiscal position.[2] But we must also ensure that the fruits of economic growth are distributed equitably and fairly in the interest of fostering a middle-class society.

Table 3: Madani Economy aspirations for Malaysia by 2033 and the current status

Aspiration (by 2033)	Current status (2022 unless otherwise stated)	Overarching theme
Top 30 globally by GDP	36th (nominal GDP), 31st (GDP PPP)[3]	Sustainable economic growth (raising the ceiling)
Top 12 globally in the Global Competitiveness Index	27th (2023)	
Fiscal deficit of 3% or lower	5% (2023 estimate)[4]	
Labour share of income at 45% of GDP	32.4%	Inclusive development (raising the floor)
Female labour force participation rate at 60%	56.3% (third quarter of 2023)[5]	
Top 25 in the Human Development Index	62nd[6]	
Best 25 globally in the Corruption Perceptions Index	61st	

Source: Malaysia Madani website (unless otherwise stated).

In accordance with these priorities, the Madani Economy has seven key aspirations to be achieved in the next 10 years, covering both sustainable economic growth and inclusive development, as Table 3 illustrates.

(i) Raising the ceiling

To raise the ceiling in order to fulfil the first three targets, the Madani Economy emphasises the need for Malaysia to be less dependent on labour-intensive investments and instead try to attract more sophisticated high technology industries and knowledge-intensive services, as the next two policy documents in this section point out. The Madani Economy also talks about capitalising on the growing trend of supply chain regionalisation amid the current geopolitical chess game.

The Madani Economy conceptualises this idea through its first focus area – Malaysia as a leading Asian economy. The framework accordingly calls for a regional agenda in trade and industry through Malaysian leadership; promoting the growth of domestic direct investments (DDI) and Malaysian champions for the local and regional markets; strengthening our advantage in the Islamic economy; and internationalising local businesses among others.

Due to the prominent role of China in the global supply chain in the past 20 years, MNCs, although based in Malaysia, were also predominantly sourcing from China. Today, "diversification" and "de-risking" have become the emphasis of these MNCs with the aim of building a shorter and more secure supply chain. They are looking to build supply chains within close proximity, in shorter distance and more secured locations. As a result, we are now seeing a massive influx of investment into ASEAN, including Malaysia.

Malaysia should tap into this opportunity where our local companies form part of the regional or global supply chain of these MNCs. We should aspire to form a vertical integration of supply chains where Malaysia is positioned as an indispensable middle. The most high-end investments, such as financial services, tend to move to Singapore whereas labour-intensive and low-skill investments go to neighbouring countries with a demographic dividend. In this new scenario, Malaysia is not in a competition with our neighbours; we complement each other. This way, the whole of ASEAN prospers together.

(ii) Raising the floor

The Madani Economy's second focus area – elevating quality of life for the *rakyat* – tackles the idea of raising the floor to meet the last four of the seven aspirations. The framework focuses on empathy and the equitable distribution of the fruits of labour. By targeting an increase in the compensation of employees as a share of income, the Unity Government considers good jobs to be a crucial component of its economic policy priorities as well.

Apart from meaningful wages, the Madani Economy also aims to develop policies to promote equal opportunities for low-income households, more expansive social protection, reforms to healthcare and education, better infrastructure and public transportation as well as universal access to basic public services.

It is heartening that through the Madani Economy, there is finally widespread recognition at the level of government, both implicitly and explicitly, that we need to build a middle-class society, chiefly by paying Malaysian workers better.

New Investment Policy and National Investment Aspirations

The New Investment Policy (NIP), which was launched three days before Parliament was dissolved in October 2022, outlines what our goal is in the procurement of investments for Malaysia. It is based on the six National Investment Aspirations (NIAs), namely:

Table 4: The list of the six NIAs

NIA	Explanation
Increasing economic complexity	The country cannot become dependent only on one or two sectors. To achieve this, local R&D capabilities and greater innovation will be enhanced. Additionally, support is to be given for industries higher up the value chain to transition into more differentiated and higher value products.
Creating high-value jobs	The country needs to reduce its heavy dependence on unskilled foreign labour through productivity gains, innovation, and automation.
Extending domestic linkages	Malaysia seeks to expand and further integrate local supply chains into global value chains, further enhancing knowledge diffusion and ensuring a greater degree of economic spillover for the nation. The country cannot continue relying on FDI alone to steer its economic upgrade.
Developing new and existing industry clusters	Clusters will continue to be a key catalyst in driving Malaysia's industrialisation. The country's investment policies will take an increasingly facilitative approach in new cluster development, focused on new high-potential industries while continuing the development of existing clusters.

NIA	Explanation
Improving inclusivity	This involves taking strong and accountable public action to dismantle geographical and other barriers, and to expand opportunities for the wider population – particularly in ensuring job opportunities, access to education and affordable healthcare. Building strong foundations through human capital investments will be essential in achieving the economic productivity needed to accelerate Malaysia's transition to a high-income nation.
Enhancing ESG practices	As policymakers, we must not view ESG as a burden. Starting with such a mindset is self-defeating because it will not take us very far beyond an incremental approach. Instead, we must be bold, and we must do as much as possible to present this as an opportunity for Malaysia. We must steer the economy and our industry towards this great transition.

The NIAs serve as the new dashboard for measuring the success of FDI and DDI, which must meet the six aforementioned requirements. While the government will still need to be friendly to investors, institutional frameworks need to be adjusted accordingly, including incentives, which must be targeted rather than broad-based. From now on, the objective of attracting investment is to create good jobs and not just investment for investment's sake.

New Industrial Master Plan 2030

On September 1, 2023, Prime Minister Datuk Seri Anwar Ibrahim launched the New Industrial Master Plan 2030 (NIMP 2030).

Consolidating all industry-related initiatives via a "whole-of-government" mindset, NIMP 2030 articulates a set of comprehensive strategies to ensure synergies at both the policy and industry levels, particularly in creating supportive ecosystems to help catalyse Malaysia's industrial development into the future.

Through NIMP 2030, the government is aiming to transform the manufacturing industry to reach greater heights, so that it can be an engine of growth and innovation again as it was during Malaysia's first takeoff in the 1980s and 1990s. It is the main reference document in charting the future of Malaysia's industrial development until the year 2030.

The plan differs from its previous iterations in that it does not adopt a sectoral approach but a mission-based approach in our pursuit of industrial development. In Malaysia's past experiences with industrial policy, the old industrial master plans often treated each sector within the broad remit of industry in isolation, which had the tendency to ignore the inevitable linkages and spillovers between sectors.

The change in policy thinking did not happen overnight. When Tengku Zafrul Tengku Aziz and I took over the reins of MITI in December 2022, we were briefed on the draft of the proposed plan. Drawn up during the pandemic years, NIMP 2030 was meant to succeed the 14-year Third Industrial Master Plan, which had expired in 2020. While the initial NIMP 2030 draft acknowledged the new global economic, social and geopolitical trends of the early 2020s, my minister and I remarked that the document focused too heavily on sector-specific action plans, losing sight of the bigger picture of what industrial policy was *for*.[7]

At Tengku Zafrul's instruction, MITI began redrafting NIMP 2030 to bring forth a new direction. Through months of intensive discussions involving stakeholders from MITI, other ministries, industry players and policy thinkers, we landed on a mission-based approach. This time around, NIMP 2030 groups all its action plans (of which there are 62) within four key missions with 17 associated strategies as well as four all-encompassing enablers, namely:

Table 5: NIMP 2030's missions and associated strategies

Mission	Strategy
Mission 1: Advance economic complexity	Expand to higher value-added activities
	Develop ecosystem to support high value-added activities
	Establish 'vertical integration' for global value chains
	Foster research, development, commercialisation and innovation ecosystem
	Increase manufacturing exports
Mission 2: Tech up for a digitally vibrant nation	Accelerate technology adoption
	Shift away from low-skilled labour model
	Spur technology innovation
	Accelerate government digitalisation and integration
Mission 3: Push for net zero	Accelerate transition towards sustainable practices
	Transition to renewable and clean energy
	Catalyse new green growth areas
	Shift towards green infrastructure

Mission	Strategy
Mission 4: Safeguard economic security and inclusivity	Develop resilient supply chain
	Foster climate resilient development
	Strengthen industrial clusters for regional development
	Empower Bumiputera participation and create inclusive workforce
Key enablers	Mobilise financing ecosystem
	Foster talent development and attraction
	Establish best-in-class investor journey for ease of doing business
	Introduce whole-of-nation governance framework

As Table 5 suggests, Mission 1 aims to increase the sophistication of Malaysian-made products, particularly for the export market, by focusing on encouraging more complex, high value-added economic activities in manufacturing and related services, such as the design of integrated circuits in E&E (see pages 89-98). Mission 2 sees the country using more automation, technology, innovation and digitalisation in its industrial and related processes, such as artificial intelligence and smart manufacturing, to improve productivity (see pages 79-88). Mission 3 is aligned with the government's goal of achieving net zero carbon emissions as early as 2050, treating the green transition as an opportunity to develop new activities in renewable energy (see pages 99-115). Mission 4 is to ensure that industrialisation provides better wages and job opportunities for the people, in addition to capitalising on the growing global appetite for resilient and reliable supply chains. These missions are not mutually exclusive – all four missions are cross-cutting for various sectors – and efforts should be made to achieve them simultaneously.[8]

This new mission-based approach is important in today's age of interconnected value chains. Put simply, sectors have become increasingly integrated and dependent on one another for success. For instance, Malaysia's E&E sector produces semiconductors in large quantities, which are used in many other sectors, including automotive (in EVs), medical devices (to power imaging machines and scanners), and aerospace (in navigation and control systems). E&E and EVs in turn depend on the efficient management of the chemical sector: semiconductors are made using materials such as silicon and germanium while EV batteries require lithium, cobalt, and manganese among others. Every value chain is only as strong as its weakest link, and a mission-oriented approach allows us to see and capture these links effectively.

Through missions, we are making it clear that we know *what* we want to achieve through industrial development. In this regard, NIMP 2030 sets holistic, impact-based targets for 2030, moving away from the old adage of simply measuring how much approved investment Malaysia manages to achieve each year. The most important macroeconomic target within NIMP 2030 is to increase the median salary in the manufacturing sector from RM2,205 in 2022 to RM4,510 by 2030, in addition to growing the output and employment of manufacturing as a whole.

In addition, at the mission level, NIMP 2030 uses the NIAs as the new dashboard for measuring success, with 12 outcome-based targets across the six NIAs (see Table 6). Each target has a specific indicator, such as creating 700,000 new high-skilled jobs in manufacturing and related services; and tripling the share of gross expenditure on R&D to GDP from 1% in 2021 to 3.5% by 2030.[9]

Table 6: NIMP 2030's targets and associated indicators by corresponding NIA

NIA	Outcome-based target	Specific indicator
Increasing economic complexity	Sophisticated exports with high value added	Share of the value added of high-tech manufacturing and services to GDP
	Regional innovation hub	Gross expenditure on R&D to GDP
Creating high-value jobs	High-skilled jobs	Number of high-skilled jobs created
	Fair income	Manufacturing median salary
Extending domestic linkages	Internationally competitive SMEs	Share of export-oriented SMEs
	Deepen local supply chain integration	Domestic value added in manufacturing
Developing new and existing industry clusters	Strategic positioning of high value tech manufacturing	Global market share in high-tech manufacturing exports
	Develop new clusters in managing growth markets (eg 4IR and digital)	Global market share in green and digital exports
Improving inclusivity	Catalysing sectoral and regional development within Malaysia	Share of realised FDI and DDI to states' GDP
	High manufacturing value added participation by less developed states	Share of manufacturing value added in Kedah, Kelantan, Perlis, Sabah, Sarawak and Terengganu
Enhancing ESG practices	Derisking economy against ESG factors	Sustainalytics ESG Index
	Drive towards Net Zero aspirations	Reduction in carbon emission intensity

A Delivery Management Unit (DMU) has been set up to implement NIMP 2030. For the DMU and NIMP 2030 not to go down the same trajectory as the ETP projects of yesteryear, the following points are crucial:

First, the DMU is formed to make the whole-of-MITI and whole-of-government approaches a reality and not to replace them. Therefore, efforts have been made to ensure the active involvement of the Ministry of Economy, Ministry of Finance, the World Bank, Bank Negara, and other institutions in the economic sector in rolling out NIMP 2030. The investments into realising NIMP 2030 can come from across the government and across MITI, meaning financing for the plan is not just confined to the amount specifically allocated to the line item of NIMP 2030 in the government's annual budget.

Second, it is very important for the DMU and MITI to be clear-eyed that NIMP 2030 is almost an industrial policy with the aim of shaping and developing the next generation of industries that are aligned with the four missions. However, industrial policy is not exactly choosing individual companies as 'champions' but building the ecosystem for the rise of industry-wide upgrade more broadly.

Third, Malaysia's industrialisation has depended heavily on funding from FDI. The banking sector has somehow not paid adequate attention to manufacturing as a whole. The DMU and MITI are keenly aware that "to move the needle", using Tengku Zafrul Aziz's words, conventional government grants with a meagre amount would not change things much. We must bring together funding sources from across the board to understand manufacturing, in the hope to drive the missions at a much faster pace.

Key imperatives

A keen observer of the Malaysian economy told me that there has not been such a period since more than two decades ago that the government of the day was so intently trying to ask tough questions and set new policy priorities and directions.

An attempt to create a paradigm shift in economic thinking, these policies echo precisely what I had called for in a speech I delivered back in 2016:

> *"I call on MITI to lead the national soul searching for a new economic model that goes beyond export-oriented industrialisation, which is now based mostly on production by low-end unskilled foreign labour.*
>
> *MITI's mission is not just about trade. It is also about industry. MITI has a role to reshape the next generation of Malaysian industries which is based on skills and technology, and generate middle class to high income for the Malaysian workers.*
>
> *Instead of just focusing on the next trade deal, MITI and the Federal Government needs to re-look at Malaysia's industries and take it to the next level."*

As outlined in the Madani Economy, NIAs and NIMP 2030, we are moving towards outcome-based targets, focusing on high-quality investments to create high-value jobs. We are aiming to be more selective, strategic and impactful in attracting investment, which should imply moving away from the race to the bottom in terms of tax cuts and related incentives. In other words, any investment that comes into this country will be evaluated not just in terms of its monetary value or how much is approved, but more importantly in terms of the impact on our economy, our people and our society.

The three documents all acknowledge, whether implicitly or explicitly, that Malaysia needs to be cognisant of "three middles" when positioning itself on the regional and global stage: (i) building a middle-class society with a well-educated, better skilled and better paid workforce; (ii) occupying an indispensable middle in the global supply chain in which we complement our less and more advanced regional partners; and (iii) embracing our role as a middle power in the geopolitical scene, in which we are non-aligned in the US-China trade war in order to benefit from companies de-risking by diversifying their supply chains out of China.

How exactly do we position Malaysia in the middle and implement the new policy documents with national, regional and global developments in mind? Moving forward, the key imperatives are for the country to: (1) ensure stronger linkages and knowledge transfer between companies; (2) drive more facilitative policies for local companies to expand and internationalise; and (3) strengthen the capabilities of local companies to develop higher value products and services. Developing long-lasting, high-skilled jobs will bring significant productivity gains. This calls for a greater emphasis on R&D, innovation, capacity building, and high-quality FDI, as well as the adoption of IR4.0 technology, automation and process improvements, the focus of Part III.

This new policy direction, if it is carried out meticulously, will allow the Malaysian economy to advance over the next few years. More importantly, it should bring us closer to building a middle-class society so that we can stand proud as an advanced nation one day, hopefully sooner rather than later.

PART III

REIMAGINING INDUSTRIAL POLICY

The government's new package of plans, from the Madani Economy to NIMP 2030, provides a new sense of economic direction for a country that had pushed reformist policy making to the backburner for decades after the crash at the end of Malaysia's first takeoff. But this is just the beginning.

The proof is in the pudding: these policy documents clearly need to be implemented well and thoroughly for us to witness the next takeoff. What they have in common, however, is the recognition of the pre-eminence of industrial policy in building a better future, which this Part III endeavours to explore.

A renewed industrial policy should have many moving parts, the most evident of which is manufacturing. Chapter 6 in this Part III gets the ball rolling by explaining how Malaysia underwent premature deindustrialisation in the 2000s and 2010s, effectively spelling an end to the euphoria surrounding the first takeoff. The chapter also talks about why we should care about deindustrialisation, why manufacturing matters and how the industrial sector provides opportunities for regional cooperation that will be mutually beneficial for us and our neighbours.

Thinking beyond our borders to see a wider market for our manufactured goods and a destination for our investment is important, but we must not lose sight of the necessity of sound domestic policies tied to industry. Chapter 7 presents a solution to our perpetual problem of low wages through technology, which if done well, can create a virtuous cycle of high pay, high productivity and high innovation. The chapter proposes a carrot-and-stick approach, using the Tech Up pillar in NIMP 2030 as an incentive and imposing a levy on foreign workers as a disincentive.

After automation, the next engine of growth that I have talked about time and again is re-industrialisation. Tying in closely with NIMP 2030's first mission of advancing economic complexity, I use Chapters 8-10 to look at ways to improve value addition in three strategic sectors, namely semiconductors, EVs, and steel.

Finally, Chapter 11 offers a different way of thinking about the green transition, presenting it as an opportunity rather than a burden. The chapter explains why green is the future and what Malaysia can do to make the most of it, once again drawing from NIMP 2030, in particular its third mission of pushing for a net zero economy.

CHAPTER 6

Rethinking Manufacturing for a Second Economic Takeoff

Malaysia's manufacturing sector: What went wrong?

Malaysia's manufacturing is sometimes marked by bizarre contrasts. As previously mentioned, Malaysia is a rare case where the median wage in manufacturing is lower than the general median wage. This stands in contrast to the trend in countries as diverse as the US and India, where manufacturing workers earn a premium compared to the average salaried employee.[1]

Manufacturing also contributes to nearly a quarter of Malaysia's GDP and 16% of total employment, but its decades-old model of labour-intensive production, low value addition and over-reliance on unskilled foreign workers have limited its potential for growth and high productivity.

In its glory days in the late 1980s and 1990s, Malaysia's manufacturing sector effectively ushered in a new middle class and transformed the country from an agrarian society into a newly industrialised economy. But since the Asian Financial Crisis in 1997, the political crisis in 1998 and China's entry into the WTO in 2001, the sector has languished amid premature deindustrialisation.

Figure 6: Manufacturing, value added (% of GDP) in Malaysia, Singapore and South Korea, 1970-2022

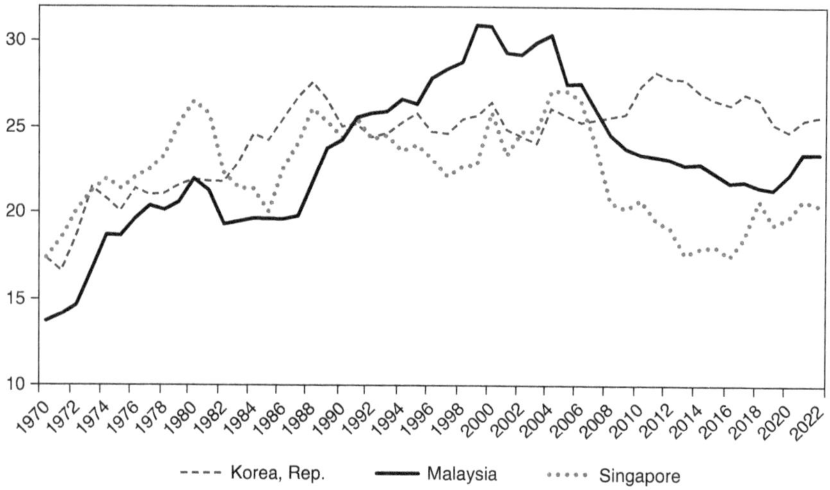

Source: World Bank (2023)

As Figure 6 suggests, Malaysia's manufacturing sector made up less than a fifth of GDP until the 1970s while the East Asian Tiger economies of Singapore and South Korea raced ahead in the path to industrialisation. Malaysia soon attempted to emulate the East Asian success stories through its own heavy industry programme in the 1980s and 1990s, which saw the contribution of manufacturing to GDP peak at just under 31% in the late 1990s. From the mid-2000s, however, the share of manufacturing shrank almost as quickly as it had previously risen, on the back of the growth of the service sector, before picking up slightly in the last few years.

While it is normal for advanced economies to deindustrialise – by replacing labour-intensive manufacturing with highly productive, capital-intensive industries, freeing up labour for high-skilled services – Malaysia appears to have experienced premature deindustrialisation.

In other words, the country's manufacturing sector declined in relative contribution to total employment and economic size without an associated increase in productivity and competitiveness, and at a lower level of economic development than its peers.[2]

This trend was particularly noticeable in the 2000s and early 2010s, with an improvement in the trajectory from 2018 onwards, but the process of re-industrialising our economy has only just started.

Why manufacturing matters

Why is premature deindustrialisation a problem? And why should we care about manufacturing so much, if at all? The McKinsey Global Institute answered these questions succinctly in a 2012 report[3]:

> *"Manufacturing industries have helped drive economic growth and rising living standards for nearly three centuries and continue to do so in developing economies. Building a manufacturing sector is still a necessary step in national development, raising incomes and providing the machinery, tools, and materials to build modern infrastructure and housing. [...] Manufacturing makes outsized contributions to trade, research and development (R&D) and productivity."*

Clearly, manufacturing matters. In the Malaysian context, for our industry to move up the value chain and be globally competitive with the ultimate goal of producing high-quality jobs and better pay for Malaysians, the government needs to lead the way in a "whole-of-society" approach to have a paradigm shift in its thinking, including moving away from the old model that no longer serves our aspirations.

Domestically, the Unity Government has begun the process of

rethinking Malaysia's industrial development policies through the Madani Economy and NIMP 2030.

In addition to more widespread technology adoption through Tech Up as Chapter 7 explains, we should focus on implementing NIMP 2030 by departing from low-cost production and moving into higher value-adding activities, such as the design of integrated circuits, wafer fabrication and downstreaming the chemical and mineral sectors among others (see pages 89-98).

Cooperation, not competition

But domestic policy is only one piece of the puzzle. We must not lose sight of where Malaysia can and should stand in the region and the world.

Herein lies the challenge for Malaysian policymakers. Should we compete with Indonesia or Vietnam, the rising star of Southeast Asia? Or should we see them as economies complementing our own?

When Prime Minister Datuk Seri Anwar Ibrahim visited Indonesia in January 2023, he was asked at a dialogue session why he was still coming to Indonesia to talk about recruiting Indonesian workers to work in Malaysia and why Malaysia was not thinking of investing in Indonesia to tap into its cheaper labour.

Malaysia will need a new mindset. For sectors which require cheaper labour, the government should assist Malaysian industries to relocate to cheaper destinations from major cities within Malaysia, and to cheaper destinations in Southeast Asia. Malaysia does not need to compete with Vietnam, Indonesia or Thailand, which all have demographic dividends. If we compete with them to be labour-intensive, at some point they will catch up and leapfrog us, just like China in the last 20 years, and we will forever be in the middle-income trap.

Malaysia should instead foster a relationship of vertical integration with these economies: Malaysian firms should invest there to tap into cheaper production costs while linking these production sites seamlessly into a single Southeast Asian supply chain. Regionally, we can help our neighbouring countries prosper together.

Rethinking Malaysia's manufacturing industry and related sectors begins at our doorstep, but it certainly does not end there. No man is an island. Accordingly, we have to position Malaysia as the indispensable middle in global and regional supply chains, and to integrate our domestic and regional approaches to industrial and trade policy in order to properly get our engine running for the next economic takeoff.

CHAPTER 7

Higher Pay, Higher Productivity and a Higher Level of Technology

To deal with economic insecurity, the Malaysian state needs to confront some old assumptions and intervene with the aim to create a virtuous cycle of higher pay, higher technological adoption and higher productivity.

A sustainable increase in wages has to be achieved through a sustainable increase in productivity. However, the economy is currently overly reliant on cheap foreign labour, the availability of which reduces incentives to invest in labour-saving technologies. Overall, this means that our labour productivity remains depressed.

According to 2021 ILO data, the productivity of Malaysia's labour force – measured by GDP per hour worked – stands at USD25.59, comparable to Bosnia and Herzegovina, Iran, and South Africa. While we are ahead of our less developed neighbours, such as Indonesia (USD12.96), Thailand (USD15.06), and Vietnam (USD10.22), we are far behind our aspirational peers, including Singapore (USD74.15), South Korea (USD41.46), and Taiwan (USD53.14).[1]

Therefore, the government needs to incentivise investment in automation in all sectors, in a staggered manner. The increase in productivity for businesses will also enable higher wages to flow to fewer but higher-skilled workers.

This will lead to a virtuous circle, where the availability of skilled labour attracts more complex (and thus, higher-margin) manufacturing and services, generating more demand and more supply for skilled workers, et cetera. For individual households, higher wages will decrease economic insecurity.

What does productivity mean?

In Microeconomics 101, students are introduced to the factors of production – inputs such as labour (workers) and capital (factories and machines) – that affect the output of a firm or an economy. More advanced courses develop this idea into production functions, which try to model and empirically test the effect of an increase in labour, capital or any other input on total output.

But intuitively, without needing to go into the calculus, the simple fact of the matter is that the more units of labour and capital we have (at least up to a certain point), the greater the output. With more hands at work and more machines, we can produce more, keeping external factors constant.

The old-fashioned way of thinking about labour as an input is in terms of the number of employees and the number of hours worked. Indeed, some businesses still expect their staff to come in early and stay in the office until the late hours of the evening under the misguided notion that longer hours would equal better outcomes.[2] Even if this were true, factors of production are finite: we cannot keep piling more workers into factories and businesses in the hope of increasing our production.

What matters more is the efficiency of production. How can one worker produce more without having to work to death? How do we work smart? The answer is to raise productivity through technology.

In simple terms, productivity is the difference between giving someone a broom to sweep the floor or upgrading to a vacuum cleaner. A vacuum cleaner cleans a larger surface area than a broom at a fraction of the effort, thereby reducing the need for more workers or more human hours. In economic terms, such an improvement in output, which is not accompanied by a measurable increase in units of labour or physical capital, is captured by 'total factor productivity' (TFP), along with other intangible factors such as economies of scale, growth in human capital or organisational improvements.[3]

What should the government do to raise wages?

Technology adoption is the way forward to reduce reliance on unskilled foreign labour and increase the productivity and competitiveness of our industry as well as Malaysia's economy-wide TFP more broadly. This also serves as an opportunity to upskill local talent, which would in turn push up wages for these skilled workers in line with building a middle-class society.

The push to raise wages has to come through a combination of carrots and sticks. In terms of carrots, the government will have to handhold the industry to automate. One could turn a task that requires 10 unskilled foreign workers into one skilled position for Malaysians at double or triple the original salary. The companies will still make huge productivity gains even after the initial technology investment.

In terms of sticks, the government should opt for measures to disincentivise the use of foreign workers by making them more expensive to hire, especially among large firms, as well as enforcing existing legislation, such as provisions on suitable lodging for foreign workers, which would make hiring them more costly overall.

(i) NIMP 2030 as the true north, with "Tech Up" as a major supporting pillar

In October 2018, the government launched Industry4WRD, the first national policy on Industrial Revolution 4.0 (IR4.0), which attempts to address the low adoption of digital technology and limited use of automation by SMEs and other manufacturing firms. As part of this policy, MITI's trademark programme to strengthen IR4.0 adoption among SMEs until late 2023 was the Industry4WRD Readiness Assessment Intervention Programme, which provided successful applicants with a grant of up to RM500,000 per firm to pursue IR4.0.[4]

When Tengku Zafrul Aziz took office as MITI Minister in December 2022, his initial comment was that this model did not move the needle for a few reasons:

- IR4.0 and automation were treated as though they were different concepts when they should both be part of an overarching effort to enhance technology adoption, automation and digitalisation, whether through IR2.5, IR3.0 or IR4.0.
- The maximum grant amount of RM500,000 per firm under the Intervention Programme was hardly enough to support the acquisition of new capital for innovation, in addition to creating a dependence on government grants as a financing option.
- SMEs had to jump through bureaucratic hurdles in order to apply for the Intervention Programme, including dealing with different government agencies. As of mid-2023, only 99 firms received the full disbursement of the grant out of over 2,000 applicants in total.

NIMP 2030 brings forth a new approach, with the cross-cutting concept of Tech Up as one of its four missions.

A shift from the hands-off approach of yesteryear, Tech Up

encompasses a set of strategies to empower SMEs to achieve greater sustainability, competitiveness, productivity and prosperity through technology upgrading as follows:[5]

- Targeting the right technology for SMEs, which must be frugal, affordable and fit for purpose at the baseline;
- Targeting suitable, scalable technology solutions for SMEs with specific needs; and
- Streamlining and simplifying SMEs' financing journey through capacity building, diversified financing options, credit assessments, and so on, in order to crowd in private sector financiers and reduce the dependence on grants.

Through Tech Up, NIMP 2030, cross-ministry collaboration and other relevant policies, the government aims to strengthen Malaysia's industrial capabilities in order to create better jobs and better pay for Malaysians in support of a vibrant middle-class society.

Ultimately, the government will have to support and provide financial incentives for firms to tech up in line with NIMP 2030, adopting automation, digitalisation and technology where possible. But to make this happen, SMEs need more financing options beyond just government grants – a successful Tech Up venture should mobilise the larger ecosystem of banks, financial institutions and the capital market to crowd in funds.

At the same time, as the government steers the nation's trajectory towards high technology and high-skilled manufacturing, the automation ecosystem needs to be streamlined with and linked to upskilling and re-skilling initiatives to ensure that workers are industry-ready.

(ii) Develop domestic workers' skills

One argument that often comes up in the debate on automation is the concern that machines and robots will destroy jobs, potentially displacing thousands of workers.

It cannot be denied that technology will create winners and losers. Greater automation will spur the need for high-skilled specialists in data analysis, machine learning and business development, as well as semi-skilled technicians to operate new machinery. But admittedly, with further mechanisation of industrial practices, there could be less demand for certain low-skilled workers, such as data entry clerks and manual factory workers.[6]

That is why skill development, such as technical and vocational education and training (TVET), should be a priority for the nation alongside Tech Up. During their studies, TVET students should be able to participate in an apprenticeship scheme in which they are linked to a company and given some form of remuneration while working. It would help if all TVET policies were streamlined and handled by just one ministry, as opposed to the current messy institutional set-up in which TVET providers are under the remit of different ministries – ranging from education and higher education to human resources, agriculture, youth and sports, health, and others – depending on their area of focus.

Jobs will have to be refashioned in the process to stay relevant and competitive. For automation to make a dent on hiring practices to push domestic wages up, it could be accompanied by a 'Malaysianisation' programme, depending on different sectors' needs.

For instance, the job of a security guard can be transformed through the introduction of CCTVs, body cameras and other technologies needed for surveillance. At the same time, the government through the police or Home Ministry can also step in to empower the workforce by introducing certain certifications and recommending a reference pay for each level of certification. If a security officer is well-versed enough to use all the technologies as well as to make proper police reports when a crime occurs, they should be paid much higher, say at RM3,500 per month to start. That way, we reduce the need to have 200,000 (and counting) mostly Nepali security guards, replacing them with fewer but better paid, better trained and more tech-savvy locals.

Additionally, with the advent of EVs, we should introduce new micro-credentials and other certifications to ensure Malaysia transitions into EVs with the highest safety standards in workmanship while creating higher paid jobs for wiremen and chargemen.

The state should provide support for workers to transition from sunset industries to new and growing sectors in demand. Upskilling and re-skilling initiatives should be expanded to ensure workers have the skills and know-how needed to work with technology. A streamlined TVET curriculum, which should be accessible to vulnerable low-skilled and unskilled workers without having to borrow to learn, could be one such avenue.

In addition, Malaysia's Employment Insurance System, which provides employment assistance to workers who have lost their jobs, may be expanded to create a safety net for employees at risk of redundancies due to automation. While they look for better jobs, it is important for such workers to have access to information on TVET training courses and qualifications as well as details on the job market in line with their profile. At the same time, employers should be able to view applicants' employment history and list of qualifications to ensure better search and matching of jobs.

(iii) Reduce the dependence on foreign workers

The government will need to set a five to a 10-year time frame in consultation with industries to sequence the reduction of foreign labour. As proposed by NIMP 2030, the multi-tiered levy system (MTLS) is one of the policy tools to not only reduce the number of unskilled foreign workers but also help the nation increase the median wage, especially in manufacturing.

Through the MTLS, the more foreign workers a firm hires, the greater the levy for each foreign worker. A schedule of five or ten years of annual steep and punitive hikes of the levy for big corporations that hire more than, say, 1,500 foreign workers should be announced at the onset. At the same time, a generous reinvestment allowance for automation should be provided. Smaller firms that hire less than 200 foreign workers should be given much smaller hikes as transition for these firms would be harder.

Imposing a multi-tiered levy is crucial in raising the cost of hiring unskilled foreign labour so as to level the playing field for Malaysian workers. Employers often cite the fact that they need to pay more for Malaysian workers who would demand more benefits, including time off while foreign workers can work non-stop, and foreign workers are so much cheaper.

Past attempts to impose such a levy failed because big corporations employing a large number of unskilled foreign workers would lobby their cause together with SMEs. SMEs tended to object to the MTLS because they often genuinely needed foreign workers due to the low-end segment they were operating in, as well as their inability to increase automation due to the lack of funding.

The current idea by the Ministry of Human Resources, as of 2023, is to base the multi-tiered levy on a "dependency ratio", i.e. the percentage of foreign workers a company hires vis-a-vis the overall number of workers. The problem with this model is that it is very hard to police or monitor.

Moving forward, there will have to be political will to implement the MTLS based on absolute numbers, placing firms into different tiers based on the number of unskilled foreign workers they hire. For instance, Tier 1 are firms that hire more than 1,500 unskilled foreign workers, Tier 2 for those who hire more than 500, and Tier 3 below 500.

The core idea is to target Tier 1 companies with a set of carrots and sticks. The "stick" is a 5-year schedule of steep annual increases in the levy. The 5-year schedule will be published and firms that hire 1,500 and above unskilled foreign workers should be made to pay a levy that increases by RM1,000 per annum over the next five years. The "carrot" is to allow for a Reinvestment Allowance for investment and other outcome-based incentives in labour-reduction automation and digitalisation tools and technologies. Tier 3 meanwhile will be required to pay a RM100 annual increase over the next 5 years. Such an arrangement will allow more time for small firms to transition and remove the political noise from these firms.

The sequence should start with manufacturing and manufacturing-related services, leaving the plantation and agriculture sectors to another time. Admittedly, it is far more difficult to automate in agriculture than in manufacturing. Finally, a biannual monitoring system should be put in place to provide guidance and ensure compliance.

Tech Up and NIMP 2030 are opportunities to create a virtuous cycle of higher pay, higher productivity and higher technology. Coupled with the proposed multi-tiered levy and not forgetting the role of continued investment in skills development, we have the chance to truly transform the scene and make Malaysia's second economic takeoff a reality.

CHAPTER 8

Thinking Strategically About Malaysia's Semiconductor Industry

One of the best-selling business books of 2022-23 is Chris Miller's *Chip War: The Fight for the World's Most Critical Technology*. It resonates so well because we are indeed in a new era which will see semiconductors as both the new oil and the new source of global conflict.

Intel founder, the late Gordon Moore, predicted in 1965 that the number of components that could be fit on each microchip would double every two years as engineers learn to fabricate ever smaller transistors. Known as "Moore's Law", semiconductors have witnessed exponential growth over the past half a century.

Today, just about everything that requires computing power would have chips fitted on it, be it a weapon, a car or a watch. Even in internal combustion engine cars, the amount of chips being used now has doubled compared to a decade ago, not to mention the chips that are fitted into EVs. And we have not really entered the artificial intelligence era yet, which will see even greater use of chips.

Amid all this, Malaysia is right at the centre of the global chipmaking supply chain.

Malaysia's semiconductor industry at a glance

The electrical and electronic products (E&E) sector comprises about 7% of Malaysia's GDP, with semiconductor devices and electronic integrated circuits (ICs) alone making up a quarter of total exports and two-thirds of E&E exports out of Malaysia, totalling RM387 billion in export value as of 2022.[1]

As the world's sixth largest semiconductor exporter, Malaysia holds 7% of global market share in the semiconductor industry and contributes to 23% of American semiconductor trade, a fact that is not widely acknowledged in the US.[2] That being said, when I visited Detroit in May 2023, I did hear it myself from US Secretary of Commerce Gina Raimando that when factories in Malaysia were shut down during the COVID-19 lockdowns, Detroit's automotive industry had to cease operating, too.

The industry came into being in the early 1970s when Intel opened an assembly plant in the northern state of Penang, where the country's first free trade zone was located. After Intel, several other MNCs, including Robert Bosch, AMD, Hewlett-Packard and Clarion, followed suit, effectively turning Penang into the E&E factory of the nation. Today, Penang and the district of Kulim in neighbouring Kedah form the backbone of Malaysia's semiconductor industry, housing over 350 MNCs and 3000 SMEs in manufacturing, including homegrown E&E manufacturers.[3]

Let me share four observations on Malaysia's semiconductor industry.

(i) Scaling higher and more complexity

Making a microchip is an extensive process with several stages along the whole value chain, starting from design and the front-end through to the back-end.

To begin with, chips are designed with several parameters in mind, such as cost and capacity, through market development, design automation software and licensed intellectual property (known as IP core).[4]

As part of the front-end, electronic circuits, complete with components such as transistors, are created on silicon discs of about 200-300 mm in diameter known as wafers. Transistors are so small such that their size is measured in nanometres, and each wafer can easily hold a trillion transistors, making this process of wafer fabrication an intricate, sophisticated activity.

After fabricating the wafers, they are packaged, cut and moulded into individual microchips – each of which consists of thousands, if not millions of transistors – for loading onto semiconductor devices. The devices also need to be tested to ensure they work properly. Assembly, packaging and testing are part and parcel of the back-end.

Completing the value chain are electronics manufacturing services (EMS). Ultimately, the aforementioned electronic components form the brain of consumer electronics and other products. EMS providers step in as contract manufacturers to assemble or manufacture electronic products, often on behalf of multinational companies as original equipment manufacturers.[5]

Malaysia welcomes more investments into both the back-end and the front-end parts of the semiconductor value chain under its industrial planning. To begin with, the country has an established presence in chip assembly, packaging and testing as well as EMS, producing 13% of global back-end semiconductor output.[6]

At the same time, the newly launched NIMP 2030 aspires to see more front-end activities, such as IC design, wafer fabrication, semiconductor machinery and equipment manufacturing. Recent announcements of investment by Intel (US$7 billion), Infineon (US$5.5 billion) and Texas Instruments (US$3 billion) show that Malaysia is well positioned to scale higher and engage in more complex activities, which is central to NIMP 2030.[7]

I would also like to acknowledge that the back-end manufacturing of semiconductors remains highly relevant as advanced packaging is increasingly a sophisticated trade, and the back-end manufacturing helps Malaysia occupy an indispensable part in the global supply chain. Local champions such as Inari, Globetronics and Carsem are notable in this area.

Some like to claim that when it comes to trade, it does not matter whether we sell potato chips or microchips, as long as our absolute GDP, inward FDI and export figures are strong.[8] That is far from the truth. As mentioned, microchips have the potential to generate far greater value addition, with a stronger multiplier effect through a boost in productivity and innovation, which is why semiconductors and the E&E sector are an important focus area in the government's plans, such as NIMP 2030 and the 12th Malaysia Plan.

(ii) Precision engineering industry is the unsung hero

The global semiconductor industry in Malaysia has also created a number of successful Malaysian companies specialising in automation, such as Greatech, Pentamaster and Walta, just to name a few.[9] Often being large local companies (LLCs) with well-established links to MNCs, these manufacturers tend to have a major stake in the precision engineering or precision tooling industry. However, because most of them produce under non-disclosure agreements (NDAs), not many people know their collective capabilities.

Unfortunately, many Malaysian companies, especially SMEs, are still dependent on unskilled foreign labour to make things by hand, and are reluctant to automate, fearing that machines from Germany or Japan are too expensive.[10] Many do not believe that we have the capability to produce automated machines or precision tools at the level of Germany or Japan.

In reality, Malaysia has manufacturers who can make sophisticated automation machines and, importantly, they form the critical and highly resilient Malaysian supply chain for the semiconductor industry.[11] To give an example, the Penang Automation Cluster – a joint venture between ViTrox, Pentamaster and Walta – designs and manufactures computer numerical controls and other high-precision tools for E&E players.[12]

The precision engineering industry deserves more attention than it currently receives.

(iii) The semiconductor industry should lead in creating good jobs for Malaysians

Admittedly, the extremely competitive semiconductor industry has been conscious of costs from its very inception, as Chris Miller explained in *Chip War*. And it was this consciousness of costs that brought the semiconductor industry first to Hong Kong in the early 1960s and subsequently to Singapore, Taiwan and Penang.

As Miller pointed out:

> *"[Hong Kong]'s 25-cent hourly wages were only a tenth of American wages but were among the highest in Asia. In the mid-1960s, Taiwanese workers made 19 cents an hour, Malaysians 15 cents, Singaporeans 11 cents, and South Koreans only a dime."*[13]

I quoted this paragraph to show that once upon a time, wages in Malaysia were higher than in Singapore.

The semiconductor industry often complains that there is not enough talent in Malaysia. Those who know me have probably heard my reply in parliament when this question was raised: "Malaysia has no talent problem, Malaysia has a pay problem".

A 2022 report by the Board of Engineers Malaysia found that over a third of recent engineering graduates had a starting salary below RM2,000 a month as of 2021 while 90% of them earned less than RM3,000 per month.[14] For a single household in Kuala Lumpur, this is scarcely enough to get by, as highlighted in a 2018 study by BNM on living wages.[15]

An unintended consequence is that students are discouraged from taking up full-time education, and by extension employment, in the science, technology, engineering and mathematics (STEM) fields. Malaysia's engineer-to-population ratio stands at 1:170 as of late-2022, below the aspirational target of 1:100.[16] Those who decide to pursue STEM often end up taking up other forms of employment, such as gig work, or choose to work in Singapore, where they can expect to make around S$2,800-3,400 (about RM9,500-11,500) per month as an entry-level engineer.[17]

While I acknowledge that we need to do more in STEM and TVET education and to prepare a more robust talent pipeline in schools and universities, the most crucial mindset shift we need now is to acknowledge that Malaysia needs to pay its skilled workers better to address long-standing issues ranging from brain drain to underemployment. As I have previously mentioned, a simple rule of thumb is that paying Malaysians two-thirds of Singapore wages would be sufficient to entice many to come back (see pages 25-30).

NIMP 2030 aspires to see the manufacturing median wage double from RM2,205 as of 2022 to RM4,510 by 2030.[18] With the aforementioned efforts to move up the value chain in front-end and back-end semiconductor activities, we can be even more ambitious and aim for engineering wages in the E&E sector to rise to RM5,000-6,000 for fresh graduates, particularly in MNCs or LLCs. I hope that with a paradigm shift, the semiconductor industry will be able to take the lead in helping Malaysians get better jobs and better pay.

(iv) Policy leadership is paramount

Until a few years ago, most governments around the world saw the semiconductor industry first and foremost as a private venture by investors.

Within the Malaysian government's structure, the semiconductor industry has been under the de facto domain of MIDA without much policy guidance from its parent ministry MITI. In effect, Malaysia has relied for the longest time on the outdated ethos of simply "welcoming investments" into semiconductor-related activities willy-nilly rather than treating MITI as the custodian of the industry with a dedicated set of strategies and incentives to strengthen the manufacturing and design capabilities of local semiconductor companies.

In the 2020s, as a result of requests from industries and due to the intense strategic competition over semiconductors and artificial intelligence, many governments are belatedly building the policy infrastructure and capabilities to coordinate policies and shape outcomes.

The CHIPS Act and the bans on export of advanced chips by the US are the most significant examples. But other countries have carried the mantle with their own packages of incentives. For example, India is investing US$30 billion to strengthen its E&E industry with a co-funding scheme in place for semiconductor fabrication, South Korea is offering up to 50% tax credits on semiconductor-related R&D while Japan is providing subsidies of up to US$3.5 billion for a semiconductor plant in Kumamoto.[19]

At home, beyond just treating the semiconductor industry as an investment, MITI and the government of Malaysia should build up stronger policy leadership in this realm. To begin with, NIMP 2030 provides some much-needed policy direction by spelling out the need for Malaysia to create global IC design champions and attract advanced wafer fabrication for the rest of the decade. But while we know *what* we want, we need to figure out *how* to make our semiconductor industry stronger and more resilient in the years to come, using the policy tools at our disposal.

One newfound avenue for more strategic thinking is government-to-government (G-to-G) dialogue. As the latest addition to our policy toolbox in recent times, G-to-G dialogue is an opportunity for Malaysia to collaborate with more advanced partner countries and learn from their experiences. In my capacity as Deputy MITI Minister, for example, I have received a policy expert on semiconductors from the Foreign Ministry of a government, whose expertise in economic security and supply chain resilience should be tapped into.[20]

Additionally, in 2022, Malaysia and the US signed a Memorandum of Cooperation on Semiconductor Supply Chain Resilience. A signal of the growing importance of bilateral semiconductor trade between Malaysia and the US, the memorandum provides "guiding principles" to strengthen collaboration, transparency and trust between the two governments.[21]

Even more recently in November 2023, the Dutch Prime Minister Mark Rutte visited Malaysia and Vietnam with 25 businesses, almost all of which were from the semiconductor and tech sectors. In his bilateral meeting with Prime Minister Anwar, it was decided that a G-to-G dialogue on semiconductors would be set up between Malaysia and the Netherlands.

While we should continue to look outward to maintain the attractiveness of our export-oriented semiconductor industry through such dialogue, we must not neglect the role of domestic policy in keeping the industry competitive.

Some areas for the government to look into include reviewing the existing ecosystem of tax incentives for FDI and DDI in order to identify more targeted benefits for the semiconductor industry, particularly in R&D. Subsidies to promote domestic manufacturing capabilities in the industry should also be considered, which must be complemented by measures to strengthen STEM education and TVET training in order to mould and retain industry-ready graduates. Further, for greater impact, it would be beneficial for MITI to undertake a mapping of the national semiconductor supply chain to identify sectoral gaps and opportunities for greater linkages among MNCs, LLCs and SMEs.

All of these measures need to be tied together by stronger collaboration among key stakeholders, preferably under the auspices of a cross-cutting Semiconductor Council, which would include MITI, its agencies, other government ministries, policy thinkers, and industry players and associations. That way, we will be able to think more strategically about the semiconductor industry, so that Malaysia can be at the forefront of the most intense, interesting and important industry of our time.

CHAPTER 9

Electric Vehicles as a Catalyst for the Next Generation of Mobility

EVs present a rare opportunity for Malaysia to pivot from internal combustion engine (ICE) cars, transition from fuel subsidies and fuel itself, and to build an industry of regional and global significance based on EVs.

Around the world, more and more countries have come up with ambitious plans to accelerate the adoption of electric and hybrid vehicles. In the region, Thailand is looking to increase the share of EVs produced within its borders to 30% by 2030 while Singapore is aiming for 100% of its vehicles to run on clean energy by 2040.[1] In the US, President Joe Biden has announced that two-thirds of new cars sold by 2032 will be all-electric.[2]

The Unity Government has begun the process of reshaping mobility in the country. In June 2023, the government established the National EV Steering Committee (NEVSC), a new cross-ministerial advisory group within the purview of the MITI-led National EV Task Force as its secretariat, which focuses on strengthening the competitiveness of Malaysia's EV industry. In October 2023, with the aim of creating a path for the exponential growth of EVs, the NEVSC updated its previously modest EV goals, increasing the target for xEV (battery, plug-in hybrid, hybrid and fuel cell EVs combined) sales as a share of total sales volume from 15% to 20% by 2030 and from 38% to 50% by 2040. The NEVSC also introduced the aforementioned 80% EV sales target by 2050 in line with the NETR's push for green mobility.

While current discussions on EVs generally focus mostly on adoption, the real prize for the nation lies in linking adoption to innovation, the future of manufacturing, climate transition, transition away from fossil fuel, or a new way of organising mobility.

Reshaping mobility for the next forty years

Minister Tengku Zafrul Aziz has indicated that MITI will review the National Automotive Policy 2020 (NAP 2020) to ensure that the policy remains relevant in the future, in line with new developments, especially regarding energy-efficient vehicles (EEV) and EVs.

All in all, the advent of EVs offers an opportunity for Malaysia to renew her trajectory for the next 40 years. We must acknowledge and harness the transformative potential brought about by EVs. With policy clarity and a dynamic, developmental approach, we can aim to do the following:

- With clear policy incentives for industries and subsidies for owners to switch to EV, a market of 1 million locally assembled and hopefully produced EV cars and 1 million EV two-wheelers could be created within five years, without significantly adding to the number of cars on the roads;
- Massive adoption by the public sector;
- A boost in EV adoption in car-sharing, public transport and commercial vehicles;
- Various aspects of the EV spectrum, including battery development, standards development and service and maintenance field, can be developed quickly.

Malaysia in the EV value chain

Adoption of EVs is only half of the story – making Malaysia a regional and global player in the EV value chain is the main prize. Malaysia should position herself in the full spectrum of the EV value chain and be a global or regional player in key segments, including:

EV batteries

Accounting for 30-40% of an EV's value, the battery is the 'heart' of an EV. Critical minerals are in turn essential to make EV batteries, making it beneficial to secure a stable supply of these minerals as EV demand soars. Research from the Minerals and Geoscience Department revealed that Malaysia contains RM1.030 trillion worth of unmined metallic minerals used in EV battery production, including nickel, manganese, copper, and aluminium.

Malaysia can develop industries along the EV battery supply chain, from mining, processing of critical minerals, production of batteries and repurposing/recycling end-of-life EV batteries. We need to view battery and EV production as a strategic sector, and develop industrial policies to support the growth of an integrated supply chain.

Component assembly

Malaysia is now uniquely positioned because an EV is both a car and an electrical appliance, powered by software and ICs. Malaysia has capabilities in both the automotive and the E&E sectors, with the semiconductor industry having a significant place in the global supply chain. In the new global landscape, Malaysia could quickly emerge as a major EV parts and components manufacturer, building linkages to the EV market through software and IC design. In fact, Malaysia's companies are already supplying parts and components to Tesla and other EV makers.

From the onset, importers should be told to move towards local assembling by say 2025, and after a period of time, say 2027, they should locally source at least 40% of contents. The aim is to assemble for the ASEAN and Asian markets. Malaysia should also take its advantage as a major transshipment hub with many shipping routes to South Asia, Central Asia, the Middle East, and Africa, to develop the export market for the EVs assembled here in Malaysia.

Other areas

Other areas with considerable growth potential include: (i) manufacturing EV 2-wheelers through subsidies for producers, conditional on a certain percentage of local sourcing; (ii) assembling and manufacturing commercial EVs and electric buses for the ASEAN market; (iii) building human capital for EV servicing and maintenance; (iv) developing national standards for EV infrastructure and battery swapping; and autonomous vehicles.

Strategies for adoption

The following are some key strategies for Malaysia to adopt EVs with an exponential growth model, and to position itself in the global EV value chain as much as possible, and as quickly as possible:

Reducing the overall cost of mobility

To repurpose the fuel subsidies, the three-pronged strategy of (i) transitioning to EVs; (ii) car-sharing and ride-sharing or incentivising people who do not own a car; (iii) massive investment into bus-based electrified public transportation, should come hand-in-hand to reduce overall cost of mobility for the vast majority of Malaysians. Reducing the total number of vehicles on the Malaysian roads should be a key objective.

Reaching cost-parity

While EVs have often been seen as being prohibitively expensive for the average consumer, EV prices are now coming down globally due to the falling price of lithium and EV batteries, and because Japanese carmakers are finally embracing EVs, thus adding a lot more competition to the global EV market. Malaysia should take this opportunity to quickly force through domestic assembling and eventual production of cheaper EVs (below RM100,000) to facilitate the transition away from fuel subsidies and fossil fuels.

Government fleet and public transportation

The government fleet must have a much quicker adoption of EVs than currently set. The current target of 50% EVs for new cars in the fleet by 2025 is too low. The government should commit to 90% EV adoption for new vehicles in its own fleet by 2025. Electric buses have also reached a point where their total cost of ownership is less than that of diesel buses in the long term.

The electrification of the government fleet, including utilities trucks, and bus-based public transport would justify the government subsidising charging facilities in semi-rural and rural areas. Such charging facilities can also be used by the public, thus eliminating range anxiety. Further, there should be incentives for e-hailing vehicles to adopt EVs, which will both reduce their emissions, fuel consumption and costs, as well as achieving promotional objectives.

Charging facilities

Often it is asked whether to have the chicken or egg first. With exponential growth, the chicken is there to lay eggs. For urban areas and highways, once businesses and banks are aware that the transition to EVs is tied to the transition away from fuel subsidies and ICE cars, they would know that charging facilities are business cases that warrant business responses.

What is needed now for charging facilities, especially those in urban areas and on the highways, is not financial assistance. Instead, government agencies as regulators, together with GLCs such as Gentari and TNB Electron as charge point operators (CPOs), should jointly develop template approval processes for rapidly rolling out charging stations so that more private sector firms may enter the business later and more quickly with less regulatory concerns.[3]

Emphasis should be placed on setting up more DC charging stations, which are faster than AC charging. The original target in the 2020's Low Carbon Mobility Blueprint of 10,000 charging stations by 2025, of which only 1,000 are DC while 9,000 are AC charging stations, is outdated. With many Malaysians living in landed property with access to AC charging at home, public spaces need more DC charging stations to catalyse an exponential growth model.[4]

Conclusion

In line with the NETR and Malaysia's new EV adoption targets, Malaysia should seize the opportunity to transform mobility for the next 40 years, to execute climate transition away from fossil fuels, as well as helping Malaysia be a global or regional player in as many parts of the EV value chain as possible.

Note: This piece was adapted, with updates and edits, from an internal memo I wrote on April 13, 2023 in my capacity as the Deputy Minister of Investment, Trade and Industry.

CHAPTER 10

The Future of Malaysia's Steel Industry

In the popular imagination, the steel industry is usually seen as old-fashioned or even a relic, certainly when compared to the high-tech glamour of semiconductors and EVs. In reality, however, steel is one of the most fundamental materials that enables the modern world, and it will remain indispensable in a green future. Any renewable energy project and EV will need steel as one of their primary inputs, all along the manufacturing supply chain.

For Malaysia, the steel sector is a strategic industry that has economic and trade significance. A key component of the construction and manufacturing sectors, the steel industry employs more than 350,000 workers with a cumulative investment of RM29 billion since 2015.[1]

All this serves to underline that the steel sector will remain a mainstay of our industrial fabric for decades. However, the polycrisis has made it difficult for the industry to chart its future. For Malaysia's steel industry to have a sustainable future, two major challenges have to be dealt with collectively by the industry and government, namely, the green transition and overcapacity in construction steel.

Overcapacity in construction steel

The overcapacity in construction steel in Southeast Asia requires all stakeholders to work together. As of 2021, the capacity of steel production in ASEAN stood at 75.3 million tonnes, with Malaysia being the third largest producer with a capacity of 16.1 million tonnes, behind Vietnam and Indonesia.[2]

Based on analysis by the South East Asia Iron and Steel Institute (SEAISI), the steel production capacity in ASEAN is expected to balloon to 147.2 million tonnes by 2026 as a result of the influx of foreign steel investments into the region, especially those from China.[3]

This can be an issue of concern as we see a slowdown in the construction sector and the subsequent reduction in demand for steel from China. The capacity of China-owned steel firms in Southeast Asia is intended for export to China.

The Chinese economy is increasingly looking like it is operating at two speeds: the construction sector is unlikely to be robust in the foreseeable future but technology, EVs and renewable energy are all doing very well.

Through determined and aggressive supply-side reform, China took out at least 150 million tonnes of steel-making capacity between 2016 and 2020, which is a commendable feat. The Malaysian Government will engage China and our ASEAN neighbours in a collaborative manner to ensure a win-win situation for all, as an attempt to address the issue of construction steel overcapacity in the region.

Moving forward, two of NIMP 2030's four missions are especially relevant to the steel industry – advancing economic complexity and the push for net zero.

In terms of the first mission, the local steel industry needs to move up the value chain by producing steel products not locally available to reduce dependency on imported steel and to ensure availability of raw material for the domestic market.

Broadly speaking, steel products can be divided into two categories: long steel and flat steel. Long steel is used in the construction sector whereas flat steel products are an intermediate raw material with downstream applications in the manufacturing of appliances, cars and furniture among others.[4]

While long products still dominate steel production in the country, MITI and its agencies have been promoting and encouraging the development of flat steel to fill the gap in the supply chain. Developing steel products would in turn support the growth and development of our local construction, automotive, E&E, machinery and equipment industries.

Green transition

The steel industry, by the nature of the business, contributes very significantly to the nation's carbon emissions.

Under the industrial processes and product uses (IPPU) sector, iron and steel industry emissions have been the fastest growing since 2014, and contribute 23% of total IPPU emissions and almost 4% of overall energy emissions in Malaysia as of 2019.[5] In other words, nearly a quarter of the emissions from manufacturing are contributed by the steel industry. Thus, it has an outsized responsibility to craft a green transition plan.

MITI and one of its agencies, the Malaysia Steel Institute (MSI), are working with the Malaysian Iron and Steel Industry Federation (MISIF) and the Malaysian Steel Association (MSA) to formulate the "Green Transition Roadmap for the Iron and Steel Industry", which will be aligned with the push for net zero under NIMP 2030.

NIMP 2030 will prepare the industry by developing a decarbonisation pathway that utilises various measures such as implementation of energy efficiency and waste management initiatives, electrification of processes, and adoption of renewable energy and technology, supported by a robust regulatory framework and programmes to facilitate access to financing for this transition.

The greening of the iron and steel industry should not be seen as a burden but an opportunity – a chance to innovate and adapt to ensure steel production aligns seamlessly with environmental stewardship. This is a win-win pursuit that provides direction to the industry's future and allows it to anchor its place in the economy.

Restructuring the industry

Lastly, to allow the steel industry to address these challenges proactively and effectively, it is also time for MISIF and MSA to consider consolidation in the sector. Scaling up and integrating various links in the value chain would make the required innovations easier and the related expenses more bearable.

In this context, Minister Tengku Zafrul Aziz has decided to establish an independent committee chaired by HSBC Malaysia CEO Datuk Omar Siddiq to look at realigning the direction of the iron and steel industry with the current policy objectives of ensuring that the industry remains relevant and sustainable.

The sooner it starts down the path of becoming greener and moving up the value chain, the quicker the Malaysian steel industry will become more dynamic domestically and competitive globally, including enhancing its appeal to ESG-sensitive markets like the EU. Far from being an industry from the past, the transformation outlined here will ensure that the steel sector secures as important a role in the green revolution as it did in the industrial revolution.

CHAPTER 11

Green Transition as a New Investment Opportunity

Batik for the climate: one small step for cloth, one giant leap for the country

As Deputy Minister of MITI, I frequently host, chair or otherwise attend meetings, courtesy calls and discussions, whether at the MITI Tower or in other government buildings. Until recently, this was not always a comfortable experience because the air-conditioning would be running on full blast.

One fine Thursday in the early weeks of my tenure, I made the mistake of wearing a short-sleeved batik shirt to work in line with a government circular designating Thursdays as batik days. I distinctly remember nearly freezing to death by the end of that day.

This is now a thing of the past thanks to a small but meaningful change by the Minister of Natural Resources and Environment Nik Nazmi Nik Ahmad on batik and building temperature.

In September 2023, Nik Nazmi announced that the temperature at government buildings would be set at 24°C. At the same time, the Chief Secretary to the Government's Circular now permits batik as daily wear for civil servants.[1]

The move sends a signal of the government's interest in promoting energy efficiency.[2] Wearing batik or a suit without a tie is no longer a mere fashion statement but a meaningful "batik4climate" action. The saving on electricity from raising temperatures to 24°C is well-documented in other countries. If rigorously implemented in Malaysia, the financial savings and the environmental benefits will be apparent.

Apart from the batik-climate action, Nik Nazmi, along with Minister of Economy Rafizi Ramli, should be commended for the work they put into the National Energy Transition Roadmap (NETR), which forms the basis of Malaysia's new energy transition journey. The green transition is often resisted by governments and businesses because it is seen as a financial burden and a cost centre. Inaction often becomes the default response.

But a mindset change is paramount. Rather than an inconvenience, the green transition should be seen as a new opportunity to build green businesses and green jobs in emerging sectors. Climate change is a cross-cutting challenge that allows us to take a fresh look at how we organise our societies while the green transition creates an ecosystem for new investments, which in turn will spur new growth for a better nation.

Complementing the NETR in this regard is NIMP 2030. Its third mission – the push for net zero – aims to decarbonise the country's industries while capitalising on new green growth areas such as renewable energy, EVs, the circular economy as well as technology and services in carbon capture, utilisation and storage (CCUS).

To achieve a net-zero carbon future for our industries, the nation must adopt comprehensive and bold policies, including green subsidies to pivot away from fossil fuels towards EVs, public transportation and renewable energy, as Chapter 13 in Part IV explains.

Financing the green transformation

As important a role as green subsidies may play, the green transition would be unattainable without a key enabler – the financing ecosystem. It goes without saying that transforming our economy and industries requires substantial financial investments to fund new technologies and innovation, and to adopt new business practices.

NIMP 2030 has identified the mobilisation of the financing ecosystem as one of its four key enablers to achieve its industrial transition goals. To this end, firms in the industrial sector should have access to financing options that will enable them to participate in ESG-sensitive supply chains (for example, through the vendor ecosystem of MNCs) and ESG-sensitive markets (for example, the European market).

At present, through BNM, the Low Carbon Transition Facility (LCTF) has been established to support small and medium enterprises in adopting sustainable and low carbon practices. SMEs in all sectors that are committed to transform their business operations towards low carbon operations and have such a plan should apply for the LCTF. The plan should include improving energy efficiency, increasing the use of sustainable material for production, and obtaining sustainability certification.

It is also encouraging to know that based on BNM's 2022 report, 50 out of 66 financial groups are already offering green products and solutions, with more than RM110 billion financing allocated for ESG until 2025.[3]

This shows that the financial market is proactively offering incentives to businesses implementing environmentally friendly supply chain management, promoting the integration of sustainability throughout the industrial ecosystem.

NIMP 2030 also looks to increase the utilisation of the capital market to cater for the different financing needs of companies across their growth cycles. Once the industry has the ability to access a wider range of capital and funding sources, it can strengthen its business practices, aligned to the goals and missions of NIMP 2030.

Industry players should also be ready to embrace the needed change, and be given adequate support. As the banks and major corporations move to focus on Scope 3 emissions, the financing of the industry will become an even larger challenge unless the industry players take proactive steps to reduce carbon emissions in all parts of the supply chain.

The future is green

According to a January 2023 report by Arup and Oxford Economics, the shift towards a net zero emissions environment by 2050 is projected to boost the global economy by US$10.3 trillion (RM48.2 trillion).[4] This growth will be driven by five major green markets, namely EV manufacturing, renewable electricity generation, clean energy equipment, renewable fuel production and green finance.

With a concerted national effort with the right set of policies, plus carrots and sticks, the country's industries may embark on the green transition at a faster pace than previously thought possible.

East Malaysia in particular is well-positioned to take the lead in this green transition. Sarawak, for instance, has quite an impressive catalogue of ideas to invest in climate change, including a strategy for the production of green hydrogen. As for Sabah, the state's energy profile is peculiarly interesting. No coal is used in the generation of electricity yet there is insufficient energy for household use, let alone industrial usage.

While some in Sabah attempted to bring coal into the mix, it is not easy as banks are now increasingly unlikely to fund coal plants. The predicament of Sabah not having sufficient electricity, even for domestic use, is thus a great opportunity for leapfrogging – to bypass coal to go into renewable energy straight away. Everyone else needs to go through the painful process of transitioning away from coal, but Sabah is ahead of the curve by default, as highlighted in the Sabah Energy Roadmap and Master Plan 2040.[5]

As the Sabah and Sarawak cases highlight, the challenge of climate change should be introduced to many old debates as a new angle so we can take a fresh look at new climate-friendly solutions, and the green transition should be articulated as new opportunities for investment.

And, on a lighter note, if this means I no longer have to worry about shivering in official meetings, that would be a nice bonus.

PART IV

RETHINKING FISCAL POLICY

Active industrial policy, the likes of which I proposed in Part III, cannot be implemented without adequate fiscal support. At the same time, for Malaysia's second takeoff to happen, the government needs to be bold in how it allocates expenditure for the betterment of the economy and society.

In Chapter 12, I emphasise that renewed calls for austerity are counterproductive and would not serve us well in building up the capabilities and infrastructure needed to realise NIMP 2030, the Madani Economy and other policies that lay the groundwork for the next takeoff. In the process, I draw parallels between Malaysia's current economic situation and the circumstances at home in 1986, where choices between austerity and growth were made. Nearly four decades ago, after a false start, we rejected austerity, and the country's first takeoff soon began. This time around, are we going to learn from history or bow under pressure from pundits who obsess over debt levels without context?

Chapter 13 revisits the green transition through the lens of government expenditure, drawing attention to the critical need for the country to pivot away from extensive and expensive fuel subsidies towards green subsidies for EVs, public transport and renewable energy. 'Subsidy' does not have to be a dirty word. Done correctly with the objective of crowding in more investment and being at the forefront of a new socio-economic agenda, repurposed subsidies can be another powerful tool in the state's development kit.

Chapter 14 concludes by focusing on one aspect of fiscal policy that comes up now and again – GST. In this chapter, I stress once and for all that GST should not come back in the near future, and will only take us further from the goal of building a middle-class society. Once again, our policy priorities should revolve around high-quality job creation and industrial development rather than reintroducing a regressive tax that would burden the already stretched population.

This Part IV thus wraps up Section I by reminding the reader of the centrality of jobs, reiterating the role of the government through fiscal policy and calling for adequate government support (as well as creating an enabling ecosystem to crowd-in private investment) to finance the new plans that have been announced.

CHAPTER 12

Pushing for Exponential Growth

With a return to economic normalcy after the tumultuous years of the COVID-19 pandemic, clamour for balancing the books and reducing the government's debts has become louder again. To do so, deficit and debt reduction advocates consistently land on the removal of all forms of subsidy and the re-introduction of the Goods and Services Tax (GST). This is despite Prime Minister Datuk Seri Anwar Ibrahim repeatedly stating that the GST would not be imposed in the near term.

Much as the debate is about more fiscal restraint, some outdated textbook ideas are being promoted, which could lead to an unnecessary self-imposed austerity that could scar our social and economic fabric.

The response of the US and EU to the Global Financial Crisis in 2008, which centred on austerity, caused permanent damage to the lives of millions and resulted in the rise of populism such as Brexit and the Trump presidency. We must avoid walking into such self-harming austerity unwittingly.

The government is not like a household: debt at a glance

First, the public purse does not run on the same logic as private households. There is a huge difference between microeconomics and macroeconomics. A crucial role of fiscal policy is to sustain aggregate demand in the event of a downturn or recession.

Private households want to avoid incurring debts they cannot repay. But for public debt, the question is not how much is owed but for what purpose. If debt is incurred and then syphoned off by despots and corrupt officials, it is criminal and a deprivation of public welfare, thus warranting the harshest condemnation and punishment.

Curb wastage and stop corruption by all means. However, if debt is incurred for productive reasons, whether to bring a depressed economy out of the doldrums or to finance much-needed infrastructure projects with a strong multiplier effect for the betterment of the people, it should be welcomed.

What matters in this case is not the absolute level of debt but the sustainability of debt, that is the ability of a government to pay the interest on its debt obligations over time without defaulting.

A true measure of debt sustainability requires sophisticated analyses and frameworks, the likes of which are undertaken by organisations like the World Bank and the International Monetary Fund (IMF). But a good proxy is the debt-to-GDP ratio.

Malaysia's Federal Government debt was RM1.08 trillion as of end-2022 according to the Finance Ministry, with total public debt including guaranteed commitments and other liabilities (such as 1Malaysia Development Bhd or 1MDB) standing at RM1.45 trillion. However, the main problem is not its size, but its relative size to the overall economic pie, measured by GDP. Currently, the Federal Government debt-to-GDP ratio is 60.4%, rising to 80.9% if we include liabilities (which may be off-budget but still require the government's support and could influence our credit rating).[1]

At this juncture, we must not forget that we can (and should) bring our debt-to-GDP ratio down by doubling down on the denominator, that is by accelerating GDP growth.

Policy sequencing should always place growing the pie as the top priority, instead of cutting deficits. When Anwar launched the Madani Economy framework, he stated the aspiration to grow at 6% per annum over the course of the next decade.

Lessons from the first economic takeoff

I would like to draw your attention to the first economic takeoff that Malaysia experienced in the late 1980s and 1990s.

In 1985, the government incurred significant debts as a result of former Prime Minister Tun Dr Mahathir Mohamad's push for heavy industry, including Proton and steel. The year also witnessed a cyclical downturn of the E&E sector and the collapse of oil and commodity prices.

Figure 7: Malaysia's GDP growth (%), 1982-2022

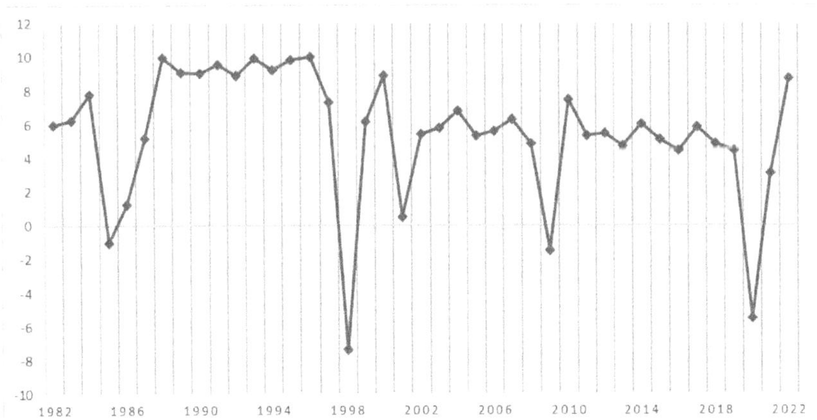

Source: World Bank (2023).

The initial response of the then Finance Minister Tun Daim Zainuddin was to impose austerity by massively and suddenly cutting government spending. The economy duly faced a recession, registering a 1% decline in GDP in 1985.

In 1986, the government switched gears. There is a reason why the Promotion of Industry Act bears the year "1986" on it. To resuscitate the economy, the government allowed for 100% foreign ownership of export-oriented manufacturing firms and established a set of incentives to promote more FDI into the economy. By 1988, the effort bore fruit: the economy took off with a spectacular annual average growth rate of 9% until the Asian Financial Crisis in 1997 (see Figure 7).

Luck had it that the appreciating yen, Korean won, New Taiwan dollar and Singapore dollar triggered a massive wave of relocation to Southeast Asian economies, especially to Malaysia. At the same time, the withdrawal of the generalised system of preferences – special tariff concessions on selected imports into the US – from Japan, South Korea, Taiwan and Singapore in 1988 helped attract capital from these countries to relocate production to Malaysia.

In 1989, as a 12-year-old boy from a struggling family, I was selling lottery tickets at a Chinese restaurant in Subang Parade, Selangor. I could see many Japanese and Korean businessmen, engineers and technicians at the restaurant every lunch hour and at dinners. They were from the industrial areas of Shah Alam and Sungai Way, and a physical embodiment of the success of the Promotion of Industry Act.

In the 2023 context, as opposed to 1986, a lot of focus should also be on domestic direct investment (DDI) and overall societal benefits. The influx of FDI into Malaysia, as a result of diversion from China, the world's factory in the previous two decades or so, is huge and unprecedented. But we must always remind ourselves that the government needs to ensure that FDI is translated into more linkages with domestic firms, as well as better jobs and better pay for Malaysians.

The growth narrative

Malaysia in 2023 has great potential for a second economic takeoff. The Unity Government has the potential to be a stable government for the long haul thus providing the basis for long-term growth.

It has been pointed out by the Prime Minister that during the heyday of the first economic takeoff between 1988 and 1997, investment as a ratio to GDP was at 40% but in the last 25 years, the ratio has hovered around 20%-25%.

Thus, growth through investment should be the primary concern for the economy. And, one cannot deny that growth would require some investment from the government too, apart from the government shaping the policy environment for investment and growth.

Industrial policy is now back in fashion with many nations ready to invest in industrial growth, more reason why austerity should not be on the policy menu.

Of course, growth should avoid exuberance, especially speculation in real estate, but should instead be led by innovation and value adding.

Over the past 25 years, especially in the last decade or so, growth has been often driven by private consumption, and quite often by debt-fuelled consumption.[2] For instance, early EPF withdrawals during the COVID-19 pandemic fuelled a short-lived consumption boost.

Any policy action would have to be cognisant of the need to sustain consumption, thus aggregate demand. Focusing on creating exponential growth whose fruits will be shared across the society will mean the government collecting more taxes from corporations and from individuals when their incomes increase. Such taxes are progressive and not regressive like the GST.

Prime Minister Anwar has chosen the right course: focus on reducing the fuel subsidy (see the next chapter) and not to pursue the re-introduction of GST now (see pages 133-138).

The Malaysian economy is at a crossroads like that of 1986. A self-inflicted and unwitting austerity drive would cause unnecessary sufferings and hold back the economy. GST is not really needed at this stage of our economic development. Just like in 1986, the nation should work hard to create exponential growth. This is the time for our second economic takeoff.

CHAPTER 13

Green New Deal: Pivoting from Fuel Subsidies to Green Subsidies

Fossil fuels are bad for the climate, and the transport sector is the single biggest consumer of energy as well as one of the largest sources of carbon emissions in this country.[1] Unfortunately, many Malaysians have no choice but to drive a car or ride a motorbike due to poor public transport (see pages 197-204). Our generous fuel subsidies, covering petrol, diesel and liquefied petroleum gas, only further compound the issue.

In 2022, due to rising oil prices precipitated by the Ukraine war, Malaysia's fuel subsidies ballooned to RM52 billion.[2] Making up 17% of the government's annual operating expenditure and 74% of the total subsidy bill, 2022's fuel subsidies even exceeded the government's allocation of operating expenditure to the ministries of health and education respectively.[3] Such is our addiction to these subsidies that Malaysia's petrol (RON95) is cheaper than oil-rich Saudi Arabia's.[4]

This is why I have been advocating for a Green New Deal: a transition from fuel subsidies to one-time green subsidies. We have a once-in-a-generation chance for the nation to implement this green transition. On the one hand, we should phase out Malaysia's substantial fuel subsidies, paying attention first to the removal of the diesel subsidy. Removing the diesel subsidy can be implemented sooner as it affects mostly commercial vehicles.

At the same time, there should also be significant one-time subsidies for the purchase of EVs, both two and four wheelers alike. Ambitious subsidies can help build up a nascent EV industry.

Meanwhile, the removal of petrol subsidies should be gradual and moderate, as it affects most ordinary Malaysians and would have more direct inflationary consequences (an increase in transport costs and by extension price levels), and paired with very rapid rollout and increase of public transport services, on top of the EV subsidy.

Here are the mechanics of and rationale for this approach, part of which has been included in Budget 2024 announced by Prime Minister Anwar on October 13, 2023.

Removing the diesel subsidy and phasing out the petrol subsidy

Budget 2024 outlines a clear path to address Malaysia's high fuel subsidies by first calling for the removal of the diesel subsidy.

As it stands, Malaysia subsidises diesel at a cost to the government of RM1.29 per litre, constituting about 40% of the total fuel subsidy bill.[5] Consumers at the pump pay RM2.15 for every litre of diesel while the average market price is RM3.44 per litre.[6]

In addition to costing the government a lot of money, the diesel subsidy has created a price gap between Malaysia's lower diesel price and that of our neighbouring countries. As a result, diesel smuggling is rampant[7] and can only be seriously dealt with through the narrowing of prices.

On the flip side, once diesel price gaps are narrowed, it could bring bounty to the Treasury in the form of more revenue from the reduction of the diesel subsidy, in addition to plugging leakages from diesel smuggling. However, admittedly, pushing diesel prices up will have inflationary consequences that have to be cushioned.

Recognising this, the Prime Minister has announced that the diesel subsidy will be removed in phases and will not affect fishermen or key segments of the logistics industry. While private and commercial vehicles not involved in logistics may be expected to pay the full market price in the foreseeable future, qualifying fishermen will continue to pay for diesel at the lowest tier subject to a quota.

That being said, care must be taken to ensure the effective enforcement of these special arrangements for fishermen and freight companies to minimise smuggling and abuse.

As diesel is mostly used by commercial users, some of the hikes would be passed on to the general consumers, but some would be absorbed by businesses, thus cushioning the impact on the general public.

If diesel affects businesses more, petrol affects almost everyone due to the heavy dependence on private cars and motorcycles. Studies have shown that in 2008, when the pump price was raised by 40% overnight, road deaths shot up as poorer car owners switched to motorcycles, and motorcyclists were far more vulnerable to accidents than those driving a car.[8]

Therefore, the government must continue to recalibrate its fuel subsidy programme with empathy, not just for the poorest of the society but also many others who are in the middle yet precariously so.[9]

The sequencing of starting with phased removal of diesel subsidies and only followed by petrol subsidies much later is the right move. A lot more effort should be made now to make the removal of petrol subsidies an opportunity to move away from fuel subsidies and fuel itself. Although there is yet any decision on petrol (RON95), I encourage all stakeholders to imagine that, at some point, as the Prime Minister signalled, the petrol price would eventually have to go up.

Instead of subsidy cuts, which will be politically and socially costly without a mitigation plan, the debate should shift from fuel subsidies to green subsidies. Imagine that Malaysia embarks on a massive green transition involving all ordinary folk through transforming mobility.

Green subsidies for EVs and public transport

Without providing a viable alternative to cushion the impact of fuel hikes, the poorer segments of the society would be the worst hit. Therefore, the cut in fuel subsidies needs to happen concurrently with the implementation of green subsidies to promote the use of EVs and public transport.

Ultimately, the stick cannot come without a carrot, and I am pleased to see that Budget 2024 will get the ball rolling on EV subsidies at the very least.

Budget 2024 introduces a one-time subsidy of RM2,400 for the purchase of new electric motorcycles under the Electric Motorcycle Usage Incentive Scheme (MARiiCas). The scheme is timely and will help increase the affordability of EV two-wheelers. The scheme targets those earning less than RM120,000 a year and could be expected to bring down the cost of purchasing the most popular urban scooters in Malaysia, such as Blueshark R1 and Ebixon TailG, by about a quarter to a third.[10]

At RM2,400 per motorcycle, assuming that one million will receive the grant over a period of five years, the scheme would cost the Treasury RM2.4 billion in total, which is a small fraction of the fuel subsidy cost. Instantly, Malaysia also creates a domestic market for one million EV bikes, which in turn would help industrial development.

Ensuring the affordability of EVs goes beyond just incentivising their sale at the point of purchase. The cost of installing EV infrastructure, such as chargers, needs to be accessible, too. In this regard, Budget 2024 calls for the extension of the income tax exemption of up to RM2,500 for expenses related to EV charging facilities, such as installation, rental or purchase.[11] A typical EV charger can cost anywhere from RM3,000 to RM7,900, so a move to bring this cost down to scale up EV adoption should be welcomed.[12]

Ideally, the scheme should be accompanied by incentives to scrap internal combustion engine (ICE) motorbikes in order to increase the penetration of EV bikes in the market.

While Budget 2024 does not allude to a similar scheme for cars and other four-wheelers, I would hope that the government introduces a similar subsidy for the purchase of EV cars in the near future. To move the needle, I would suggest a one-time subsidy in the form of a significant amount of tax relief for new locally assembled EV cars which are below RM100,000 bought within a five-year period from 2025 to 2029.

A significant amount of public funds should also be channelled to improve public transport, which may be financed through the savings from the fuel subsidy rationalisation. We need to address long-standing issues concerning first and last-mile connectivity once and for all. A massive bus-based public transport (and catamaran-based ferry services where applicable) system, electrified wherever possible, is the answer. Such a network can be rolled out across the nation very quickly if there is political will.

Besides, the government does not need to own the whole fleet of buses. The current Stage Bus Service Transformation (SBST) programme or ride-sharing Kumpool-like services and other suitable mechanisms can be enhanced with a massive injection of funds from the savings through the removal of fuel subsidies.

There must be an acceptance that public transport is not generally a profit-making endeavour, and so it deserves considerable subsidies for the sake of enhancing mobility (see Chapter 19 in Part VI).

Other green subsidies

The government may also provide substantial subsidies for households and corporations to install solar panels and battery storage to reduce their energy costs.

Once the transition away from subsidies for fuel and energy can be articulated as a one-time subsidy for a massive national green transition in a period of three or four years, it becomes a positive agenda that would be embraced by rating agencies, the financial markets and, most importantly, the public.[13]

This is a clear instance in which the state, through fiscal policy, can play a powerful role towards capitalising on the increasingly important green agenda for the betterment of society.

CHAPTER 14

Putting the GST Ghost to Its Final Rest

Any pundit that still thinks of GST as a revenue generator never learnt from history and has no understanding of the economic factors that defeated Barisan Nasional (BN) in 2018.

GST was announced to the Parliament in October 2013, after the 13th General Election in May 2013, when the then Prime Minister and Finance Minister Dato' Sri Najib Razak presented Budget 2014. GST was scheduled to be implemented on April 1, 2015 amid a drastic slump in oil and commodity prices.

Such was the economic cocktail that helped Najib's defeat in May 2018. A week after capturing Putrajaya, the then newly elected Pakatan Harapan government shelved GST, re-introducing the Sales and Service Tax (SST) on September 1 the same year. The SST regime remains in place today, though murmurs about GST's revival come up time and again.

If GST was the silver bullet for the next economic boom, there would have been boom years between 2015 and 2018 when the tax was in place. If GST was the solution to raise government revenue, it would have shown the result between 2015 and 2018, yet there was no such evidence. Instead, both government and tax revenues have generally been increasing over time, except for the pandemic-stricken years of 2020-2021 (see Figure 8).

Figure 8: Malaysia's total government revenue and tax revenue, 2012-2023 (RM billion)

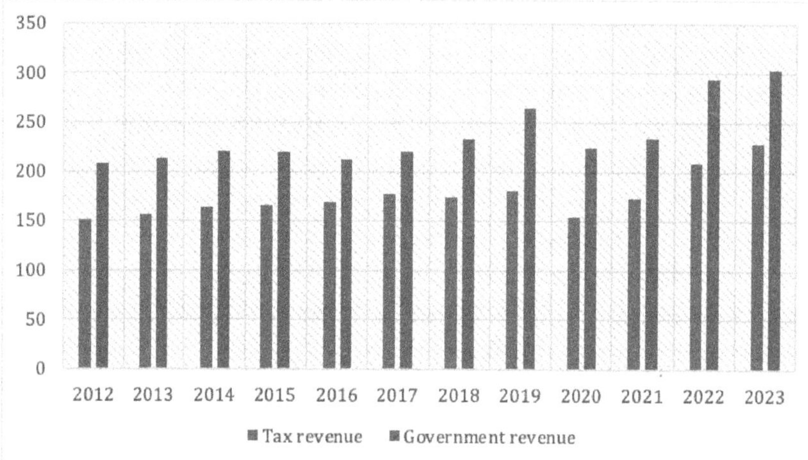

Source: Author's tabulations based on the Ministry of Finance's annual budget documents.

Those who argue that GST is good for businesses are not wrong. Businesses can claim back the input tax and only the final consumers pay for GST.[1] Unlike now, sales tax is paid by businesses.

Herein lies the trouble: what is good for businesses is not good for the final consumers, and once the final consumers are forced to pay GST, the resulting cutting of consumption is akin to the killing of the golden goose.

Wrong cure for the wrong problem

The promoters of GST have argued that Malaysia's tax base is too small and there are too few Malaysians – less than 17% – subject to individual income tax. Therefore, by implementing GST, the promoters are hoping to expand the tax base, as everyone needs to pay it whenever they consume.

But why are so few Malaysians paying income tax? Admittedly, there is some tax evasion. But the tax authorities have enough tools to deal with it. The bigger problem here is, Malaysians are simply too poor to pay income tax. Their income just does not qualify them to pay income tax.

To pay income taxes, one needs to have a gross income of around RM4,000. With median wage in 2022 at RM2,424, it means half of Malaysian workers are earning less than RM2,424, only about half of the RM4,000 threshold.

To further corroborate this, one just has to go back to the thinking behind the introduction of BR1M in 2012. Under political pressure from the then Pakatan Rakyat, Najib and his then deputy Tan Sri Muhyiddin Yassin pushed for this band-aid idea to give 60% households a bit of money once a year to help tide them over. The 1Malaysia People's Aid or BR1M is a recognition that 60% of Malaysian households are not doing well economically.

Juxtaposing these two facts – that under 17% of Malaysians pay income tax and 60% of households are deemed poor – it should be evident to everyone that GST, which taxes consumption at a flat rate, is the wrong cure for the wrong problem.

GST is a regressive tax: the poor and low- and middle-income families pay more GST as a proportion of their income than their richer counterparts.

What the Najib administration essentially did was to pay out BR1M to 60% low-income households using the right hand, and then using the left hand to collect back a larger proportion of their income from this particular group. That was the GST.

GST and similar consumption taxes in general have been proven to trigger a sharp drop in consumption after the introduction, at least temporarily. Under former Prime Minister Shinzo Abe, Japan twice attempted to raise its consumption tax. Each time the tax was raised, there was a sharp drop in consumption and therefore the raise threatened to reduce already fragile growth.

GST became a political shorthand for Najib's lack of empathy from the eyes of the voters due to a combination of economic factors: first, oil price and commodity prices slumped drastically from October 2014 for an extended period into 2016; Najib followed some ill-advised neo-liberal ideas to cut budgetary outlays in 2015 and 2016 when the economy was hard-hit by the oil slump, exacerbating the sufferings and anger; and the GST was introduced in April 2015.

What should the government do?

There is no magic formula or a quick fix. The government should restructure the economic model so that in a decade's time at least 60% of Malaysian households would earn enough to pay direct income tax.

In the meantime, I hope enough policymakers pay attention to the proposal by Tan Sri Yong Poh Kon, former President of the Federation of Malaysian Manufacturers, on reforming SST without bringing back GST. In a report published under the Malaysian Institute of Economic Research, Yong calls for the introduction of a harmonised SST (HSST), which unifies the separate sales and service taxes while ensuring appropriate exemptions from input taxes.

According to Yong's calculations, GST was collected from 480,000 companies, with an estimated net contribution of RM35bil to the Treasury after refunds (in gross terms, GST brought in RM44bil). HSST meanwhile can collect RM28bil from just 80,000 eligible companies, effectively providing 80% of what GST promised to deliver while targeting just 16% of companies who would have previously paid GST.

In other words, HSST could free 400,000 SMEs from becoming

collection points, saving these enterprises a total of RM10bil (at RM25,000 per company per annum of compliance cost) whilst only sacrificing an additional RM7bil in foregone tax revenue, making HSST far more efficient and less onerous to businesses and consumers.[2]

In the long run, there are other alternatives to GST and consumption taxes in general. For instance, we can make our income tax system even more progressive by raising the marginal tax rate for the highest earners. In 2019, the Pakatan Harapan government introduced a new maximum tax bracket, where annual earnings above RM2,000,000 would be taxed at a marginal rate of 30% from 2020 onwards, a 2% point increase compared to the maximum taxable rate in previous years.

While this was a small step towards making the wealthiest of the wealthy pay more tax, we can do more to ensure the middle class does not bear a disproportionate share of the tax burden. Currently the marginal rates on earnings above RM50,000 and RM70,000 a year are 11% and 19% respectively while it is only 28% for those making between RM600,001 and RM2,000,000.[3]

There are also many foreign investors in Malaysia getting huge tax holidays for many years, often at a disadvantage to domestic SMEs. Some of them no longer deserve those tax holidays as they are no longer "pioneers". The Finance Minister can tell these foreign firms that to continue to enjoy tax holidays, there needs to be a new "contract": that these firms invest heavily now to upgrade technologically and increase productivity, to reduce reliance on unskilled foreign workers and to create jobs for Malaysians, and to pay Malaysians better. If not, their tax holidays would be gradually wound down.

Ultimately, when corporations are making a profit while Malaysians are doing very well in their jobs, as well as when the country has a 60% middle class society that qualifies to pay income tax, it is a virtuous cycle for all Malaysians.

As I have established, the fundamental challenge facing this nation is the vicious cycle of low pay, low skill, low technology adoption and low productivity.

Lest we forget, the GST is the tax that punishes the poor, kills consumption at all levels, does not increase government revenue efficiently, and does not benefit the overall economy.

SECTION II

CHANGING THE WAY
WE MEASURE SUCCESS

For the longest time, Malaysia's unidirectional pursuit of GDP growth, high FDI figures and heavy industry for its own sake have been to the detriment of our socio-economic structure. It was assumed that this growth would trickle down and improve the general well-being of society. Instead, as we have established in Part I, the low-wage model of the 1980s and 1990s has resulted in an unequal society and a precarious middle and lower class.

At the same time, the quality of life of successive generations of Malaysians has suffered due to the very same set of policies. In the name of narrow growth, the environment was neglected and urban landscapes were developed in a haphazard fashion. The consequences of poor planning are clear and visible: from destructive floods to longer traffic jams and increasingly unaffordable housing, many Malaysians are deprived of a "good life", not just in a monetary sense but also in social terms.

It is not just government dashboards that should change but individual measures of success as well. With the help of an entrepreneurial state, we need to effect a mindset shift around home and car ownership as purported measures of success. After all, the government, in some form or another, informs and is informed by its people. And right now, the people are still motivated by the 4Cs – cash, car, condominium (or home) ownership and credit card.

To some extent, this is the outcome of decades of urban sprawl, car-centric city planning and industrial policy. The idea that everyone must own a house and a car is not self-evident or a natural part of the national DNA; it emerged as a direct response to policies from the 1970s onwards.

Not coincidentally, the 1970s and 1980s also marked the emergence of neoliberal thinking around policy making, that is the idea that "government is the problem" and that corporations should endear themselves only to shareholders.

But times have changed, with the rise of the stakeholder economy and ESG practices. And the government must follow suit. Malaysia needs to reverse the last 50 years of urban sprawling to bring people back to the inner cities, build affordable and efficient public transit everywhere in the country, and deal with deforestation with greatest urgency possible. If Section I of this book was motivated by Mazzucato's *Mission Economy*, this Section II is inspired by Jane Jacobs' classic *The Death and Life of Great American Cities*, which I urge all policymakers to read.

Malaysia's second takeoff requires building a middle-class society, and a middle-class society needs a good life. To achieve this, we must update both our state-wide and personal dashboards, effectively changing the way we measure success.

At the institutional level, we must clearly define what ESG is for the sake of not just sustainability but also equity (see pages 151-155). And as the stakeholder economy becomes the new way of doing business, we need to ensure our country's large contingent of GLCs follow suit and prioritise the pursuit of a good life (see pages 157-168), including healthcare.

We also need the whole of society to buy into, literally and figuratively, better cities (pages 175-181), better housing (pages 183-190), better transport (pages 191-204), more balanced regional growth (pages 205-210) and a stronger climate mitigation agenda (pages 211-

213). Policies should be geared towards making available affordable public transport and decent rental housing in the major cities. Remember that 80% of Malaysian citizens in formal employment earn less than RM5,500 per month. Expecting them to own a car or a house, or face calamity when illness hits, only adds to precarity.

To reduce the mental state of economic precarity is, in part, to have more assurances through sound public policy and the public provision of high-quality services. In other words, beyond just the wage problem, the way our economy organises the dynamics of urbanisation, housing, transport, and a strong care economy will have to change to make Malaysians feel more secure.

PART V

REPURPOSING THE STATE IN A STAKEHOLDER ECONOMY

In the 1970s, Milton Friedman talked about the purpose of a corporation. He argued that a corporation had only one purpose – to make profits for its shareholders. For over three decades, this was the prevailing logic in the global economic system: the world was conditioned to think that weak states with no regulation, low taxes, free movement of money, the financialisation of housing property, and cheap labour were good for capitalism.

Across the US, Western Europe, East Asia (excluding China) and Southeast Asia, upward mobility halted, more movement of capital instigated more financial instability, more outsourcing caused more loss of well-paid manufacturing jobs, and more movement of low-end labour across the globe drove wages down in most societies.

But while these conditions made some capitalists rich, it has resulted in unequal societies with a widening rich-poor gap, and it is terrible from the point of sustainability as the environment is destroyed. With its unfettered capitalism and corporate profits over the legitimate interests of other stakeholders such as workers and the climate and the environment, this world order was far from perfect, and not missed by many.

Indeed, today, after the Global Financial Crisis in 2008, and especially after the COVID-19 pandemic, the world has come to realise that corporations cannot focus solely on making money without being responsible to anyone else. These days, even business-linked advocacy groups like the World Economic Forum and the US-based Business Roundtable talk about a stakeholder economy.

The stakeholder economy redefines the role of a corporation: while companies remain responsible to their shareholders, they must also take into account the impact of their activities on their customers, their workers, and their stakeholders at large, including future generations through climate change, for example.

Chapter 15 explores this stakeholder economy through the lens of ESG, a framework that calls for greater sustainability and corporate responsibility. Given that ESG increasingly guides the operations of businesses the world over, the state should carefully define and enforce good ESG practices to ensure that firms do not resort to 'greenwashing' or false reporting.

We also need to define the national mission of Malaysian corporations. Do we only maximise profit as propagated by Milton Friedman, or should we place significantly higher emphasis on the stakeholder economy and ESG?

As Chapter 16 highlights, Malaysia's expansive ecosystem of GLCs and government-linked investment companies (GLICs) provides the perfect breeding ground to apply the principles of the stakeholder economy and ESG. As large state-owned enterprises run with commercial objectives, GLCs must fulfil the overarching goal of creating a positive socio-economic impact. The state should lead by example, mobilising resources to ensure that GLCs contribute in creating a better life for all.

It is hoped that this redefinition will encourage a generation of enlightened capitalists who will campaign for strong states, a just regulatory framework and a decent-wages-decent-work model, for capitalism to continue to survive.

CHAPTER 15

Harmonising ESG Practices

In 1929, capitalism was on the verge of collapse amid the Great Depression. It was Franklin Roosevelt's New Deal and Keynesian economic ideas that gave capitalism a new lease of life.

Eight decades later, the Global Financial Crisis of the late 2000s spelt the end of the so-called Great Moderation, with its promise of cheap credit and a property boom that would crash in 2007 and 2008. We did not learn sufficient lessons from the crisis and were not bold enough to change the neoliberal institutional framework that caused the 2008 economic meltdown.

Employment was no longer the primary economic concern, not for governments, and not even for economists. The primary concerns of treasuries and central banks became growth rates, interest rates and assessments by rating agencies.

In 2020, the COVID-19 pandemic threatened the survival of capitalism once again. This decade has since been marked by a recognition of the crucial role that governments play in boosting aggregate demand and strengthening livelihoods.

Clearly capitalism is in the process of being redefined. For the sake of the continuation of our economic and social fabric, we must ensure that what is good for capitalism is for the benefit of the many, and not merely what is good for capitalists. This is where ESG comes in.

Enhancing ESG practices

ESG is framed within the context of the stakeholder economy – that corporations are not there just to make money, but they also have to be responsible to their stakeholders. Initiatives around ESG have become a part of regulatory requirements and procedures for production, trade and investment, especially those who want to enter the EU market.

The government's latest policy documents take cognizance of the stakeholder economy, and ESG more specifically. NIMP 2030's third mission talks about the push for net zero while the overarching dashboard is enhancing ESG practices.

As policymakers, we must not view ESG as a burden. Starting with such a mindset is self-defeating because it will not take us very far beyond an incremental approach. Instead, we must be bold, and we must do as much as possible to present this as an opportunity for Malaysia. We must steer the economy and our industry towards this great transition.

The government's role is to unlock potential and lead the industry with new ideas, not to be behind the industry. Any possible avenues to help industries transition should be explored. Whether it is in terms of funding, policy, or processes, our role is to provide a framework and that possibility, to change what is not there yet. On October 2, 2023, MITI launched the National Industry ESG (i-ESG) framework for exactly this purpose.

The i-ESG framework comprises four pillars, namely standards, financing, capacity building and the market mechanism, to assist and prepare manufacturing companies for the ESG transition. The first phase of the framework (from 2024 to 2026) focuses on awareness, training and financial support for micro-enterprises and SMEs, followed by the second phase in the latter third of the decade) geared towards mainstreaming ESG practices.[1]

Once there is economy-wide adoption, there will be economies of scale. For example, we are pushing for net-zero technologies, and the more people that adopt these technologies, the cheaper they would be. We must be able to think beyond the noise. And we must be able to see beyond what is existing, and go for the highest and boldest ambition.

For the government to play this role effectively, there is a need to harmonise efforts within a single platform in order to develop Malaysian standards. Together we can lead and set standards for the region and the world.

It is not an unprecedented idea: if we look back into our history, there were two interesting developments in the 1980s through which Malaysia set standards for the world, perhaps unwittingly. The first are the halal standards,[2] and the second is Islamic financing.

Defining ESG

How do we define ESG? At first glance, people might associate ESG with sustainability or reducing carbon emissions. But ESG is more than that.

To start with, the 'E' may seem easy enough to define as it can be quantified through emissions. However, the 'E' does not just cover the transition from fossil fuels to renewable energy. Given that transport accounts for a quarter of energy-related emissions, making it the sector's second largest individual contributor, we cannot neglect the importance of looking into transport and urban planning and its relationship with climate change.

We need to relook into how we can organise our society better and how we can reduce emissions so that we can transition faster, as covered in the next chapter. If we transition on the energy side but not in transport, we will still not get there. Therefore, it is important we radically think through the 'E'.

Next, the 'G' covers good governance, anti-corruption and integrity, which are about effective execution and implementation. This is an overarching endeavour that cuts across all of government and society, informing both the 'E' and 'S' as well.

The real challenge for every one of us is defining the 'S', not only in Malaysia but also for the world. We are shifting away from the neoliberal economic structure in which employers are not prepared to pay fairly and work standards are not taken seriously. We must go beyond just thinking about labour standards and foreign workers.

Are our workers being paid well? Are they working in an appropriate environment? Is their productivity boosted by adoption of technology and automation? These are questions to be addressed when we discuss ESG principles.

The 'S' must be broadly defined with measures to carry and handhold the industry in support of a more equitable economic structure, in line with Ekonomi Madani's aspiration to increase the labour share of income.

In this context, we must not lose sight of the bigger picture, that is to create a middle-class society. It is only when we have a society where the middle is bigger than the bottom that we will have long-term societal stability. This has to be eventually captured in the ESG framework. Defining the 'S' is a test for everybody.

I hope that with such steps we will be able to move forward as a nation, into becoming much more sustainable, equitable, and greener in the way we operate our business practices. As the government, we need to acknowledge the importance of a "whole-of-society" approach in introducing and implementing an ESG framework to ensure a unison effort towards realising our collective responsibility for the environment, society and governance.

CHAPTER 16

From Land Capital to Tech Capital: Rethinking GLCs in a Time of Stakeholder Capitalism

MITI Minister Tengku Zafrul Aziz likes to say that "Malaysia has no liquidity problem; Malaysia lacks good investable projects with decent returns." GLC and GLICs can be key to resolving this problem.

GLCs are essentially Malaysia's brand of state-owned enterprises, being "companies that have a primary commercial objective and in which the Malaysian government has a direct controlling stake",[1] such as Sime Darby and Petronas. GLICs cover sovereign wealth funds and institutional investors like the Employees' Provident Fund (EPF), Khazanah Nasional Berhad and Permodalan Nasional Berhad, which support GLCs by "allocating some or all of their funds to GLC investments".[2]

For better or worse, GLCs and GLICs play a substantial role in Malaysia's economy, thanks to their significant size of capitalisation (at over RM400 billion)[3] and breadth of activities in many sectors. GLCs and GLICs have a responsibility to stakeholders, i.e. ultimately the Malaysian general public, and not just to make profit. In the context of the second takeoff, the GLCs and GLICs are uniquely positioned to graduate from land and resource-based capital to tech-based capital.

Since GLCs and GLICs[4] are such a big part of the country's ecosystem of companies, there are three fundamental questions that we need to ask ourselves as far as they are concerned:

- First, should the state get involved in the economy?
- Second, should GLCs, which are essentially agents of the Malaysian state, act as if they were private actors?
- Third, what purpose should GLCs serve in the new era of stakeholder capitalism?

First, should the state get involved in the economy?

There is one school of thought that claims that the state, as in the government, should stay out of the economy as much as possible and not interfere with the free market. From this perspective, GLCs have no role at all to play in the economy, which should be solely driven by private actors. In particular, an oft-made argument is that public investment from the government crowds out private capital.

However, from the world's recent experience, especially during the COVID-19 pandemic, it is clear that the government plays a major role in the economy. The state is the regulator, without which we would not have known which vaccine was safe. More strikingly, the government resuscitates the economy in times of crisis.

As the largest consumer of goods and services in most societies, and the insurer of last resort, the state is always called upon to rescue banks, businesses and workers. During the pandemic-induced lockdowns of 2020-22, when aggregate demand collapsed, businesses shut down, workers were furloughed and many people lost their livelihoods, even the usually fiscally conservative IMF urged states to spend more to save lives.[5]

On a more positive note, the state is often also a crucial angel investor. Without state funding, technologies like the Internet, GPS, smart voice assistants like Siri or medical research that provided the basis for the vaccines we needed would not exist. Private investors are far less likely to invest in long-term innovations and basic R&D, which have high risks of failing. Yet, when they succeed, they bring huge benefits to the public.

Therefore, all things considered, should the state get involved in the economy? The answer is yes.

Over forty years ago, Ronald Reagan famously said at his inauguration that "government is not the solution to our problems; government is the problem". Today, nations are searching for enlightened and empathetic states to deal with the grave challenges brought out by the age of polycrisis. The world is currently writing the obituary for the Reagan-Thatcher worldview.

By now, I hope we can put an end to the silly idea that the state has no role in the economy, and move on to debate the question of how the state should get involved for maximum benefit to the public.

Second, should GLCs, as agents of the Malaysian state, act as if they were private actors?

We must be very candid about the state of affairs of state-owned enterprises, statutory bodies, and GLCs in Malaysia. It is time for a major rethink.

For instance, what are the most common businesses that the GLCs are engaged in? If we leave out Petronas, it is either property development or palm oil or both, followed by banking and private healthcare. These are all established and well-developed sectors that would have no issue in attracting private capital.

That does not necessarily mean these sectors should be entirely out-of-bounds for GLCs. But a huge chance is missed when they hire cheap foreign labour to maximise profit, and then turn some of their land into private houses to be sold to the masses. The same applies to those GLCs that perpetuate a two-tier healthcare system, where we see government hospitals have 58% of specialists for over 70% of admissions, while private hospitals have 42% of specialists for 30% of admissions.[6]

Instead, GLCs should be trailblazers in developing new production processes and new business models. They should be looking for palm oil production processes that are more efficient to move up the value chain and develop new crops that can replace palm oil. They should be looking for ways to bring state-of-the-art healthcare to everyone, instead of building more private hospitals for the few. And in the process, they should always look to create good jobs for Malaysians. As agents of the state, GLCs should pursue not only a profit-maximisation objective, but also a broader objective for the public good, that aims to address our big societal challenges of today.

It is time for us to rethink and rewind. The GLCs should stop acting merely as private players trying to extract maximum profits out of sectors such as property, private healthcare, and commodities. Instead, they should also be run with social objectives in mind, minimising damage to the environment, mitigating climate change, creating good jobs for Malaysians and generally working towards a prosperous and fair society for all.

Third, what purposes should GLCs serve in the era of stakeholder capitalism?

By now, you can see that I am all for the state's involvement in the economy, but at the same time we are critical of the reality that the Malaysian GLCs today are concentrated in sectors which are bad for the climate, bad for Malaysian workers, bad for health equity, and enabling too much financialisation. There are also accusations that some GLCs practices lack integrity and are prone to be abused by politicians, which must be dealt with.

However, let us not throw out the baby with the bathwater. We must reorient the GLCs to achieve common societal goals, not call for their total demolition.

We are indeed in an interesting time, marked by the shift from shareholder to stakeholder capitalism. The survival of capitalism is now deemed to be dependent on firms paying their workers better, taking care of the climate, and providing its consumers the best quality of services and products. Perhaps more importantly even, firms now have to reckon with the collective conscience of better informed and more vigilant consumers, who will call out products produced by slave labour or by burning the forest.

The uncomfortable spotlight shone on Malaysian glove makers by international news outlets in 2021 for their use of exploited foreign labour is just a small taste of things to come. Increasingly, firms are being held to a higher standard and asked to play their part in ensuring that inequality is reduced for example, thereby reducing the risk of capitalism being disrupted, challenged and toppled.

This is of course what the ESG principles are all about – firms acting with environmental, societal, and governance responsibilities in mind, in addition to profit.

In such a context, we should examine the role and purpose of the Malaysian GLCs. If private enterprises are now being asked to think about their existential social purposes and their stakeholders' well-being, the Malaysian GLCs have no excuses to ignore their public purpose. If private firms around the world have to grapple with ESG principles, they should top the agenda for a state-owned firm, whether a GLC or a GLIC.

The purpose of the GLCs is not only, and perhaps not even primarily, to make a profit, and certainly not at the expense of ordinary Malaysians. The providers of state-owned capital should enshrine "economic security and economic dignity of Malaysians" as their existential purpose. The state should play an activist role in the economy to mobilise societal resources, particularly those of GLCs, to address the biggest challenges in our society and to create an ecosystem conducive to both public and private investment. For Malaysia to move forward, we need to take into consideration the stakeholder capitalism debate and the ESG principles when we re-assess the GLCs.

Further, a systemic challenge confronting the GLCs and GLICs is how not to be over-dependent on land and resource-based businesses and to move towards tech-based capital.

Here are some examples, although the list is far from exhaustive.

(i) Climate change

Climate should be introduced to the remit of GLCs in the fullest possible manner, particularly in terms of transitioning from fossil fuels to clean energy.

Khazanah Nasional Berhad, a GLIC, serves as an appropriate example of this stakeholder capitalism in practice. I was particularly honoured to launch their report titled "Mobilising Investments for Clean Energy in Malaysia" on September 12, 2023, as I have been trying to impress upon various stakeholders that the green transition is not necessarily a burden but an investment opportunity.

Khazanah is leading the way in providing a framework for its investment strategies; preparing the sovereign fund for the green transition in alignment with the Unity Government's recent policy documents; and mobilising capital to solve societal problems, in this case the push for net zero emissions by 2050. Given Khazanah's significance across the sphere of GLCs, the report also serves as a guide to others.

Khazanah's report explores four areas of investment, namely solar and storage; coal retirement; transmission and distribution; and carbon capture, utilisation and storage (CCUS). The report outlines CCUS as a project that fellow GLC Petronas will champion through the establishment of Malaysia's first national CCUS hub. Meanwhile, the Unity Government's NETR, which was unveiled in August 2023, explicitly identifies the decarbonisation of TNB generation plans through the co-firing of green hydrogen and ammonia in collaboration with Petronas as one of the steps forward.

But those initiatives are only one small part of the bigger picture. Building on this, Petronas should be directed to embark on a large-scale R&D programme for clean energy for Malaysia within the remit of actions to reduce carbon emissions across all segments of Petronas' value chain. A successful outcome in the transition would be beneficial both to Petronas (by diversifying from a non-renewable resource) and to the nation as a whole.

(ii) Housing and industrial parks

The GLCs and GLICs that own huge plots of land in and around Kuala Lumpur must be told not to effect more urban sprawl, but to invest in creating more housing in inner-city Kuala Lumpur. Further, they should espouse a mixed model, meaning not all houses are for sale, but many of the units should be for long-term rental for the middle class. There is also an urgent need for the GLCs and GLICs to lead the way to avoid the financialisation of industrial parks. In other words, land should not be sold for the sake of speculation; instead, industrial ecosystems and supply chains should be consciously and carefully built to last, with a focus on turning land into tech capital.

Also, GLCs and GLICs that own empty office buildings in the inner city should examine the possibility of converting these old unused office towers into rental urban housing for the youth, for example (see the following two chapters).

(iii) Plantations

My parliamentary colleague Ngeh Koo Ham has an insightful view about the future for the palm oil sector. He recalled that the transition from rubber to oil palms meant a great productivity gain, as the same plot of land would need seven persons to grow rubber, while only one is required for palm oil.

But what worked for us in the late 20th century is no longer viable. Indonesia and other oil palm planting countries have a much cheaper labour cost structure than Malaysia. Further, our soil, at least in the peninsula, may not be as fertile as that of our neighbouring countries anymore.

It is time to have a 20-year plan to gradually diversify and transition from palm oil into other crops. Having a diversified balance of cash crops and food crops would help strengthen our food security as well as smoothing out fluctuations in export earnings due to the vagaries of palm oil commodity prices.

Apart from high-yielding food supplying agriculture, Ngeh is of the view that high-value timber planting may be a way out, not least because it enables a leap in productivity similar to the shift from rubber to palm oil. With a long-term plan, planters can shift from palm oil to timber when the time for replanting is due. Our globally acclaimed furniture industry should be part of this conversation, so that a sustainable downstream industry is engineered. In line with the NIMP 2030 and NIAs, there is scope to strengthen domestic linkages across the supply chain by linking the upstream timber industry with our well-established midstream E&E cluster and downstream furniture industry in the realm of smart furniture.

Moreover, with a thriving timber-planting sector confined only to the already existing palm oil estates, the authorities can move very firmly to ban all forms of logging in natural forests. A no-deforestation rule in gazetted areas – coupled with widespread adoption among Malaysian companies of international standards such as the Programme for the Endorsement of Forest Certification (PEFC) Chain of Custody – would ensure that sustainable timber is not an oxymoron, as well as simplifying the process of exporting to the EU among others.[7]

Who should make the first move? This should be the explicit mission for GLCs that own palm oil plantations. Their mission should be to create a long-term plan of sustainable land usage to benefit the Malaysian economy, workers, industries and environment, and lead the way for the private sector in implementing it.

(iv) Healthcare

The GLCs or GLICs that own hospitals or other health-related enterprises should be directed to work on a new model for health financing that will ensure great quality of healthcare for all Malaysians, in anticipation not only of another pandemic, but more importantly to cope with our ageing society.

We have three different systems of healthcare providers at the moment: the government hospitals; the private hospitals owned by GLCs (such as KPJ Healthcare Berhad and Sime Darby Berhad) and major conglomerates; and the ubiquitous private clinics or polyclinics owned by individuals and small players. In early to mid-2021, the Ministry of Health did not properly tap into the private hospitals and clinics in the fight against COVID-19. It is no coincidence that we handled the ensuing wave of infections badly: at its peak in August 2021, we had over 20,000 new cases and 300 deaths daily. But once we mobilised public and private healthcare, particularly in our successful vaccination drive, we made it out of the woods and could safely lift our lockdown by late 2021.

COVID-19 will not be the last health crisis Malaysia will face. We need to find a way to somehow integrate all three systems into a platform that can collectively meet Malaysians' healthcare needs. As of now, I do not have a firm answer as to what that looks like. Is it an IJN (National Heart Institute) model – incorporated but prioritises public interest? Is it an insurance scheme? Or funded by public-private matching payment? The GLICs, particularly EPF and perhaps SOCSO, should be tasked to find an answer given that the health of their contributors has a bearing on the funds' future financial position.

Whatever model our healthcare system adopts, GLCs play a constructive role in complementing the public healthcare industry, investing in breakthrough medical technologies and upgrading the overall standards of healthcare in the country.

(v) *Banking*

As for any other GLC, state-owned banks should not be governed just for profit, especially if that were to contribute to a credit bubble and resulting property glut. Obviously, banks should not serve anyone's personal interest, thus any politician or board member who wants to misuse the banks' loans for personal favours must be prosecuted aggressively.

More widely, state-owned banks must apply ESG principles in their lending and investment decisions. Malaysia is no stranger to such constraints through its leading position in Islamic banking, stipulating which industries to avoid and even the structure of financial instruments. In future, banks should make it a badge of honour to avoid any loans that would cause pristine forests to be felled or the environment to be polluted by a toxic industry.

It is also my hope that the banking sector finally gets to understand the manufacturing sector again. There has been a long-term neglect of the manufacturing sector since the Asian Financial Crisis. The manufacturing sector has largely depended on foreign investments or production that was "subsidised" by the availability of cheap unskilled foreign labour. It is time the sector became the main concern of the banks again.

As mentioned, if the banks decide not to act, their depositors, investors and the general public will be more conscious about these issues in the years to come. Banks should recognise this and act accordingly now.

Conclusion

To sum up, I find the current Malaysian debate about GLCs a bit stale. It remains stuck on whether the state should intervene in the economy or not. One side argues the state should get out of the economy. The other side defends the GLCs either as Malay champions or as efficiently-run private entities providing much-needed revenue to the state. Both arguments miss the point.

With the Global Financial Crisis and the COVID-19 pandemic, the debate over the state's involvement in the economy is closed, and the answer is a resounding yes. The debate now is over what shape that involvement takes. We deserve a smart state. We deserve an enlightened and empathetic state, just as we reject a corrupt state, a heartless state, and an incompetent state. The point now is to get down to discussing what the state should do to create the conditions for land and resource-based capital to turn into tech capital, and for stakeholder capitalism to thrive. Malaysians need to feel economically secure, living their lives with dignity, in prosperity and in an empowering, self-confident, dynamic society.

PART VI

RE-ENVISIONING A GOOD LIFE FOR ALL

In a middle-class society, a dignified life entails more than just stable, gainful employment. Malaysia's success as a nation also rests on its ability to offer ordinary Malaysians a decent standard of living with sustainable and comfortable living conditions.

To a large extent, this requires us to have a new vision for our urbanity. According to the 2020 census, three quarters of the population – that is, over 24 million people – now live in cities and towns.[1] As a comparison, only 33.5%, 42% and 49% of Malaysians lived in urban areas in 1970, 1980 and 1990 respectively.[2] Urbanity has become a defining feature of Malaysian life, and so the second takeoff necessitates a model of urbanisation that is efficient, accessible, equitable and resilient.

Our cities are currently not space-efficient, and on that front, we can be much better organised. As Chapter 17 articulates, we suffer badly from urban sprawl due to policy decisions made in the 1960s and 1970s, and we need to re-examine our ideas about zoning. We are accustomed to compartmentalising human activities into agriculture, commerce, industry and housing, which has given rise to long commute times and mobility issues central to life in the Klang Valley and other urban areas today.

Chapter 18 zeroes in on Malaysia's housing situation, in particular the financialisation of the sector. Owning a home has become a big part of the 'Malaysian dream', a barometer of success for middle-class Malaysia, which is symptomatic of our love affair with landed suburban properties and cars. The consequence is that ordinary Malaysians have become increasingly indebted, with a large chunk of their monthly earnings going towards servicing housing and car loans.

Whether knowingly or unknowingly, we have adopted the US-led model of suburbanisation, in effect becoming American before becoming rich. We need to challenge the notion that everyone should own a house by pushing for affordable public and private housing in the inner cities for young people to rent. We must reimagine public space as a whole, if we are to live in it, work in it, and play in it comfortably and confidently.

Another obsession that we need to drop is the conviction that car-ownership is a measure of national progress, and of personal success. As Chapters 19 and 20 highlight, Malaysia's urban planning is decidedly car-centric, creating a skewed transportation system dominated by single-driver cars. Our cities are peppered with a tangled mess of highways, slip roads and cloverleaf interchanges. Congestion is a mainstay of urban life.

Public transport, which will help us resolve our mobility issues, is improving, but the debate remains focused on trains and metros. We need to change the perception that driving is a necessity by building up a bus-based multimodal public transport system. This is because buses are cheaper from the point of view of the government and the individual, as well as being more adaptable in plying routes close to residential areas that cannot be suitably served by rapid transit. An advanced nation is one where the rich and the middle class take public transport, and that is what we should aim for as part of our second takeoff.

Being home to a fifth of the country's population, the Klang Valley naturally dominates discussions of urbanisation. But we must not lose sight of the potential of other metropolitan areas to catalyse the next takeoff in their own way, chiefly the Greater Johor Bahru region in the south of the peninsula. Chapter 21 talks about why Johor Bahru's proximity to Singapore is a tremendous opportunity for meaningful job creation, mutually beneficial economic cooperation and more balanced regional development.

Finally, in Chapter 22, the spotlight shifts to climate change. While flooding is not a new phenomenon in Malaysia, it is becoming increasingly disruptive and damaging, particularly in our cities. Urban areas are also likely to be more vulnerable to future climate disasters, such as sea level rises. We need to reverse decades of indiscriminate construction and haphazard urban planning in order to create climate-friendly cities for the sake of our lives and livelihoods.

It is only once we have these crucial ingredients for satisfactory urban living, on top of a middle-class society with fair wages and a more equitable income distribution, that we can truly take to the skies and call ourselves a fully developed nation.

CHAPTER 17

Bringing Malaysians Back to the Cities

It has been said that "the 19th century was a century of empires; the 20th century was a century of nation states. The 21st century will be a century of cities."[1] Economic growth is increasingly driven less by capital and more by the density and availability of talent. Cities that possess the right physical, cultural, economic and social conditions will become a magnet for talent.

With the right set of policies, the city can provide many with opportunities for upward mobility and be a great level playing field for all to thrive, which rural and agricultural areas may not be able to do. Without such policies, cities can exaggerate the gap between the haves and have-nots, and make it worse, especially when the societies are organised to benefit the top few at the expense of the rest.

Are our cities ready to capitalise on the promising conditions for Malaysia's second takeoff? Probably not. Accordingly, there is a need to re-examine our urban development model – to rethink cities and housing – as Malaysia embarks on the mission to build a middle-class society.

There are three major symptoms underlying our current disjointed approach to the development of cities and housing as described below. The common thread is the "garden city" idea of separating where we live and where we work. The rest of the article explains why this is a problem and how we should bring Malaysians back into the cities for the sake of our future.

The garden city idea

The first problem is the garden city movement, which started with British urban planner Ebenezer Howard in 1898. It was essentially a response to the poor condition of industrial cities in 19th century England, such as those portrayed in the writings of Charles Dickens, Karl Marx and Friedrich Engels. They wrote about cities of contrast, of messiness, of crowdedness and of many other problems.

In the UK, cities were always treated with ambivalence and doubt. Therefore, the idea of a garden city was an attempt to maintain the benefits of the cities while enjoying the perks of the countryside, which were thought to be more noble and virtuous.

What we did not realise is that the garden city idea degenerated into a situation in which the city centre became the place of work while the townships around it became "dormitory cities" or "commuter towns". Such a garden city essentially separated us from where we work to where we stay and play.

Without realising it, we have entrenched the idea of zoning and treat it as a norm, to the extent that we have forgotten that these are just man-made ideas for us to challenge, and to change for the better.

Who says industrial zones have to have industrial parks only, and without residential areas? Who says business centres mean people cannot live in their vicinity?

In the case of Malaysia, particularly Kuala Lumpur, this idea that cities are congested and therefore there is a need to build satellite cities started with Petaling Jaya. Petaling Jaya was born in 1952 because Kuala Lumpur was thought to be congested with traffic and people. That was how the garden city movement influenced our thinking.

That was taken to a different level in the 1970s. My father was from the cemetery area in Kuala Lumpur behind Jalan Dewan Bahasa while my mother grew up in the squatter area where Sun Complex now stands. After they were married, they moved to Subang Jaya, which at that time was an area for the less affluent. I was just a month old.

This developer-, architect-, planner-planned city model of Subang Jaya turned out to be extremely successful. The idea of having cities entirely planned by private enterprises and not by the government was extended to many other places because of a major incident that happened in 1981.

That year, Tun Dr Mahathir Mohamad became the prime minister. Two months after that, with the petrodollars earned since the 1973 oil crisis as well as the establishment of Petroliam Nasional Bhd in 1974, the government launched a surprise major international takeover via the London Stock Exchange known as the Dawn Raid. The Malaysian Government "nationalised" Guthrie and other British plantation interests in the country.

To maximise profits in the shortest time span, these government-linked companies turned the plantation estates into housing estates. The Guthrie corridor, UEP and USJ are legacies from those years.

Urban sprawl

My second point is about sprawling and how Malaysians have inadvertently become Americans before we even get rich. We now see the hollowing-out of the Kuala Lumpur inner city. That means the city has become a "doughnut city" where the centre is hollow. We have the best public transport system in the country in the heart of Kuala Lumpur, but few people live in the city's inner core.

Sprawling has exacerbated our dependence on cars to get around, and so we have to start thinking about revamping our cities to complement ongoing measures to reduce our fuel subsidies.

There is also an added element to sprawling in this country. Due to arrangements dating back to the formulation of the Federal Constitution, the state governments have limited revenue from land and natural resources while the Federal Government collects income taxes.

As a result, states have few incentives to promote economic development apart from that related to natural resources and land, meaning that state governments have to sell logging, development or reclamation rights for extra income, contributing further to sprawl. Clearly, we need to rethink the federal-state fiscal relationship, as Chapter 23 in Section III explains.

Financialisation of housing

The third point is the financialisation of housing. I meet many people who tell me that buying a house or owning a house is our tradition, a part of Asian culture. The problem is, it is not true.

As I mentioned earlier, my father used to live next to a graveyard. His family owned a wooden house but not the land. It was the same with other squatters in Kuala Lumpur. When my father was in his early adulthood, he stayed in one of the rooms above a shop-lot in the Petaling Street area in Kuala Lumpur.

The way we understand housing and housing financing is quite recent, not more than 60 years old. Mass ownership of housing by ordinary people is also a very recent phenomenon.

Even in the UK, it was only during the administration of Margaret Thatcher in the 1980s that we saw widespread house ownership for ordinary people. After witnessing nearly five decades of financialisation of housing, we got used to thinking that every piece of housing has to be owned even if you are in the poorest strata of society.

We will have to think about how to move away from or at least rethink financialisation, which I explore in more detail in the next chapter.

Industrial parks

In my position as Deputy MITI Minister, I am worried about the potential excess construction of industrial parks. We are now seeing a massive increase of manufacturing investment into this country because of the US-China conflict.

At the same time, the massive glut in the housing market that we have seen in the past few years means developers are switching to building industrial parks instead. Uncontrolled development of industrial parks will eventually lead to their being excessive and underutilised.

I would like to use the shopping mall analogy on industrial parks. Twenty-five years ago, shop-lots in shopping malls were sold to individual owners, and the mall had no say over the type of business being run. Nowadays, all the successful malls no longer sell the lots to individual owners but instead to a real estate investment trust (REIT), which would eventually lease them to individual tenants, and the tenants have to bring together a coherent shopping mall.

Likewise, industrial parks have to be thought through in this way, where we will have to think of a new way of financing industrial parks and build clusters among them.

I am also challenging the idea that the industrial park can only be an industrial park, and people do not live in these places. I go back to the idea of a garden city, and to ask a question. Of course, these questions are somehow challenging and there are some in-between solutions.

Today, many industrial park developers are building foreign worker housing or centralised labour quarters (CLQ) inside industrial parks. But does our economy need more foreign workers? Or do we need more young Malaysian engineers and provide them with housing near the industrial park where they work, so that they do not have to travel for hours to get to work? Providing housing for Malaysian engineers and technicians would also help reduce the outflow of Malaysians seeking work in Singapore due to the wage gap between Malaysia and Singapore.

Envisaging a new future

These are the issues we have to deal with in the next five, if not 30 years. We will have to start envisaging more expensive fuel prices and how we are going to adapt, and see it as an opportunity for a green transition.

We will have to start thinking about building houses for people to come back to the inner city of Kuala Lumpur, and not necessarily having to own them. They can rent and we can retrofit some of the old buildings in KL inner city. We can build some rental housing without car parks, so that no one needs to drive because they can take public transport.[2]

These are the ideas that we will have to come together to think about, to envisage a new future for Kuala Lumpur, for the Malaysian industry and the Malaysian economy.

As I have previously mentioned, global conditions are favourable for Malaysia's second economic takeoff. But just as an airplane needs to overcome drag to ensure a successful lift-off, Malaysia needs to rethink its entire model of urbanisation, housing, transport and the built environment to take advantage of the opportunity for its second takeoff. This is something we should ponder upon.

CHAPTER 18

Thinking Beyond the Current Housing Financialisation Model

Housing is the most important expenditure of the average Malaysian household, making up nearly a quarter of mean monthly household spending at RM1,193 in 2022.[1] Especially in cities, where most of the population now lives and property happens to be more expensive, efforts need to be made to offer quality affordable housing to everyone who needs it.

The first step is to dispel the myth that everyone feels like owning a house and that owning a house is in our DNA. This is not true: owning a private house in its current form, especially landed property in a suburb, is only a new idea in Malaysia. It has been in our collective consciousness for not more than 60 years. To show this, we just need to think back a generation or two.

A brief history of housing

During his twenties in the 1960s, my father shared a room with five or six other young men in one of the shophouses on Petaling Street. Each of those shophouses consisted of dozens of rooms partitioned by walls made of thin wood planks.

Back then, most Malaysians lived in rural houses. Those in urban areas, much like my dad, lived on the upper floors of shophouses, which they did not own, and worked downstairs. I joke that such living has almost zero carbon footprint.

Before World War II, as automobiles were scarce, even Pudu was considered too far away from the core inner city, which is why its Chinese name (半山芭 or Bànshān bā) means "half jungle".

Suburbanisation soon followed, beginning with the development of Petaling Jaya as a satellite town to Kuala Lumpur in 1952. The thinking then was that living in the suburbs was superior to living in the inner cities, as cities were congested, filthy and beyond repair, so whoever could afford a car should just move out.[2] The rarely questioned policy imperative became to "spread" the population to the suburbs, so as not to "choke" the centres.

Across the Klang Valley, developers turned rubber and palm oil estates into housing estates. In the 1970s, my own hometown of Subang Jaya was developed this way. Subang Jaya was then the largest housing scheme developed by a single property developer. In the years that followed, the authorities essentially outsourced and conceded their entire town planning and oversight role to private developers while passive government authorities took a step back.

The perceived success of Subang Jaya as a model for property development prompted forays into even bigger township developments by mining and plantation interests that owned large tracts of adjacent land, such as Sime's USJ, IOI in Puchong, Sunway, and the Guthrie corridor in the 1980s.

Compounded by the Dawn Raid in 1981, the pace of turning plantation estates into housing estates hastened. The appointed managers of these plantation companies could make huge windfalls for their organisations just by conversion of land use. Around the same time, the massive growth of export-oriented industrialisation brought in huge investments and growth, which in turn resulted in a huge influx of rural-urban migration, giving rise to further need for housing.

The 1980s also saw the development of Proton, Malaysia's first national car, which further entrenched Malaysia as a society highly dependent on private vehicles for mobility. Since then, a vicious cycle has persisted: the more our cities sprawled out, the more we relied on private cars, and the further we spread the cities, the more we needed to build highways.[3]

Housing financialisation: current problems

It is time for us to unwind, change and repair the 50-year history of housing in Malaysia. The Malaysian economy is stuck with housing financialisation, urban sprawl and a private car culture, of which there are four major symptoms as highlighted below.

First, among Malaysian banks, as of August 2023, nearly 40% of their loan portfolios are related to properties and car loans, as they are deemed "low risk" until a bubble bursts.[4] Both are non-productive and, in many ways, a distraction from the bank's role in boosting economic growth in productive sectors, such as giving loans to new and emerging industries.

Second, Malaysian GLCs and GLICs are heavily involved in the property market, both directly (operationally) and as shareholders of major property developer companies. The construction sector is heavily dependent on private developers for projects.

GLCs and GLICs have become prime movers that contribute to further urban sprawl via the "plantation estate to housing estate" model. Developers, including those owned by GLCs, have been too focused on developing faraway suburbs. They should instead set themselves as the leaders supporting the return of Malaysians to sustainable housing in inner cities, including supporting a rental housing model for the M60 group (the middle 60%, or those outside the top 20% and bottom 20% of the income distribution).

Third, Malaysia's property market has not been too good for an extended period of time. This is the result of the massive residential property construction spree between 2012 and 2014, which was fuelled by cheap and very easy credit, and the effect of the COVID-19 disruption. To some extent, we are still dealing with the aftermath of the earlier building spree, though the challenges have evolved in unexpected ways due to global macroeconomic trends.

For one, the GLICs are stuck with huge investments into tolled highways that are difficult to extricate – one just has to drive on the NPE, NKVE, or KESAS highways to see my point. Second, from cheap credit in the mid-2010s, we are now in a high interest rate environment, which does not bode well for construction costs.

Where consumers are concerned, the result is escalating housing prices beyond the means of the median Malaysian household and at the same time, ironically, a massive property glut. At its core, there is a huge (and growing) mismatch between house prices and income affordability. According to BNM's estimation, house prices were 4.7 times the median household's annual income in 2020, making housing 'seriously unaffordable'. To make matters worse, from 2014 to 2020, average house prices rose by 4.1% annually, nearly double the associated increase in household income across the same period.[5]

The geographical mismatch caused by the financialisation model is another problem: those who work in the inner city often cannot afford to stay in the inner city and have to spend hours behind the wheel each day to commute. Meanwhile, those who can afford to own units there are often not staying in them. They are often not even interested in renting it out. Our rental market is not properly protected and not properly regulated for that to be attractive. Often, those units are bought for investment, or to be more precise, for speculative purposes.

As things stand, there is really no point in encouraging and pushing people to buy houses. Our homeownership rate, at 72.5%, is higher than that of developed countries such as the United States (66.5%), United Kingdom (67.4%) and Australia (68.1%) as of 2010.[6]

Finally, the property sector relies to a considerable extent on domestic private investment, such as families purchasing one or two investment units. Should the property bubble burst due to overleveraged households, it would not only have a direct impact on GLCs and GLICs, but it would also introduce significant extra risk to the entire banking and financial system, which would stress the economy further.

The economy will have to either pay Malaysians a lot more very quickly or we will have to find new ways to dispense with the houses that are already built.[7]

The past 50 years of Malaysia's housing financialisation also coincides with the financialisation of housing in the Anglo-Saxon world. Even *The Economist*, which usually champions deregulation and the free market, talked about housing financialisation as a "horrible blunder", calling home ownership "the west's biggest economic policy mistake" in a January 2020 cover story.[8]

Remedying the problems

It is about time that Malaysia's policymakers challenged their outdated intuitions around urban sprawl, which can often be the enemy of progress. Counter-intuitive thinking is sorely needed here: the more people living in cities, the better it is, and not the other way round; the denser a city (as long as it is well-managed), the more efficient it is economically and the more sustainable it is environmentally.

Instead of building privately-owned new housing stocks in faraway suburbs which are bound to face overhang, GLC-owned developers such as Sime Darby should lead in constructing and developing rental housing in inner cities. In Sime Darby's case, its landbank outside Kuala Lumpur, which is currently still dominated by plantations, can be the catalyst for high-yield and technologically intensive agriculture as opposed to yet more housing developments.

Within Kuala Lumpur, there is currently plenty of vacant office space, which is estimated to make up a third of the city's total office space, particularly after the completion of the Merdeka 118 skyscraper and Tun Razak Exchange, along with the reduced appetite for large offices amid the post-pandemic normalisation of hybrid and remote work.[9] Rather than letting hundreds of thousands of lettable square feet go to waste, the possibility of repurposing at least some of this space for residential use should be explored.[10]

A shift from owning property to renting for the M60 group should be engineered. This would involve building rental housing with superior amenities in central locations for the M60 group to walk, cycle or commute a short distance by public transport to work instead of undertaking a long and stressful car commute. For one, this would minimise or eliminate the need to build car parks, which would save at least 30% of costs.[11] Further, it would make our cities more liveable in the process, and in fact change the face of Malaysian capitalism.

Rental housing for M60 urban workers can be financed in many ways. Well-managed inner-city rental housing for the M60 group can be financed through a rental REIT, as long as there is sufficient yield for the investing parties.

Figure 9: 118-TRX-Bandar Malaysia: Kuala Lumpur's new golden triangle?

Source: Google Earth (2023).

The future of Kuala Lumpur lies in whether the three-square kilometre area with Merdeka 118, Tun Razak Exchange and Bandar Malaysia at each corner can develop a new lifestyle based on rental housing (see Figure 9), paving the way for the entire inner city to be home to middle-class people who take short train rides and enjoy extensive coverage of a bus-based multimodal transport system.

Outside of Kuala Lumpur, the housing model is no different. Across the country, renting is not fashionable yet, but it is a way out of the contradiction of our time. Therefore, we need to look into how to protect those who rent out and those who rent. One recently established body that has the potential to do this is the Johor Housing Development Corporation (PKPJ). In my capacity as a Johor assemblyperson, I proposed to the Johor State Assembly in June 2022 that PKPJ work on creating laws and rules to protect both owners and tenants to facilitate renting. By providing rental income for owners, renting may also help prevent a fire sale in case the hike of interest rates becomes too high for owners to continue paying instalments.

All in all, efforts need to be made to offer quality affordable housing to everyone who needs it. For our economy to leapfrog, rethinking housing financialisation, urban sprawl and the private car culture has to be an important and integral part of the effort.

CHAPTER 19

A New Paradigm Is Needed in Public Transportation

For cities to function, transport is the key underpinning factor. Efficient public transport is the key to well-run cities, and affordable and accessible options for mobility should be the policy objective of any good government.

At the end of the day, no amount of road construction can cater for the increasing number of cars and population; petrol is a finite resource, and cutting carbon emissions by reducing its use is a shared responsibility of all to help ease climate change.

Sadly, Malaysia is a case of not getting transport right and hence the nation suffers collectively, both economically and in terms of quality of life.

Moving people or moving cars?

Malaysia has more private vehicles per capita than far richer economies, such as Australia, Canada, the EU and the US.[1]

In 2004, the total number of registered vehicles in Malaysia of all categories was 13.7 million, with a population of around 25 million. As of 2021, there were 33.6 million registered vehicles in Malaysia, exceeding our population.[2] The same year, Malaysia's vehicle ownership

Figure 10: Total number of vehicles sold (TIV) in Malaysia, 2018-2022

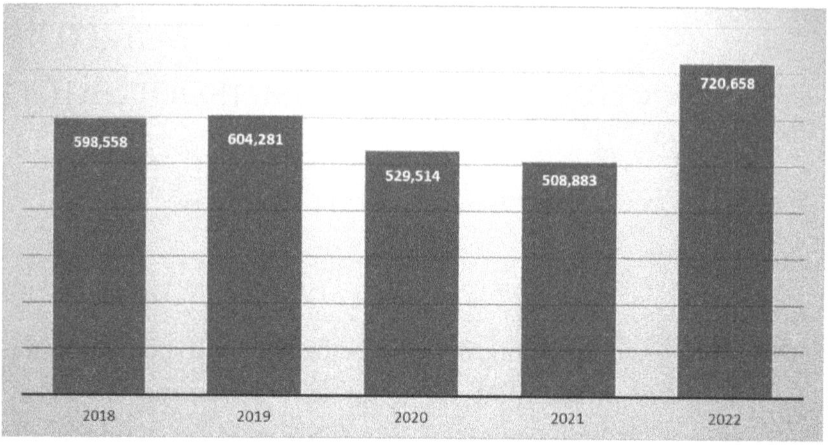

Source: Malaysian Automotive Association (2023).

reached 1,030.5 registered vehicles per 1,000 inhabitants, the second highest in Southeast Asia after Brunei at 1,052.5.[3] As early as 2014, a Nielsen survey found that 93% of all Malaysian households owned at least one automobile.[4]

This car-centric growth trend shows no signs of abating. Indeed, the total annual number of vehicles sold in Malaysia reached an all-time high of over 720,000 in 2022, a 20% increase from just under 600,000 sales in 2018, following the pandemic-era lull in 2020-21 (see Figure 10).

Malaysia is also a strange case where the poor own cars. Enrique Peñalosa, the former Mayor of Bogotá, Colombia said: "An advanced city is not a place where the poor move about in cars, but it is where even the rich use public transportation."[5] We have turned that around, misguided by the notion that more cars on the roads meant a more prosperous nation.

The consequence is simply more spending on car loans, petrol and maintenance and less disposable income that can be spent in other parts of the economy. Universiti Malaya and EPF estimated in mid-2023 that vehicle ownership cost a single household in the Klang Valley about 1.5 times more every month than taking public transportation (where applicable).[6]

Very few adults do not own a vehicle, yet the mobility needs of many are unmet, traffic congestion is rife[7] and road accidents are one of the five leading causes of death among Malaysians. Climate crises and severe flooding are further ramifications, with transport representing the second highest category of Malaysia's carbon emissions in the energy sector at 25.1%. This should be a matter of concern to any government.

Here is an exploration of some of the key issues in our transport model.

More vehicles, more problems

Every year, Malaysia records over 6,000 deaths in road accidents (three-fifths of whom are motorcyclists) and many more are injured severely.[8] The country's road-related mortality rate is the third highest in Asia – after Thailand and Vietnam – comparable to much poorer countries such as Angola, Nigeria and Senegal.[9]

The government takes the approach that road accidents can be reduced purely by teaching people how to behave properly, but the truth is that motorcycles are more susceptible to accidents and injuries than those behind the wheel, period.

Back in 2008 when I was the MP of Bukit Bendera, I learnt that a constituent of mine, Hisham, had become permanently paralysed as a result of a motorcycle accident in 2000 when his son was only a year old. On the eve of Hari Raya 2016, I was devastated upon hearing that the very same son, now 17 years old, had been injured in a motorcycle accident. When these things become multi-generational, it is heartbreaking.

Social and economic costs

We hardly talk about the economic and social costs of caring for those permanently injured. Yet, if everyone who rides a motorcycle today owns a car tomorrow, the number of cars on the roads will double. With the cities choked to no end, the nation's consumption of oil will double, too. Building more roads does not even address the issue of congestion, because of the phenomenon of induced demand (see page 200).

Of course, there is also the economic cost of owning a car. Loans for the purchases of private cars form a significant portion of private debt. BNM reported that in mid-2023, total household debt stood at RM1.5 trillion, the two biggest sources of which were housing (60%) and car loans (13%), followed by personal financing.[10] Car loans to pay off a continuously depreciating asset are especially unproductive but a lucrative and relatively straightforward business for the banks.

How does this impact petrol prices? Research has shown that there is a clear correlation between higher petrol prices and road deaths in Malaysia, because people switch from driving cars to riding motorcycles, which are more economical but also more dangerous. But can petrol prices be permanently subsidised at the expense of other expenditures and at the risk of bankrupting the treasury? Perhaps not.

Therefore, as a society, we need to make hard political choices over resource allocation. To cater for the transport needs of a growing population without everyone having to resort to private cars and motorcycles with the economic and social costs, public transport is the only way out.

The purpose of public transport

For the last few decades, public transport in Malaysia has usually been planned by vendors, driven by real estate interests, and structured as profit-driven entities that then often end up needing government restructuring (see pages 197-204).

In rethinking public transport, we need to accept that it is not always (or often) a profit-making endeavour. Instead, the government should pay for public transport as a service to the people. We have to put the "public" back in public transport.

Strangely, the government has had no problem funding the construction of roads, yet public transport is expected to pay for itself one way or the other. And because public transport is expected to pay for itself, vendor-driven schemes, cannibalisation, and real estate considerations are allowed to set the course of transport planning in Kuala Lumpur and other cities.

While it may seem like common sense, I cannot resist saying that the primary purpose of public transport all over the world is to get people to work and back home on working days during peak hours. It should not revolve around bringing people to shopping malls.

There is a misguided belief that public transport infrastructure can be funded through a "Hong Kong model" of "transit-oriented development" through selling land around a transit station for property development such as shopping malls and condominiums.

KL Sentral and other "Sentrals" around the country testify that such property plays alone do not improve the quality or increase the usage of public transport. KL Sentral, for instance, was opened in 2001 at the expense of the old railway station as a fantastic site for evolving real estate. Its purpose as an interchange station seemed like an afterthought, given that it took the eventual construction of the NU Sentral mall with an associated walkway in 2014 to properly link the commuter and light rail services in the main KL Sentral building to the namesake monorail station across the busy Jalan Tun Sambanthan.

Transforming public transport in Malaysia is my passion in part because my father was once a taxi and minibus driver, and since the time I was taking public buses to school 30 years ago, I thought we could improve our public transport.

For the nation, the debate about transport will only increase in importance as we grapple with increased transport needs of a growing population (as well as other cities outside Kuala Lumpur), energy efficiency, reducing road deaths and accidents and other economic and liveability choices.

As the next chapter explores in more detail, we need a new paradigm for public transport for all.

Note: This piece was adapted, with updates and edits, from three articles on public transportation that I wrote between 2010 and 2022 as follows:

(i) Chin Tong, Liew (2010). "A new paradigm needed in public transportation". *The Edge*, 16 November. Available at: https://theedgemalaysia.com/article/new-paradigm-needed-public-transportation;

(ii) Chin Tong, Liew (2017). "Public transport is more than big toy infrastructure". *Malaysiakini*, 20 September. Available at: https://www.malaysiakini.com/news/395737; and

(iii) Chin Tong, Liew (2022). "Malaysia's Skewed Transport System: Rising Costs Demand Bolder Solutions." *Fulcrum*, 29 June. Singapore: ISEAS-Yusof Ishak Institute. Available at: https://fulcrum.sg/malaysias-skewed-transport-system-rising-costs-demand-bolder-solutions/.

CHAPTER 20

Malaysia's Skewed Transport System Demands Bolder Solutions

The economic implications of Malaysia's skewed transport system will deepen with high petrol prices and rising interest rates. The country's heavy dependence on private passenger cars and penchant for rail-based "big toy" public transport projects are coming home to roost. With fuel subsidies growing, the need to build a highly connected and bus-centred public transport system has never been greater.

Economic and governance problems

The skewed transport system imposes three major economic problems.

First, fuel subsidies burn a huge hole in the federal budget. The Ministry of Finance has flagged the fiscal challenge, with the Unity Government acknowledging the need to reduce Malaysia's dependence on fuel subsidies, starting with the diesel subsidy. As previously mentioned, in 2022, fuel subsidies reached an all-time high of RM52 billion, an explosive rise from RM13.2 billion in 2021 and RM6.1 billion in pre-pandemic 2019.

While generous subsidies are untenable, measures to reduce fuel subsidies are unpopular and need to be approached with caution. In

June 2008, the then Prime Minister Tun Abdullah Badawi was badly advised to increase the petrol price at the pump by 40%. This effectively signalled the beginning of the end of his time in power. Pages 127-132 cover my proposals on how to taper off Malaysia's fuel subsidies by pivoting towards more sustainable green subsidies.

Second, transport-related public infrastructure projects constitute the bulk of the nation's off-budget debts. Over the past decade or so, many big-ticket transport projects were implemented, consisting of highways, city rail networks and inter-city electrified double tracking, and megaprojects such as the East Coast Railway Line (ECRL). Most of these projects were funded through off-budget channels with government-owned special purpose vehicles (SPVs) raising government-guaranteed debts. Should these SPVs become unable to service their off-budget debts, the government will be required to undertake the payments.

The most recent data show that government guarantees for DanaInfra Nasional Berhad, Prasarana Malaysia Berhad, Malaysia Rail Link Sdn Bhd, and Projek Lebuhraya Usahasama Berhad summed to RM171.6 billion, or 54% of the RM318 billion of guarantees provided by the Federal Government (Table 7). Several of these guarantees, including DanaInfra and Prasarana, are considered committed guarantees as these companies are already unable to service their debt without direct financial assistance from the government.

The majority of projects covered by these government-owned companies involve existing transport infrastructure, including the Klang Valley Mass Rapid Transit Projects (MRT1, MRT2), Light Rail Transit Line 3 Project (LRT3), Pan Borneo Highway Project Sarawak, PLUS North-South Highway, as well as operations of the LRT, MRT, KL Monorail, and bus services in various cities.

Table 7: Major recipients (>RM10 billion) of government loan guarantees (end-June 2023)

	RM million	Share of total guarantees (%)	Share of GDP (%)
Largest transport entities			
DanaInfra Nasional Berhad	82,860	26.1	4.5
Prasarana Malaysia Berhad	42,869	13.5	2.3
Malaysia Rail Link Sdn. Bhd.	34,886	10.9	1.9
Projek Lebuhraya Usahasama Berhad	11,000	3.5	0.6
Sub total	171,615	54.0	9.3
Largest non-transport entities			
Public Sector Home Financing Board	41,950	13.2	2.3
National Higher Education Fund Corporation	41,030	12.9	2.2
Others	63,115	19.9	3.4
Grand total	317,983	100.0	17.2

Source: Ministry of Finance Malaysia, Budget 2024, Chapter 5 (2023).

The fundamental weakness of these "big toy" projects is that they still do not solve the issue of first and last-mile connectivity challenges. They do not cover areas beyond the Klang Valley, leaving other parts of the country even more dependent on private vehicles. Having spent or committed so much to "big toy" public transport, the onus is now on Malaysia to make the pricey infrastructure work better and to be commercially viable, or at least less anaemic than the current 24% public transport use rate.[1]

Subsidising public transport in a big way, especially through supporting bus services nationwide, would be more sustainable – both financially and for the climate – in the long run, rather than prolonging cheap fuel forever.

Since Penang pioneered free buses in 2008 (the then Penang Chief Minister Lim Guan Eng and I came up with the idea as a response to the Tun Abdullah Badawi administration's petrol price hike on June 4, 2008), other schemes at various levels of government followed suit. One of the first programmes implemented by Anthony Loke during his first tenure as Minister of Transport was to introduce the My50 and My100 unlimited monthly travel passes on January 1, 2019 to keep fares low and encourage more public transport use. As proof of its popularity, the administrations of Tan Sri Muhyiddin Yassin and Dato' Sri Ismail Sabri continued the programme, and My50 remains in place today.[2]

However, not all schemes have been conducted in a coordinated and consistent manner. In June 2022, the then Prime Minister Ismail Sabri announced an ad-hoc arrangement, promising a RM155 million outlay for one month's free public transport in Kuala Lumpur. Just a month earlier, Ismail's administration had approved proposals to build three more highways around the Klang Valley,[3] one of which was later cancelled by the Selangor state government in July 2023.[4]

Building more highways is not the solution to congestion. It will only lead to a situation known as "induced demand", where more supply leads to more demand. The more highways or roads that are built, the more cars will be on the road, and the more congested the city will be.

Third, as I have previously highlighted, households have become increasingly indebted as they take on more housing and car loans (see page 194). Within the region, Malaysia's household debt-to-GDP ratio is relatively high at 81.9%, almost on par with Thailand (87%) but exceeding China (61.5%), Indonesia (15.7%) and Singapore (56.1%).[5]

In sum, the failure to build an efficient and functioning public transport system has a price tag: a huge fuel subsidy bill, sizable accumulated public debts via "big toy" transport infrastructure, and a high level of household debt partly caused by car loans.

Rethinking our transport system

When I talk about a middle-class society, I do not just mean one where ordinary people enjoy high-quality jobs with fair pay. Upward social mobility is certainly important, but mobility in the literal sense matters too in the overall quality of life equation.

Policymakers and political leaders must therefore first agree that transport cost is close to the heart of Malaysia's various economic questions. We must then be bold to think out of the box.

The notion of 'paying' people to take the bus is not as outlandish as it may seem. Much more can be done to subsidise bus-based public transport and incentivise the public to take public transport, guided by three key elements.

First, public transport is unlikely to generate profit and thus must be largely paid for by the public coffers. Public transport offers many benefits – known as positive externalities in economics jargon – not just to those who use it but to society and government at large. Some examples include fewer private cars on the roads, better mobility, savings on fuel subsidies, and a reduction in carbon emissions.

Second, public transport must go beyond "big toy" infrastructure. Strangely, Malaysians now think of trains when they think of public transport. Sadly, our deep prejudice nowadays is that buses are for poor people and foreign workers. The truth of the matter though, is that buses are much cheaper, faster and easier to run than trains, as well as being flexible where destinations are concerned.

Our disdain for buses is such that at the time of writing, the Klang Valley is served by only 724 active buses daily, which according to Minister Anthony Loke is a far cry from the 4,000 buses needed to run the network efficiently.[6] To bring the network up to mark and address first- and last-mile connectivity concerns once and for all will arguably cost us less than the prevailing fuel subsidies.[7]

The wise thing to do is to mix our modes of mass transport. A bus-based multi-modal public transport system, with trains, buses, bus rapid transit and related modes of transport complementing one another, is the way to go. Having many buses running on time is crucial in linking up the network and running it efficiently. For towns without sufficient density or demand for a railway network, buses are good alternatives. For Kuala Lumpur, the rail system will remain inefficient and inconvenient if it is not complemented by an extensive bus network.

Third, sequencing is crucial. Our society will have to envisage several years of transition during which public transport becomes a great alternative to driving and driving becomes a luxury. As with all luxuries, one pays for it not as a necessity but as an unnecessary enjoyment. By that point, the full petrol price can be charged without subsidies.

Just as we need to challenge the myth that everyone should own a house, we must challenge the idea that everyone needs to drive. If there are better alternatives, not everyone will want to drive everywhere. Things are already starting to change, with the expansion of the Klang Valley's rapid transit network, the advent of ride-sharing as well as e-hailing bus-pooling services like Kumpool. Many young Malaysians in urban centres no longer choose to own a car. As Figure 11 suggests, public transport ridership in the Klang Valley is rising, approaching 30 million passengers across all Prasarana-run services for the month of October 2023.[8]

Figure 11: Ridership across various Prasarana-run public transport systems in urban areas (left) and total Prasarana ridership, January 2022 - October 2023

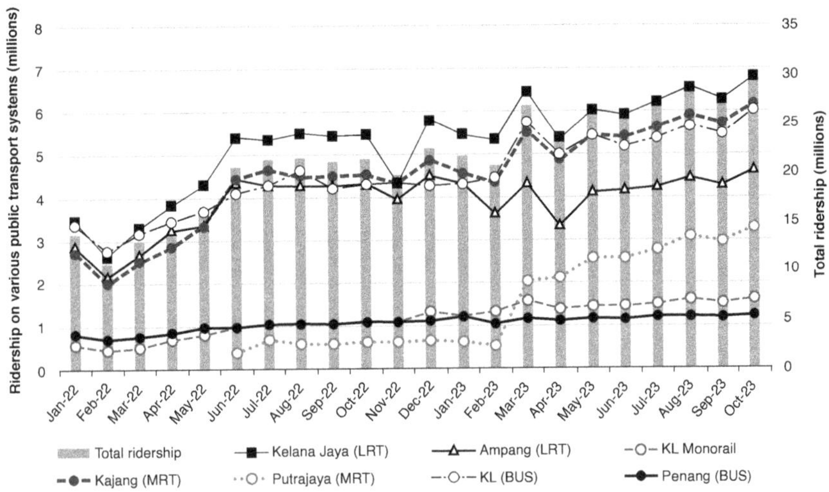

Source: Prasarana Malaysia (2023).

Mindset change does not happen overnight, but we must continue to build momentum and move away from the car-brained, car-centric approach to city planning. Beyond the obvious benefits to commuters, what is in it for the state? The answer is that well-organised and sustainable cities are more resilient. Climate-friendly cities, which do not succumb to urban sprawl, are more likely to withstand climate disasters. Cities that organise themselves better and offer reliable transport and mobility are also better at responding to emergencies.

The transport question in the Malaysian economy is huge and serious. Doing more of the same is a recipe for disaster. Let us therefore organise our transport, and by extension our cities, better so that Malaysia can be resilient on all fronts.

Note: This piece was adapted, with significant updates and edits, from an article I wrote in the journal *Fulcrum* published by the ISEAS-Yusof Ishak Institute on June 29, 2022. See Chin Tong, Liew (2022). "Malaysia's Skewed Transport System: Rising Costs Demand Bolder Solutions." *Fulcrum*, 29 June. Singapore: ISEAS-Yusof Ishak Institute. Available at: https://fulcrum.sg/malaysias-skewed-transport-system-rising-costs-demand-bolder-solutions

CHAPTER 21

Greater Johor Bahru as the Second Metropolitan Region

A fresh look at the immense potential of Greater Johor Bahru, also known as the Iskandar region, would serve as the catalyst for Malaysia's second economic takeoff. Greater Johor Bahru should be positioned as the nation's second metropolitan region after the Klang Valley, and to achieve this end, be given adequate resources and policy support.

Political structure

Unleashing the potential of Greater Johor Bahru requires us to first understand the history of the political structure governing Malaysia's urban areas.

Before Independence, as a result of the decentralised governing structure of the British colonial administration, Penang, Ipoh, Johor Bahru/Singapore, and Kuala Lumpur, were of similar levels of economic importance. According to the last census conducted by the colonial government in 1957, Kuala Lumpur had a population of 327,000 while George Town, Penang and Ipoh, Perak were not too far behind at 235,000 and 126,000 inhabitants respectively.[1]

Merdeka brought forth a powerful central government intent on nation-building. Tunku Abdul Rahman, Malaysia's first Prime Minister, went on a building spree to define the nation in Kuala Lumpur. Icons and monuments built during this period include the Merdeka Stadium, National Stadium, National Mosque, National Monument, Parliament House, National Museum and the University of Malaya.[2]

The government's revenue increased further in the 1970s and 1980s with the expansion of the oil and gas sector and a more diversified economy through rapid industrialisation. Tun Dr Mahathir Mohamad, Malaysia's fourth Prime Minister, went on not only to vastly improve the country's infrastructure but also to replace Tunku's monuments in Kuala Lumpur by building a new capital in Putrajaya in the 1990s.

As political power became more centralised in the hands of the Federal Government, so did economic activity become more concentrated in the capital region – the Klang Valley. Kuala Lumpur became the nation's unrivalled commercial centre, as well as a primate city, while the disparity between Kuala Lumpur and the nation's other cities grew wider.

Outside Kuala Lumpur and Putrajaya, the ethos was to devote resources to develop the rural sector, often to the detriment of the country's other urban areas. Nevertheless, by the 2000s, there were disparate attempts to strengthen urban development outside of the capital region, with mixed results at best.

Dr Mahathir's successor Tun Abdullah Badawi created new federal "corridor" agencies, such as the Iskandar Region Development Authority (IRDA), with the objective of developing the greater Johor Bahru region with federal resources and projects. However, the approach is now generally regarded as merely adding a "corridor" layer of bureaucracy without the intended benefits of the agglomeration effect.

With the end of Barisan Nasional's hegemonic rule in 2018 and the growing recognition of the power of the states, now is the chance to give more attention to the needs and potentials of the Greater Johor

Bahru area, beginning with the governance model of the corridor agencies.

Progress is underway, one step at a time. At the time of writing, Prime Minister Datuk Seri Anwar Ibrahim has instructed MITI to streamline the country's overlapping investment promotion and regional corridor agencies in line with NIMP 2030. But ultimately in the long run, IRDA should be "returned" to the state of Johor and synchronised with the state authority.

What's so great about Greater Johor Bahru? The Singapore factor

At this juncture, we might ask ourselves what Johor Bahru has to offer, and whether it is important enough to serve as a secondary metropolitan region, given the longstanding pre-eminence of the Klang Valley in economic and political decision-making. The answer to both these questions lies in the "Singapore factor" – the increasingly symbiotic relationship between Johor Bahru and its southern neighbour Singapore.

Since the fall of the Berlin Wall in 1989, which symbolised the collapse of Communism, the world entered a period of hyper-globalisation. Coupled with the containerisation of transport, which only became the dominant form of freight in the last half-century, outsourcing of manufacturing under the ethos of "just-in-time" was the rule of the game until COVID-19 hit the world in 2020.

Singapore was the poster child of hyper-globalisation. As a global city and regional financial hub, firms from Europe and North America set up regional headquarters in Singapore while locating their main production lines in China and other low-cost countries around the globe. For some decades, Singapore needed no hinterland.

What has changed? COVID-19, as well as health challenges such as an ageing society, means firms have to price in disruption. Likewise, wars and geopolitical tensions, climate change and climate-related disasters, and financial instability, are disruptions that can no longer be ignored.

The world has now moved from "just-in-time" to "just-in-case", from the sole pursuit of economic efficiency, i.e. low production cost to economic security. The key phrase now is "a shorter and more secured supply chain". Nowadays, the word "resilience" is used by businesses as often as defence ministries, if not more.

In such a context, the Greater Johor Bahru provides Singapore with a production site. Investors investing in Singapore are demanding to see their factories within a couple of hours of flight time. Johor is within sight, and reachable by roads, very quickly.

Housing costs, especially rental, have increased tremendously over the past few years in Singapore largely due to the influx of investors relocating from China for various reasons. The high housing costs in Singapore are juxtaposed with a glut of apartments, condominiums and high-end residential properties in Johor Bahru. Singapore and Johor Bahru may be each other's cure as far as the housing question is concerned, provided commuting is smooth.

The separation of Malaysia and Singapore in 1965 was not entirely cordial, creating a sense of competition between the two neighbours. It was real with the older generation of leaders who knew each other personally but tended to compete with each other, such as Dr Mahathir and the late Mr Lee Kuan Yew. Today's leaders may have less sense of animosity and suspicion between them.

Rethinking Greater Johor Bahru

An important mindset shift is that the federal government would need to recognise that if any parts of the nation are thriving, such as Johor Bahru, the result is inevitably beneficial to the country as a whole.

There is a need to see Greater Johor Bahru as the second metropolitan region of the nation, after the Klang Valley. The region is huge and sees economic migrants from as far as Sabah and Sarawak, as well as northern and eastern states, relocating to find better opportunities, whether in Johor Bahru or in Singapore.

Once Greater Johor Bahru is seen in different lights from other state capitals, resources and policy support could be channelled to fulfil human development needs, such as schools, hospitals and care facilities, and other economic requirements.

My parliamentary seat of Iskandar Puteri and the state seat of Perling are both in Greater Johor Bahru, and I can see very clearly the needs for more resources for human and social development. The current planning does not take into account the huge number of Malaysian economic migrants who congregate in the region.

More resources should also be channelled to provide decent public transport for the region, especially bus and water-based modes of transport. Many Johoreans are familiar with Singapore and therefore can easily become accustomed to taking public transport if sufficient services are available.

A Greater Johor Bahru-wide transport master plan that takes into consideration cross-border traffic should be commissioned. The advent of the Johor Bahru-Singapore Rapid Transit System (RTS) Link – a 4km rapid transit shuttle service linking Bukit Chagar in Johor Bahru to Woodlands North in Singapore – is a good start to make commuting more convenient once it is completed in late 2026. But it should not end there.

More efforts should be made to make immigration checks easier with the introduction of newer technology and speed. Special arrangements should be made for holders of Malaysian and Singaporean passports, or at least regular users of the crossings, to cross borders with minimal checks. If there is a fear of crime, the authorities on both sides, especially the police, have already had extensive cooperation to deal with it.

The KTM Tebrau Shuttle – the existing commuter shuttle service between Johor Bahru and Singapore since 2015 – should not cease service after the coming of the RTS. And, more catamaran-based ferries should be introduced, such as between Forest City and Jurong, and between Pasir Gudang and Changi, to provide more options besides the Johor-Singapore Causeway and the Second Link. Making walking across the Causeway a more comfortable experience with travelators and roofs, as announced by the Prime Minister in January 2023, should be pursued as a low-hanging fruit by the Home Ministry and its counterpart in Singapore.

With more commuting links, firms could set up shop in Greater Johor Bahru while continuing to maintain a presence in Singapore. When more businesses locate some parts of their operations in Greater Johor Bahru, they still can save on other operational costs even when paying their workers at least two-thirds of Singapore's pay. It will help shift the wage structure of Greater Johor Bahru, with more employers having to pay higher wages across the board.

When many more Malaysian workers get better pay in Johor, less will need to travel to work in Singapore while consumption in Greater Johor Bahru will thrive further through integration and a general population that has better income.

If done well, Greater Johor Bahru as the second metropolitan region will be one of the engines of growth that will power Malaysia's second economic takeoff.

CHAPTER 22

Climate Change and Floods Require Immediate Attention

Climate change: now in our backyard

Floods are not new, but flash floods have become more regular and have caused greater damage. Their regular occurrence is both a manifestation of the effects of climate change and a reflection of our collective failure in flood mitigation.

In December 2021-January 2022, the Klang Valley and its surroundings were hit by the worst floods in over five decades, resulting in 54 deaths and up to RM6.5 billion in property damage across Kuala Lumpur, Klang, Hulu Langat, Petaling, Bentong and other districts.[1] In 2022, floods besieged the east coast states of Kelantan and Terengganu, with losses of over RM600 million.[2] In 2023, Johor was hit by the worst floods in 17 years which displaced 40,000 people.[3]

It is clear to me that some floods are caused by poor urban planning, which became more evident when I visited flood-affected neighbourhoods in my state constituency of Perling and surrounding areas. The urban sprawl over the past 50 years is not just inefficient from the point of view of infrastructure, but it is increasingly problematic from the perspective of climate change.

For instance, when the Evergreen housing estate in Taman Tampoi Indah, Johor Bahru was built in the 1990s, it was surrounded by greens.

Many other housing and commercial projects were developed in surrounding areas in the past two decades, but the authorities have somehow neglected to link the drainage system in Evergreen to an outlet into the larger waterways, thus resulting in closed water circulation within the drainage of that area only.

The cleanliness of our drainage system is a major concern. Flow in most of the drains is not optimised in part because of irresponsible citizens who litter and sediments that build up, and on the other hand, cleaning by the authorities is not done regularly as scheduled.

One problem that seems obvious but has not been dealt with is the concealed drainage system. To some people, it is as if concealed drains can be conveniently overlooked even if they are filled with garbage and sediments, as they go unnoticed and hidden beneath the covers.

I have also visited urban villages such as Kampung Pasir, Johor Bahru which have no proper drainage system and some of its nearby rivers are filled with garbage. These villages should not be neglected and left to their own devices. Flood mitigation in these villages will also reduce the risk of flooding in surrounding urban areas.

State governments, local authorities and federal agencies such as the Department of Environment and the Department of Irrigation and Drainage must work together to ensure that our drainage system and waterways are well planned, regularly cleaned and well maintained.

Galvanising the whole of government and society

Flood mitigation is just one part of the whole picture. Climate change will continue to affect us in a multitude of ways, ranging from sea level rises to rising temperatures and unpredictable weather patterns on the back of greenhouse gas emissions (GHG) and deforestation.

We cannot address flooding and climate change without also dealing with our GHG emissions. In 2021, the Malaysian Government articulated its intention to achieve net-zero GHG emissions by "as early as 2050". Subsequent policy documents, such as the 12th Malaysia Plan, the National Energy Policy 2022-2040 and the NETR, have formalised this net-zero statement as a commitment with associated strategies to diversify away from fossil fuels.

Whatever side of the political divide one finds oneself, no one can run away from the issue of climate change. Back in June 2022 in the Johor State Assembly, as the then state opposition leader, I proposed to the Chief Minister of Johor Dato' Onn Hafiz Ghazi that the assembly set up a bipartisan committee on climate change, urban and rural planning. I am glad that the bipartisan committee chaired by the State Assemblyman for Pemanis Anuar Abd Manap has been established and some of its recommendations have been accepted by the state government.

Bipartisanship in this matter remains crucial at the state and federal levels. State governments in particular play a major role in providing leadership as well as coordinating the public, local councils and government agencies.

State governments must make all stakeholders see climate change as a major challenge, have a clear plan to mitigate floods, and make our cities and communities resilient to potential disasters.

SECTION III

THINK SYSTEM

Back to basics, we must ask what the policy objective of the state would be. In Sections I and II, I have established that the government needs to step in and promote progressive policies in the name of good jobs and a good life for a middle-class society. I have also established that the government, whether through GLCs, GLICs or agencies, does not just have a regulatory purpose but also an entrepreneurial and a developmental role through a mission economy.

But if we want 2023 to be remembered as the beginning of Malaysia's second takeoff, there is still one piece of the puzzle that needs to fit into place: the role of effective governance in our young democracy. Even the loftiest of plans would fail without a strong, competent and kind state that is committed to upholding the interests of its people.

Put simply, the Malaysian state needs to update the system for the 2020s. The legacy of the past authoritarian state has not been completely undone despite multiple changes of government in the last five years. Tun Abdullah Badawi summarised it best when he remarked that Malaysia had "first-world infrastructure and a third-world mentality" over two decades ago.

On May 9, 2018, the world's then longest-serving elected one-party state was defeated in a peaceful election, but a new compromise or compact has not emerged as yet. Immediately there were talks of a "New Malaysia" and hopes for reforms, including to improve the federal-state relationship; to bring about effective decentralisation of some forms of decision-making away from Putrajaya; to strengthen the autonomy of Parliament and the separation of power across the branches of government; and to update our foreign policy and security apparatus for the challenges of the new decade.

The 2018 General Election has caused the UMNO hegemony to fall, but the new political order is only beginning to emerge. There is no more presidential premiership, yet many have not fully come to the realisation that prime ministers are just first among equals.

Granted, some changes were made, but 60-odd years of mismanagement could not be corrected in just a few months. The ensuing COVID-19 pandemic and Sheraton Move in 2020 brought a stop to the momentum we had built just 22 months earlier.

As the 2022 General Election made clear, the new era is marked by a 50-50 electorate where no party can win an outright majority without forming a unity or coalition government. More than ever, this calls for a spirit of bipartisanship as today's winners could be tomorrow's losers. To make this happen, we must strengthen our parliamentary democracy together.

The parliament, the judiciary and other institutions need to be allowed to carry out their constitutional functions without fear or favour. The general civil service needs more technical expertise and competence. Reforms are needed to our security and defence landscapes to safeguard our territorial integrity and guarantee the continuity of our state. There is no more Big Brother in Putrajaya watching over the states, but a new equilibrium between the centre and the states has yet to emerge.

All great democracies are not created through textbooks but a work-in-progress through political battles and their settlements. In the UK, for example, the modern party system in Parliament grew out of fights at different stages of the industrial age, from the need to accommodate the new urban rich against the old landed rich to accommodating mass industrial workers, culminating in the first Labour government in 1924.

A hundred years on, now is the time to think system, using the lessons we have learnt both during the era of one-party dominance and the subsequent changes of government following the collapse of the old order. Any piecemeal or band-aid solutions are not going to help much because otherwise we will continue to be trapped in the same vicious circle. Malaysians deserve better and the Malaysian democracy deserves better.

PART VII

RENEGOTIATING THE FEDERAL-STATE RELATIONSHIP

In general, sovereign countries can be classified as federal or unitary states. A federal state has, as its name suggests, a federal government that shares power with second-tier state or provincial governments. A unitary state meanwhile features a central government that governs the nation as a single entity. Such a state may or may not consist of smaller administrative divisions, but any power that those smaller units have is ultimately under the auspices of the central government.

For all intents and purposes, Malaysia lies on the federal side of this divide. At the very least, this was the intention when the country was born. The Constitution makes repeated references to Malaysia as a federation. However, decades of what amounted to one-party rule effectively eroded the power of the state governments to the benefit of an increasingly centralised federal government.

Politics certainly played a role in Malaysia's weakening federalism, but as Chapter 23 points out, the contribution of economics cannot be ignored. The Federal Government coffers are filled through the collection of income, corporate and other related taxes while the states have relied on revenue from natural resources and land to fund their operations. This was a deal struck when the Malaysian economy was dominated by commodities in the early days after Independence. It was reasonable then, but today the country's economic structure has shifted while the federal-state fiscal relationship is unchanged, resulting in fiscally weak state governments.

There needs to be a new deal for Malaysian federalism where states and the federal government share revenue in a more equitable manner. That way, state governments will be empowered to carry out affairs such as education, community policing, healthcare or just maintaining all roads within their state borders, on their own terms in line with their policy priorities.

Chapter 24 delves deeper into federalism from a historical perspective, talking about why it matters and what we can learn from the experiences of Australia and India, whose systems formed the basis of our own model of federalism.

Finally, in Chapter 25, I stress the long overdue need for Kuala Lumpur to have a state government, and how it is a strange case among the world's federal territories due to its complete lack of a state-like legislature, which has left the capital without a voice in policy making.

An ideal model of federal-state relations would allow both levels of government to pool their resources and capabilities for the sake of the states' prosperity, thereby moving away from the old model where states would often be forced to kowtow to Putrajaya's wishes.

What does this have to do with Malaysia's second takeoff? To begin with, it is important to note that the next takeoff is not just about higher income in the aggregate but also a more equitable distribution of income. With this in mind, by correcting the policy blunders of our past and giving states the resources and power they deserve, we will help nurture more balanced regional development, which is essential for sustained growth.

With the Minister of Investment, Trade and Industry, Tengku Zafrul Aziz during a factory visit. February 2023.

Participating in the Asia-Pacific Economic Cooperation (APEC) Ministers Responsible for Trade Meeting held in Arequipa, Peru. It was an opportunity to align trade policies among member economies and I proposed the idea of APEC economies to work together on a collective industrial policy to solve common challenges such as climate change, instead of having national industrial policies which would lead to further trade wars. This was also my inaugural trip to Latin America. May 2024.

ASEAN Economic Ministers Meeting in Luang Prabang, Laos. March 2024. Malaysia will be taking over as ASEAN Chair from Laos in 2025.

Sharing a light moment with H.E. Katherine Tai, US Trade Representative; H.E. Mary Ng, Canada's Minister of Export Promotion, International Trade and Economic Development; and H.E. Tim Ayres, Australia's Assistant Minister for Trade and Assistant Minister for Manufacturing at the APEC Ministers Responsible for Trade Meeting. May 2024.

Prime Minister Datuk Seri Anwar Ibrahim launched the New Industrial Master Plan 2030 (NIMP 2030) on 1 September 2023. NIMP 2030 is different from the previous Industrial Master Plans as it takes a mission-based approach, instead of a sectoral approach. It aims to increase the median manufacturing wage to RM4,510 by 2030, from RM1,976 in 2022.

At the opening of the Johor Democratic Action Party (DAP) State Headquarters in Kulai, with DAP Secretary-General Sdr Anthony Loke. The Johor DAP State HQ is an "office in a park" designed by my architect friends Dr Tan Loke Mun and Ng Sek San. September 2022.

Enjoying the King of Fruits – durian with H.E. Gan Kim Yong, Singapore's Minister for Trade and Industry when the Singapore delegation visited Kuala Lumpur for the Annual Ministerial Dialogue. June 2023. Gan was appointed Singapore's Deputy Prime Minister in May 2024.

Speaking at the National Resilience College with military leaders on the key ideas of the Defence White Paper, of which I was involved in crafting in my capacity as the Deputy Defence Minister for the Pakatan Harapan Government. September 2023.

Accompanying China's Vice President H.E. Han Zheng for his visit to Proton's manufacturing facility in Tanjung Malim. It is my fervent hope to see more localisation and creation of good quality job opportunities for Malaysians whenever we receive foreign investments. November 2023.

At the finale ceramah for Iskandar Puteri, the parliamentary constituency that I contested and won in the 15th General Elections. I am grateful for the support received, and very honoured to have taken over the baton from Sdr Lim Kit Siang, who represented this seat for two terms since 2013. November 2022.

Carrying out parliamentary duties, replying to questions from Members of Parliament and Senators, in Dewan Rakyat and Dewan Negara, respectively.

CHAPTER 23

A New Deal for Malaysian Federalism

Malaysia was established as a federation of states, but over the years, it has become a highly centralised polity. Across the country, states have repeatedly expressed their dissatisfaction with the concentration of power and resources in the hands of the Federal Government, and the resultant lack of economic and infrastructural development.

Political structure: how did we get here?

According to the Malaysian constitutional framework that was conceived in 1957 and 1963, the Federal Government receives its revenue from income taxes while the state governments control and derive revenue from natural resources and land. Back then, income taxes were not as important a source of revenue as in current days. Providing the states with sole power to manage land and natural resources was deemed a fair deal as the main economic drivers were mining, plantation and agriculture.

However, over the decades, the federal coffer expanded many folds due to the expansion of the modern economy. As the country industrialised and discovered oil, both since around the 1970s, the

Federal Government's revenue increased at a much faster pace. And with the enlargement of federal collection revenue, the roles and responsibilities of the Federal Government swelled.

Today, the poorer and resource-based states rely on mining and logging rights to gain revenue while the more prosperous states depend on housing developments that sprawl the cities or allow for reclamation. Meanwhile, the Federal Government collects corporate and personal income taxes, in addition to indirect tax, duties, and investment income. As a result, the revenue of the Federal Government (projected to be RM291.5 billion in 2023) is more than ten times greater than that of Malaysia's 13 states combined (estimated at RM27.3 billion in 2023).[1]

Political structure was one of the many underlying factors that resulted in the widening federal-state gap. Until 2018, the Federal Government was able to cajole and compel states into following federal edicts mostly because BN, led by UMNO, controlled most of the states.

UMNO was the dominant party that provided the candidate for the Prime Minister while almost all states on the peninsula were governed by an UMNO Menteri Besar, who was most likely a state liaison UMNO chief appointed by the UMNO President, who also wielded powers as Prime Minister. Under such tacit institutional settings, the state governments tended to acquiesce to most of the Federal Government's dictates.[2]

However, since the end of the BN's one-party state structure in 2018, states have become important power centres. Even if the states' chief ministers are from the same party, the Prime Minister and the Federal Government have to be more consultative with them.

Renegotiating the federal-state relationship

The federal-state relationship should be renegotiated to provide adequate resources for the state governments.

The existing arrangement, as stipulated in Article 109 of the Constitution, is that the Federal Government must provide two types of funding to state governments: a "capitation grant" (based on population size) and a "state road grant" (for the maintenance of state roads based on total road length). The latter is by far the largest grant given to state governments, making up over 60% of the total transfer of funds from the Federal Government to the states as of 2020.[3] However, federal money may also be distributed to the states through other grants as stated in Table 8 below.[4]

Table 8: Types of discretionary federal government grants available to state governments

Type of grant	Purpose
Revenue growth	Distribution to all states of up to RM250 million a year if federal government revenue grows by over 10% year-on-year, excluding tin duties and road traffic-related taxes
Grants to local authorities	Grants to state governments to assist in the operations of their respective local authorities
Service charges to the state	Compensation to state governments for their involvement in federal projects
Concurrent list	Operating expenditure provided to state governments for areas with overlapping federal-state responsibilities, such as social welfare, culture and sports, irrigation, etc.
Economic development, infrastructure and welfare	Grant to states for development projects focused on economic development, infrastructure and welfare

Type of grant	Purpose
Other grants	Deficit grant to states running a current account deficit; tourism grant; special and compensation grants to Sabah and Sarawak; special grants to Selangor and Kedah over historical territorial changes; financial assistance to local authorities for the payment of electric bills for street lamps and traffic lights.

Source: Mahmood, J. (2021) and Gooi, H. L. et al. (2022).

In 2023, the Federal Government allocated a total of RM8.7 billion in grants and transfers to the thirteen states for 2024.[5] Some states have argued that the amount received from the Federal Government is disproportionately small compared to their contribution to the federal coffers. The state government of Johor, for example, received an estimated RM865 million from Putrajaya in 2022, a far cry from the RM13 billion the Federal Government collected from the southern state in tax.[6]

The ideal situation is that in the years to come, the Federal Government will provide adequate resources for the state governments by sharing income tax revenue with the states. This is much better than having the different levels of government sharing income from natural resources, such as oil, or restricting the states to revenues from environmentally destructive activities, or only giving states access to puny federal grants.

The taxes collected are not a zero-sum game. Sharing tax revenue collected in the states will incentivise the states to do more to grow their share of the national economic pie since they would gain directly from it. This will foster federal-state coordination in economic developmental matters. The more the economic activities that are generated in a state, the more taxes there will be for both the eager state and its federal master.

With more revenues coming in, states would consequently be able to play a larger role in local policing, education, healthcare and possibly even defence. This would put us closer in alignment with Australia and India, which have almost the same constitutional frameworks as Malaysia, where community policing, hospitals and most educational institutions are the domain of the states, not the Federal Government.

Having a state-level government system in our constitutional structure is now an obvious blessing which Malaysia should make full use of. The question now is whether we can find a new political compromise to empower the states under a new deal for Malaysian federalism.

It is time for the federal and state governments to create a Malaysian federalism that is more balanced and just, which will then contribute to the prosperity and well-being of ordinary Malaysians.

CHAPTER 24

The Future of Federalism

How we arrange and rearrange the institutions of our three-tier government – federal, state and local governments – will remain an important subject for Malaysia for the years to come with huge implications.

We have to first ask ourselves, why do we want to strengthen federalism? Federalism is not necessarily normatively superior to a unitary state. We must avoid devolution for the sake of devolution. Any discussion about local elections without looking at strengthening the state governments' roles and responsibilities is not helpful in improving democratic governance.

Federalism is a very relevant arrangement to accommodate identity politics within a larger unit of nationhood. But identity politics should not be an end in itself. Federalism, decentralisation and devolution have to come with material benefits in terms of well-being and welfare to the people.

Devolution is good only when it makes democracy work better for the people. There are two folds:

- First, the type of devolution that should be promoted must facilitate public participation and thus improve democracy at the subnational level; for instance, the authority to manage public transport and environment can be devolved or at least shared between federal and states in the hope that locals can participate in the decision-making process. It is strange to design bus routes from Putrajaya. And with environmental consciousness, locals hopefully can help monitor environmental degradation better.

- Second, devolution must be protected by democratic accountability. There is no point to devolve powers to the states if there are no checks-and-balances at the state level to prevent despots or corruption, for instance, in environment enforcement. For example, it is well and good to grant immigration control to Sabah and Sarawak, which I do not dispute. But I was barred from entering Sarawak and turned back on the same flight during the 2016 Sarawak state elections. That is not the best use of devolved power.

Balancing democratic participation and accountability is crucial in designing what to devolve and what not to devolve. Malaysia is not going to be well served if we swing from a highly centralised system to one that is fragmented with corruption and abuses.

From the point of organising our society and nation better, whatever we do to rearrange our institutions, we need to ensure that we remove silos too and not add to islands of disconnectedness.

Where do we start?

Much as many think that Malaysia inherited a British model of governance, to be precise, the Malaysian federalism is very much modelled instead after the Australian and Indian constitutional arrangements, especially the following features:

- The states – the UK has no concept of states; the idea of states came from the US;

- The Senate as the House of States – the UK has no concept of a Senate conceived as the House of States; and
- Local governments, whether elected or appointed, are within the purview of states.

The UK was very much a unitary state until devolution in the 1990s.

To strengthen federalism in Malaysia, we may look to the Australian and Indian models for ideas.

In the current institutional arrangements, if the local government is shut down today, the public will soon notice it as soon as they realise that their garbage is not collected. But no one would notice that if a state government is shut down.

I remember back in around 2001 when Indonesia was trying to grapple with the question of decentralisation. It was then said that federalism was an "F" word, something which was disliked and even a taboo. But today, Indonesia is a very decentralised state, for good and for bad. Indonesia was highly centralised and militarised under Suharto and thus it was said that Indonesia had to sail the decentralisation water while building the ship of subnational authorities.[1]

Malaysia does not have that problem. We can work on strengthening the state authorities through devolving roles and responsibilities from the Federal Government and consolidating some local government functions into state levels.

I am among many who have advocated for local elections but I have always done it with a caveat: local elections should only happen when the roles and functions of the state governments and local authorities are re-looked at, reorganised and reduced at once.

By design, the Local Government Act 1976 frames local authorities as an extension of the state governments. Today, some local councils in Selangor, Penang and Johor are larger in fiscal size than the Perlis state government and around the size of Malacca. For example, Majlis Bandaraya Petaling Jaya's (MBPJ) budgetary allocation for 2022 was RM410.7 million while Majlis Bandaraya Pulau Pinang (MBPP) tabled a budget of RM405.2 million for 2023, nearly double the state budget of Perlis (RM293.4 million) and comparable to the estimated operating expenditure of the Malacca state government (RM455.4 million) as of 2023.[2]

If the realignment of local governments can be done so that they are balanced in fiscal, geographical and population size, local elections can be a good way of improving democratic participation. Otherwise, once we have local elections, state governments will cease to operate in the eyes of the public. This is a very important point which unfortunately eluded those who are for local elections. The debate about local elections in Malaysia is unfortunately political and often racial, without those who are pro and against talking facts and thinking through.

Indonesia was once militantly against federalism and decentralisation very much due to its history during independence in which the breakaway of provinces was a perennial concern and worry.

So, history matters. Malaysia's current institution was very much created in 1948. It was structured as a federation to respond to the dissatisfaction against Malayan Union in 1946. But 1948 was also the year in which the Malayan Emergency was declared against the Communists. The police was the first full-fledged national body, even before the federal civil service was fully formed.

We can now look at the Australian and Indian federations and see how we can gradually devolve powers in comparable services. For instance, states play a very strong role in Australia and India as far as community policing, health and education. We can experiment with, for instance, states getting to form some auxiliary police (*polis bantuan*) units to carry out some policing functions which do not have to be centralised, such as traffic police. Health and education can also be devolved as much as possible.

At the same time, we will have to acknowledge that there would not be complete devolution as even in very decentralised nations such as the US, there is still a need for some forms of federal policing.

Of course, states do need to pay for these services if they run some parts of them. One of Malaysia's weaknesses in fiscal arrangement is that states' revenues come from land and natural resources. The big debate on federalism still does not go beyond the debate of oil royalty, just like other natural resources, which is essentially lottery money and not necessarily good for the environment.

Income tax from individuals and corporations in a particular state can be shared in different proportions subject to the new shared roles and responsibilities agreed upon between the Federal Government and the said state.

Finally, national representation of state voices is an important subject. Both India and Australia designed the Senate as the House of States. India elects its senators through state parliaments while Australia directly elects its representatives to the upper house from every state (each state elects 12 senators for a six-year term on a staggered basis).

Meanwhile, Malaysia has three categories of senators: first, 26 to represent 13 states and indirectly elected by a state assembly motion; second, four to represent the federal territories; and third, 40 appointed by the King at the recommendation of the Prime Minister.

My hope is that one day, we will elect most of our senators directly by voters through the ballot boxes, as is the case in Australia. They should represent the interests of their respective states, with Sabah and Sarawak having a higher weightage of perhaps one-third of senators. The campaign for one-third of Sabah and Sarawak representation should be in the senate and not in the lower house, which should as much as possible represent the one-person one-vote standard.

In conclusion, the discussion of how to rearrange our institutions will continue to dominate headlines, such as discussion on local elections or state nationalism in Sabah or Sarawak. It is time for us to look at the issues with fresh eyes and perspectives so that we are not caught in clichés but actually move forward one step at a time in the right direction.

CHAPTER 25

State Government for Kuala Lumpur?

On February 1, 1974, Kuala Lumpur was declared a "Federal Territory". The Federal Government reasoned that Kuala Lumpur, as the federal capital, would be better governed when placed under its direct rule. Malaysia was initially conceived as a three-tier democracy with elected federal, state and local authority (local elections have not been held since 1965). In contrast to the residents of other states in the country who elect their federal and state representatives, the two million KL residents only have the right to elect an eleven-member delegation to the Federal Parliament.

As much as those of us working in KL might enjoy having Federal Territory Day as a holiday, we should examine what the status of KL means for our right to representation. In particular, I would like to discuss three issues to support the argument that the residents of KL should no longer be deprived of their right to elect a sub-national government.

First, "federal territories" in other countries actually elect their own local governing bodies. Second, given the creation of Putrajaya, the function of KL as federal capital has lost its meaning. Third, and most importantly, immediate measures should be taken to ensure transparency and accountability of KL City Hall (DBKL), by far the most populous sub-national government in the country. Given these reasons, the people of KL should be allowed to elect their own state government. I first made this point in 2004; by the time this book goes to the press, the argument will have been 20 years old.

The concept of FT elsewhere

The government's use of KL's federal capital status as an excuse to deprive the democratic rights of its citizens started a long way back. In 1961, fearing that the ruling Alliance Party's grip on KL would be eroded in the municipal elections, the government decided to transfer authority from an elected council to an appointed Federal Commissioner, who was responsible solely to the Interior Minister. An Advisory Board consisting of eleven members assisted the Commissioner. This is the origin of the double deprivations of KL citizens: not only could they not elect state representatives like all the other cities in the country, but they also had no appointed local council members (with decision-making power) to serve them.

Kuala Lumpur was originally part of Selangor. In the 1969 elections, the Alliance Party won only 14 of the 28 seats in the Selangor assembly. This resulted in a hung parliament. The opposition won most of their seats in the vicinity of KL. Thus, the Tun Razak government, determined to prevent any future possibility of losing the Selangor legislature, decided to turn Kuala Lumpur into a federal territory in February 1974, a few months before the general elections of that year.

The concept of "federal territory" is a slightly modified version of Washington, District of Columbia (D.C.) and the Australian Capital Territory (ACT) in Canberra. Like Malaysia, both the American and Australian governments are federal systems. However, the argument that local representation is not needed under direct federal rule does not hold water as these two examples demonstrate. The 690,000-population of Washington, D.C. has an elected mayor and a 13-member council. Meanwhile, the 460,000-population of Canberra has a territorial assembly with 25 members, from which a chief minister and a cabinet of ministers are selected.

Kuala Lumpur's population of 1.982 million (according to the 2020 census) is almost double that of D.C. and the ACT combined. Among Malaysian states, it ranks seventh in terms of population size. It is, therefore, legitimate for a KL resident to ask why KL cannot have a state government if the residents of the miniature Perlis, with less than 300,000 inhabitants, could elect a 15-member legislature.

The case for KL to be made into a full state has become stronger with the opening of Putrajaya in June 1999. Today, most major government offices have been relocated to the planned city, including the judiciary, with only three federal ministries remaining in KL.[1]

Expenditure outlays

The most compelling case for an elected Kuala Lumpur state legislature is to ensure accountability in one of the largest sub-national governments in Malaysia.

One of the best ways to compare the size of the governments is to compare their expenditure outlays. DBKL's budget for 2023 was RM2.6 billion, making it the third largest budget, next to Sarawak's RM10.8 billion and Sabah's RM5.1 billion. The DBKL budget is slightly bigger than that of Selangor, the country's most populous state, which has an allocation of RM2.5 billion, and is eight times that of Perlis' RM293 million budget.[2]

All state budgets are subject to the scrutiny and approval of their state legislature. Yet because KL does not have a state legislature, the

KL Mayor (Datuk Bandar) is not obliged to disclose the full extent of the government outlays.

Moving forward, an elected state legislature of around 45 seats (each seat representing roughly 45,000 residents), with a chief minister and a state cabinet chosen from the elected representatives should be considered. This will ensure greater democratic accountability, giving KL-ites the representation they deserve.

Note: This piece was adapted, with updates and edits, from an article I wrote in *Malaysiakini* on January 3, 2004. See Chin Tong, Liew (2004). "State government for Kuala Lumpur?" *Malaysiakini*, 31 January. Available at: https://www.malaysiakini.com/opinions/22554.

PART VIII

REFORMING PARLIAMENT IN THE SPIRIT OF BIPARTISANSHIP

Politics can sometimes be a lonely journey. Max Weber (1864-1920) wrote that politics is a vocation for someone "who is certain that it will not break him when, from where he stands, the world looks too stupid or mean for what he wants to offer it – that in spite of everything he will be able to say 'but, still!' – only he has the 'call' for politics".

We need every politician to recognise that their role is more than just giving handouts. They are elected to think, deliberate, and decide on good public policies for the society and the nation.

Democracy needs to deliver progress and improvement to daily lives, and the people's well-being. It means we should appreciate differences as strengths, and not as weaknesses. In democratic countries, parliaments are never established to force uniformity. On the contrary, they are built to accommodate differences.

To think system means we need to co-exist. We need to build bipartisanship and respect our opponents. And Parliament is the avenue for such civilised engagements. Accordingly, Chapter 26 draws attention to the functions of Parliament, which go beyond just making laws, being an institution that should provide checks and balances through co-governing.

Chapter 27 explains the much-needed reforms that would strengthen the effectiveness and fairness of Parliament. The aim is for the government and opposition to reach long lasting consensus on various policies that will survive the changes of government.

The long-term challenge for Malaysia is to get all key political actors to be serious participants of the parliamentary processes and turn their ideas into laws in a bipartisan manner as much as possible. As the saying goes, it takes two to tango: we need governments that provide room for the opposition, we need also a responsible opposition whose primary focus is not to plot outside the parliamentary processes but to develop credible policy positions inside the parliamentary framework.

The good news is that the Malaysian Parliament has never been more relevant than under the current Unity Government. Prime Minister Datuk Seri Anwar Ibrahim subjected himself to a test of confidence vote in the Dewan Rakyat on December 19, 2022. As the head of government, he has appeared in Parliament more often than any other prime minister on average in the last 40-odd years. There is also now a 30-minute Prime Minister's Question Time on Tuesdays during sitting days, which is a breakthrough instituted by Anwar.

In the name of bipartisanship, let us continue the momentum of parliamentary reform in the months and years to come.

CHAPTER 26

Key Agenda for Parliamentary Reform

I first became involved in championing parliamentary reforms when I assisted Lim Kit Siang in organising a forum on the "Agenda for First World Parliament" in May 2004 attended by Datuk Seri Nazri Aziz, who was made the first-ever Minister responsible for Parliament. At the time, Kit Siang had just returned to the Parliament after a one-term break, and there was a new Prime Minister, Tun Abdullah Badawi, who campaigned on the reform platform.

Nazri was able to promote some international causes via the Parliament, such as democratisation in Myanmar, for which I am grateful, but there were few reforms to the actual workings of Parliament.

During the tenure of Tan Sri Pandikar Amin Mulia as the Speaker of the Dewan Rakyat from April 2008 to April 2018, the only substantive change to the parliamentary institution was the establishment of a second chamber aimed at creating more parliamentary time for MPs to speak. Regrettably, nothing much beyond that was done in his 10 years as Speaker.

Following the 2018 general election, the two years of the 14th Parliament under the Speakership of Tan Sri Dato' Mohamad Ariff Md Yusof finally started the ball rolling on modernising our parliamentary institutions. The momentum should continue as much as possible under Speaker Tan Sri Dato' Johari Abdul in the 15th Parliament.

Keeping Parliament up-to-date

What do we seek to achieve through parliamentary reforms?

The Parliament is a living institution that should be the centre of rapidly changing national public life. Practices of the Parliament should reflect the changing needs. Malaysia adopted the Westminster Parliamentary framework of government at its Independence in 1957 and the first Parliament convened in 1959.

It is interesting to note that a permanent set of ministerial select committees scrutinising the functioning of ministries only came into existence in Westminster in 1979 after Margaret Thatcher's victory. The second chamber was first "invented" in the Australian Parliament and later adopted by Westminster.

In the 14th Parliament, for the first time there were serious efforts to promote parliamentary reform. I recall my many conversations with Mohamad Ariff. His eyes would shine with excitement when sharing the practices he had learnt from overseas visits or seminars conducted by experts, or preparing to adopt new ideas.

My deputy minister colleagues and I met Mohamad Ariff several times and each time he listened attentively to our views and subsequently some practices were changed immediately, with the help of Datuk Roosme Hamzah and the parliamentary service. I felt particularly grateful to him because I had lobbied for some of these changes for years with the previous Speaker but to no avail.

One such example was to restrict the time of each question-and-answer to 6 minutes to allow for approximately 15 questions to be replied in each of the daily one-and-half-hour sessions. The 6-minute rule allows for more questions to be answered, and for ministers to know exactly which day of the week their ministries have to answer questions in Parliament.

One of the major pieces of work which is still ongoing is to present a Parliamentary Commission Bill for Parliament to have its own parliamentary service commission rather than to be part of the general civil service. Much as we talk about reviving the Parliamentary Service Act 1963 which was abolished in 1992, Mohamad Ariff is right with his idea that the Malaysian Parliament deserves a new Act to govern its administration.

An independent parliament should have the institutional, administrative, and financial autonomies to manage its own affairs under the aforementioned commission.[1] The establishment of this commission needs to be part and parcel of a new and improved Parliamentary Service Act. The Act should empower the Speaker of Dewan Rakyat, the Yang di-Pertua of Dewan Negara, leaders of the government and opposition in both Houses to jointly manage the commission.

Co-governing: The functions of Parliament

Forming governments and testing their legitimacy

The primary role of a Westminster parliament is to enable the formation of a government, and to allow for the legitimacy of the government to be tested through a vote of confidence or other forms of bills and motions.

A functioning and independent parliament allows for attempts by its members to test the legitimacy of the government. Former prime ministers Tun Hussein Onn and Abdullah Badawi tested their legitimacy in Parliament after taking over from their respective predecessors. More recently, the incumbent Datuk Seri Anwar Ibrahim successfully tested the Unity Government's legitimacy through a motion of confidence in Parliament on December 19, 2022 after the 15th General Election had resulted in a hung parliament.

But Parliament should not be put aside to become a rubber stamp after a government is formed. This is what happened throughout the history of the Malaysian Parliament until 2018.

Making laws

The Parliament is where laws are made. But in the Malaysian context, MPs are expected to just rubber stamp in haste bills drafted by the Attorney-General's Chamber and approved by the Cabinet. MPs are not given sufficient time to read and review the bills that are usually tabled in a parachuted form just a few days before they are due to be debated and passed in Parliament.

Parliamentary reforms must therefore focus on enhancing the mechanism for MPs and the parliamentary institution as a whole to fulfil their law-making roles. Some possible tweaks include:

- Parliament should have its own parliamentary draftsmen to work alongside the Attorney-General's Chamber, and sometime provide an alternative to the draft from the AG's chamber;
- Having the Parliamentary Special Select Committees conduct more hearings across the country and even via online platforms, to solicit views from stakeholders and the general public before a bill is finally laid on the table of Parliament for debate;
- Providing MPs with their own research officers with the cost wholly borne by Parliament (instead of the current practice of having a pool of parliamentary research team to be shared among 222 MPs).

Preferably, a bill should be drafted in consultation with MPs in a committee setting, and scrutinised thoroughly, before its eventual passing in the Chamber.

Providing checks and balances

Parliament is also to serve its check and balance function vis-à-vis the executive. Parliamentary time and mechanisms should be made available to fulfil this function. Ultimately, governments need to see Parliament as partners in co-governing to enable the flourishing of parliamentary committees as well as high quality debates and questions in the chamber.

Ministers will not know everything that happens under their watch. The time of government knows best is long gone. Transparency and accountability by ministers to Parliament and by civil servants to parliamentary committees would help ensure that the government is run with the people's best interests in mind.

Co-governing through parliamentary committees would also help nurture a bipartisan group of MPs who will be subject matter experts on policy areas they devote their time to. This would allow successive governments from both sides to draw talents to be promoted to the front bench. Their interactions with bureaucrats in committee works would also help foster a strong whole-of-government ethos. Committee works would also strengthen collegiate bipartisanship which is important to the functioning of a democracy.

More needs to be done to expand mechanisms for co-governing. In the years to come, as we first saw in the 15th General Election, I do not foresee a single dominant party winning more than one third of the seats in Parliament. Future governments will be formed by coalitions of parties with similar strengths and there will be more changes of government. If one takes a long view, co-governing is good for the nation and good for all sides in Parliament.

Expanding time and space for MPs

One important role of the MPs is to speak on behalf of the voters they represent specifically and the general interests they champion. It is important that Parliament makes space and time for MPs to carry out this important function to keep Parliament relevant to the lives of ordinary people and to ensure that the powers that be in high places hear the voices of the people through their elected representatives.

Let us be frank. To a certain extent, each parliamentary chamber is a theatre. We cannot stop some MPs from theatrical performances. For the longest time, the Malaysian Parliament has faced a double whammy – not enough time for MPs to speak and once an MP has the opportunity, he or she would load everything at one go especially during the debate of the Royal Address and the Budget.

For the nation's sake, more should be done to expand the time and space for MPs to bring the voice of the people to Parliament.

CHAPTER 27

Let Us Speed Up the Remaking of Our Parliament

As someone who has cared very much about parliamentary reform since I was elected as a Member of Parliament in 2008, I believe there is a need to accelerate the changes, particularly in making committee work a primary task for all MPs.

In parliaments around the world, the real policy work is mostly done in committees. In Malaysia, for decades there was practically no committee to examine policy matters, except the topical Public Accounts Committee, which was anaemic in the days of the 1MDB scandal. Hence the reason for the media to focus on the shouting and quarrels as well as throwing insults among our MPs in the main Chamber.

This should serve as a trigger to the government to remake our Parliament more extensively than what has taken place since 2018. Some areas for reform, which I proposed in 2019, are as follows.

Parliamentary Special Select Committees

Under the leadership of Speaker Tan Sri Dato' Mohamad Ariff Md Yusof in 2018-20, Parliament introduced 10 committees on various policy areas, such as the Defence and Home Affairs Select Committee.

The incumbent 15th Parliamentary Session under Speaker Tan Sri Dato' Johari Abdul continues the practice of having departmental select committees, including two headed by the Opposition. Many policies can be deliberated in these committees with participation from both the government of the day and the opposition.

Through these committees, backbenchers and opposition members who are keen on policy details can help foster a sense of bipartisanship as most of what governing is all about is common sense.

With a robust committee system in place, it is important to learn that the Main Chamber is not the only place in which MPs have to be. MPs who are not sitting in the Chamber may be sitting in committee meetings. The media people either are not aware of this or not reporting on their work, and of course the committees have yet to allow for live telecast.

For these committees to work, sufficient media space will need to be given to reporting the work of committees. Most parts of committee work should be telecast live on the Internet, and the work of the Public Accounts Committee should get some air time on national television. While the MPs must improve their knowledge and understanding of policy matters, friends in the media too need to do the same to ensure accurate and easy-to-understand news.

To ensure quality committee work, these committees need a very strong secretariat and MPs need to be given better research backing. Thankfully, Speaker Johari Abdul indicated in June 2023 that the select committees would be provided with an allocation, research staff and an office – an improvement from the state of affairs under the previous parliamentary session.[1]

Repurposing the Main and Special Chambers

The Special or Second Chamber was created during Speaker Pandikar Amin Mulia's time in 2016. Inspired by the Australian and British parliaments, I can claim a bit of credit for its creation as it came through my lobbying work with Pandikar Amin.

However, for the most part, the Special Chamber remains somewhat limited in its functions, i.e. to allow for the previous "adjournment speeches" and "emergency motions" to be taken off the main Chamber.

The roles and time of the Special Chamber should be that more motions and speeches can be made by MPs there, parallel to the Main Chamber's sitting. Previously, only two speeches of seven and a half minutes each by backbenchers or opposition MPs with replies from government of equal time were permitted, amounting to only 30 minutes each day. With the latest amendments to the Standing Order in 2023, four speeches could be made on each sitting day, and motions could also be debated, expanding more debate time for MPs.[2]

A full-fledged Second Chamber should take away all constituency-specific issues from the Main Chamber and move them to the Second Chamber so that the main chamber focuses only on the most important things.

With an active Second Chamber for constituency matters, there is a need to ensure MPs speak in a more concise manner in the Main Chamber. Each minute in the Main Chamber costs the nation thousands of ringgit, thus it should be focused on the most important subjects. The days of expecting MPs to sit in the Main Chamber from 10 am to midnight should be behind us: we should maintain the current schedule that does not go past 5:30 pm, with late sessions conducted only when absolutely necessary.

Committee stage, not committee of the house

Currently, after the Minister of Finance presents the annual budget, there will be a policy debate stage. Parliament then spends up to 15 days debating each ministry's budget specifically at a "committee stage". The initial idea was for bipartisan committees of about 10-15 MPs each, comprising government backbenchers and opposition MPs, to look into the ministerial budget in detail.

Instead, in the last 60 years, we have had the "committee of the house", which means everyone sits in the same main chamber, calling the speaker by a different name, i.e. chairman. It is the most inefficient way of utilising Parliament's precious time.

We should allow for committees to debate the ministerial budget during the "committee stage" instead of the current practice. Such a move would give MPs ample time to scrutinise ministerial budgets instead of the current speed train that does not do justice to the billions of ringgit approved within a couple of hours. These arrangements will help make Parliament a co-governing body with ministers, and it will provide more detailed scrutiny and checks on the civil service running the ministries. Such an institutional arrangement will also create a talent pool with policy knowledge on both sides for future ministerial appointments.[3]

To make the country's fiscal policy direction even more transparent, a well-staffed Parliamentary Budget Office (PBO) would be a great change. The idea of a PBO was proposed during a Cabinet Special Committee on Anti-Corruption meeting in January 2019 chaired by then Prime Minister Tun Dr Mahathir Mohamad. A PBO could help prepare MPs and Senators for more meaningful economic debates.

No more *ketua pentadbir* and no more minister of parliament

At the time of writing, the administration of the Parliament is placed under a department run by the Ketua Pentadbir (chief administrator), a bureaucrat assigned by the Public Services Commission (JPA). To date, this administrator has been responsible to a minister in the Prime Minister's Department (usually with a portfolio revolving around parliamentary affairs) rather than the speaker of the Dewan Rakyat or the president of the Dewan Negara.[4]

Moving forward, there is a need to end the Ketua Pentadbir's role in Parliament and return the scope of responsibilities of administering parliamentary affairs to the secretaries of the Dewan Rakyat and Dewan Negara. As stipulated by the original Federal Constitution in 1957, the Dewan Rakyat secretary should serve as the chief administrator of Parliament (*setiausaha bagi parlimen*) while the Dewan Negara secretary should serve as the deputy chief administrator of parliament (*timbalan setiausaha bagi parliament*).

With the prospective tabling of the Parliamentary Commission Bill for the 15th Parliament and the possible return of the Parliamentary Service Act, the parliament should be governed by the Parliamentary Service Commission, with the Dewan Rakyat and Dewan Negara secretaries as the chief executive and deputy chief executive respectively.

The Parliament, with a functioning and inclusive committee system, must be an avenue for the government and opposition to build consensus and to find compromises. It also needs to get feedback from the wider public, and to have checks and balances to prevent the government from making mistakes that are too grave to repair. Let us speed up the remaking of our Parliament. The time for reform is now.

PART IX

STRENGTHENING GOVERNANCE IN A YOUNG DEMOCRACY

This period of newfound dynamism under the Unity Government is the perfect chance to work on setting democratic rules. These rules should stay regardless of who is in power. We need to think system and not personality.

Therefore, all parties should come together and work out fair rules to ensure a level playing field. Clearly, corruption is something we should not sidestep. How to transform the institutions to avoid decay and inertia is also crucial.

That is where Chapter 28 comes in, proposing wide-ranging reforms in various sectors, including the police service, the defence sector, the civil service and the media. Good governance would not only prevent the abuse of power, but it would also lend legitimacy and longevity to responsible policy making in pursuit of the next takeoff.

To think system also means to break silos, and nowhere is this more evident or urgent than in security. Chapters 29 to 32 therefore dive deep into the security sector, emphasising the need for a whole-of-government approach to policing (Chapter 29) and defence (Chapters 30 to 32) in our pursuit of a better, stronger and safer Malaysia. Along the way, the role of the state governments in policing powers (Chapter 29), the importance of innovation and long-term planning in defence (Chapter 30), the expansion of the notion of security to include economic considerations (Chapter 31), and the necessity of having civil servants who are specialists (Chapter 32) are touched upon, bringing many ideas in this book full circle.

The relevance of security to Malaysia's second takeoff is self-evident: all the hard work to strengthen our manufacturing capabilities, attract high-quality investment, export sophisticated goods and services beyond our borders, and build resilient cities will be in vain if we take national security for granted, given the growing geopolitical tensions in our neighbourhood and beyond.

With this in mind, domestic policy is certainly important, but we must not forget the importance of securing Malaysia's position in the world, particularly in light of conflict elsewhere. The final Chapter 33 explains how we should orient our foreign policy to ensure that Malaysia has room to navigate in a contested world.

All in all, throughout this book, I have emphasised the need to redefine the role of the state as an essential participant in the economy. By now, it should be clear that I would like the Reagan/Thatcher-inspired "government is the problem, not the solution" idea to be thrown out of the window.

For the sake of a prosperous and secure middle-class society, we need a state that is both smart and kind. It is time to build a long lasting new economic, social and political order for the decades to come.

CHAPTER 28

A Reform Agenda to Remake Democracy

In December 2019, just as the first cases of the then unknown COVID-19 virus were popping up around the world, I took stock of Pakatan Harapan's first (and, as it would soon emerge, only) full year in power:

> *"What happened in Malaysia on 9th May 2018 was a democratic uprising through the ballot box. It ended the 61-year rule of the semi-authoritarian Barisan Nasional regime, by then the world's longest continuously serving elected government.*
>
> *However, consolidating democracy is probably more difficult than defeating authoritarian rule. If Malaysia can remake our democracy, we will lead the world in bucking the democratic deficits and decline in recent years. It will take time, will and determination but also patience and a more collegiate approach."*

Even as we were trying to push through reforms to strengthen the role of the Parliament and reduce the consolidation of power at the hands of the executive, it was clear that addressing all the systemic issues in our mode of governance would not happen overnight.

Less than three months later, we were embroiled in a triple crisis – health, political and economic – that pushed our nation and its people to the brink. In the name of fighting a deadly pandemic, reforms were pushed to the backburner while the Perikatan Nasional government-of-the-day was preoccupied with its own survival.

With the pandemic behind us and a new government in power, now is the time to pick up where we left off in 2020. If we want to keep the reformist zeal alive, we need wide-ranging reforms across a range of other areas, including in the police force, defence sector, civil service and media, which I have been pushing for since my time as Deputy Defence Minister and earlier.

Police reform

Take police reform as an example. For me, it has to be a comprehensive reform that appeals to a wider spectrum of society beyond a legal agenda to enact laws. Law-making is important to set new rules for democracy but needs to be complemented with holistic reforms.

For one, the Royal Malaysian Police (PDRM) needs to be made more accountable for its actions, such as custodian deaths and corruption, prison reforms and reducing overcrowding, immigration and the management of foreign workers and refugees. In this context, police reform is not a new idea. In 2004, the then Prime Minister Tun Abdullah Badawi set up a panel chaired by the former Chief Justice Tun Mohamed Dzaiddin Abdullah to investigate these challenges. The following year, the panel commissioned the 2005 Report of the Royal Commission to Enhance the Operation and Management of the Royal Malaysian Police Report (commonly known as the Tun Dzaiddin report).[1]

Though the cited data in the Tun Dzaiddin report is dated, many of its 125 recommendations remain sharp and relevant today. The 600-page report's central spirit is best captured by the second paragraph of the Strategic Objective:

> *"It must continue to uphold the law, maintain law and order and combat crime, but must pursue these ends in compliance with human rights, restricting and infringing upon them only when necessary and permissible in law. PDRM must see itself more as a 'service' than as a 'force' and the guardian of the people's rights though it will need to retain some of its paramilitary capabilities and characteristics. Finally, PDRM must be more transparent and accountable, especially to independent bodies established by the Government and to the people."*

In short, the Tun Dzaiddin report calls for a more people-centric PDRM through a people's *police service*, not a *police force* that only serves the interests of the state. The report advocates the democratisation of the police service for the sake of the service as well as the people.[2]

Such a mammoth task of democratising the police service will take statesmen, police officers, civil society leaders, security experts, victims of police misconduct and many other stakeholders to acknowledge that change is needed. This pursuit of democratisation requires all these stakeholders to negotiate the various trade-offs in a transparent and participatory manner.

Re-envisioning PDRM as a service rather than as a force will mean changing doctrine, organisational structure, and therefore resource allocation, according to policing operations that we as the *rakyat* value the most. Similarly, ensuring that PDRM is developed, trained, and equipped along these lines will resolve their logistical concerns over the next few years as they acclimate to their new mission and motto. Potential reforms to this end are addressed in the next chapter.

Eventually we want to see a PDRM whose beat officers and patrol cars are welcomed and known in the communities that they work in. We want a PDRM that can process criminals quickly and correctly, and uphold the law justly and fairly. We want it to become a service that cares for the communities and protects them, rather than just another uniformed force carrying guns.

The final outcome of this exercise should mean a dignified police who no longer have to serve narrow partisan interests but to be the guardians of Malaysian democracy. At the same time, the professional and economic lives of police personnel will be improved when democracy accords them a louder voice, respect and dignity.

Defence and security reform

While the democratisation of the police service is still a slow work in progress, the defence sector has witnessed the dawn of such democratisation in the form of the Defence White Paper (DWP). As former Deputy Minister of Defence for 22 months, I was closely involved in the formulation of Malaysia's first DWP to reform and modernise the defence sector.

Presented by the then Minister Mohamad Sabu to the Parliament on December 2, 2019, the DWP was the labour of love of about 50 military officers, civil servants in the Ministry of Defence, and academics. They sat together for a total of 50 days in 2019 to deliberate, discuss and prepare the document, a break from the typical approach of outsourcing the government's policy thinking to consulting firms.

The core idea of the DWP is to define Malaysia as a "maritime nation with continental roots" (for which my friend Professor Dr Kuik Cheng-Chwee deserves credit), given the country is surrounded by the South China Sea (arguably the most contentious body of water in the world) and the Straits of Malacca (the world's busiest shipping lane).[3]

The DWP calls for the drafting, debating, and later publishing and enacting of several important plans, namely:

- A joint capability development plan between the three service branches of the Malaysian Armed Forces (MAF) – the Army, Navy and Air Force – to outline the specific equipment and service needs of the organisation for the next 10 years;
- A defence investment plan to clarify how much money would be spent in the period of 10 years for various selected defence projects aligned with these other plans; and
- A defence industrial policy to set clear rules of the road and create a competitive environment for local firms to participate in the market under the government's guidance.

Accordingly, the plans should be rigorously discussed and tested within Cabinet, and then brought to Parliament for further deliberation. Allowance for robust debate and discourse will ensure that the end result will be reflective of the outcomes we want to achieve with this endeavour.[4]

In September 2022, the MAF released its National Military Strategy 2.0 document, which has the DWP as one of its sources of reference. The MAF has therefore expressed willingness and readiness to play ball on implementing the DWP. Beyond the defence sector, the entire security apparatus – which also covers the portfolio of the Home

Ministry on immigration – needs to get its act together. Security needs a "whole-of-government" approach, which Chapters 30 to 32 cover in more detail.

Ultimately, Malaysia's defence sector can be of more relevance economically if we could build up a defence and security industry that is not captured by agents but driven by innovations. The goal is not to produce everything in Malaysia for self-sufficiency's sake, which is unrealistic for a small country with a small defence budget. It is about building expertise and irreplaceable niches in some selected areas, which can then be also for civilian usage and help spur domestic R&D efforts across the board.

Civil service

The civil service also needs to be guided by democratic principles. We should aspire to develop a world-class civil service that serves the democratic interests of the Malaysian population so that no more mega scandals such as the 1MDB fiasco would ever happen again.

One of the key concerns is how to build a very competent cohort of middle-level officers with subject matter expertise. The Malaysian civil service rotates officers who are trained as generalists across ministries and agencies. However, as government and governing becomes a lot more sophisticated, expertise among officers is so crucial in determining the outcome of a policy or a decision.

At the same time, the public must feel genuine benefits of a reformed civil service through improved service and performance via collegiate public debate.

Ultimately, democracies need to build, survive and thrive on democratic institutions such as a reformed parliament, electoral system and media; and a democratic culture that starts from young in schools.

Media reform

Media reform is particularly important. We need to negotiate a new grand bargain between society and the media for a nascent democracy.

To build a more resilient democracy, the role of state media, the role of partisan-owned media, and the role of media that racialises debates, apart from handling fake news via social media, should be examined and re-looked at. In fact, the governance of social media in a democratic but rule-based setting is important too.

To change that, the public must come together to desire the change in the interests of preserving Malaysian democracy for all, and not for the government of the day.

If democracy cannot bring better economic well-being for ordinary folks, it is a recipe for disaster. The case of Europe is quite indicative that austerity breeds right-wing populism that tends to dismantle democracies. At the end of the day, if democracy cannot put food on the table through better jobs, better pay, better living standards, democracy itself would fail sooner than later.

The Malaysian democratic change in 2018 can only be preserved if the majority of the society embrace democracy and become democrats to preserve the gains actively.

CHAPTER 29

Turning the Police from a Militarised Force to a Community Partner

Since the release of the Tun Dzaiddin Report in 2005, the debate on police reform has mostly centred on the Independent Police Complaints and Misconduct Commission (IPCMC) bill, almost as if it was the miracle cure. Actually the idea was only one strategic thrust of ten identified by the Report.

Essentially, the polemic is on the one side a sole concern about police accountability, and on the other side a sole concern about whether police are fully equipped with powers to get the job done. There does not have to be such a divide. The progressives should be concerned about the welfare of the police and the effectiveness of policing, too.

In any discussion of police and enforcement reforms, we need to consider a more fundamental premise first. What role should PDRM play in our society? How does it view itself in relation to the rest of society?

This might seem like an easy question at first but we cannot forget that PDRM's history in the immediate post-colonial era required it to be a fundamentally different organisation than what we would expect it to be today.

The immediate threat to public order and safety at the time was the subversive activities of Communist insurgents. Thus, the police force of the time necessarily took on a paramilitary and counter-espionage nature. Police field force units were trained essentially as light infantry to carry out deep jungle raids and other kinetic operations to eliminate the Communist fighters. Meanwhile, the Special Branch took on the role of counter-intelligence, combating the clandestine activities of Communist infiltrators.

The legacy of this experience is prevalent today. There are currently five brigades' worth of General Operations Force units (the field force equivalent today), each composed of anywhere between two to four battalions. At Lahad Datu, they were among the first to respond to the incursion in 2013. The Special Branch is heavily involved in political surveillance that is often controversial and obsolete. Be that as it may, the special branch is still an important element of national security when it comes to countering violent and extremist groups.

So it is clear that PDRM was first structured as an armed force in its early days, but it must now transition to a smart and community-driven service to reflect the needs of today's Malaysia. This is in fact the first recommendation made by Tun Dzaiddin in his report, under the first strategic thrust on modernising the roles, functions, and organisation of the RMP. Once this premise is accepted, and the wider context of the reforms needed to fulfil this is understood, then we can appreciate why IPCMC alone is insufficient.

We need to be mindful of the fact that the police to citizen ratio in Malaysia is still largely unfavourable. In a briefing conducted in October 2019 by PDRM to the Parliamentary Special Select Committee for Consideration of Bills, nationally there is one police officer to 356 people when looking at personnel posted to police contingents by state (i.e. not including those in Bukit Aman). By comparison, Interpol suggests that the ideal ratio should be closer to 1:250.[1]

To put this statistic into perspective, consider that in 2017, the former Chief Justice Tun Arifin Zakaria once witnessed the same investigation officer having to attend three back-to-back court cases in a single day.[2] In 2013, then Deputy Minister for Home Affairs Wan Junaidi Tuanku Jaafar noted that in one extreme case, an investigation officer had to contend with 100 cases.[3] The rule of thumb is the fewer cases an IO has to deal with, the more time he could devote to each case, thus the quality of investigation would improve.

Being bold in revamping PDRM

We cannot expect our police officers to be able to satisfactorily investigate and resolve cases under these conditions. The government needs to consider bolder initiatives. It needs to start considering modernising PDRM, making it more data-centric and facilitating its adoption of technologies that will help to optimise and process its operations more quickly. A rationalisation exercise may also be in order between PDRM's various departments to give more headcount and resource space to its investigations and community-centric units.

Specifically on the issue of narcotics, the government also needs a completely different approach. On the one hand, it needs to consider a more rehabilitative approach for addicts, who are also victims of the product. Doing so will also help to reduce overcrowding in prisons.[4]

PDRM should not completely cast away its paramilitary and counterintelligence capabilities. The special branch as well as the paramilitary units should be drastically reduced in numbers but increased in capacity to become elite units dealing with very specific tasks. Such capabilities should be retained but organised more specifically, given the ever present and growing non-traditional security threats in the form of transborder crimes (both on land and at sea) and a rise in violent criminal and / or extremist activities.

Furthermore, these capabilities also need to be synchronised and integrated with other national security agencies, such as the Armed Forces, the Research Division, and the National Security Council, to foster a whole-of-government approach to cross-sectional problems.

Meanwhile, specifically for the Special Branch, roles such as domestic political surveillance and monitoring should be cast aside to enable it to better focus on these duties. Domestic politicians are not terrorists and enemies of the state. They should not be treated as enemies of the state.

Nonetheless, eventually we want to see a PDRM whose beat officers and patrol cars are welcomed and known in the communities where they work. We want a PDRM that is able to process criminals quickly and correctly, and uphold the law justly and fairly. We want it to become a service that cares for the communities and protects them, rather than just another uniformed force carrying guns.

There is also a deeper question about how Malaysia organises its federal institutions vis-à-vis the states. Policing powers in many other countries are the domains of provincial or state governments or even that of municipalities. For instance, do we need a centralised traffic police system or can we devolve the powers of traffic police to the states? With the roles of the state governments becoming more important in the years to come, devolving some less critical policing powers should be on the table for federal-state negotiations.

In a similar vein, if we expect the new PDRM to take on these missions that are driven around protecting and serving our communities, then we must also consider the logistical implications of such a mission set.

Tun Dzaiddin's report indicates that much of the PDRM's equipment, such as patrol vehicles and even computers, of the time were either obsolete or in need of serious repair, owing to a lack of funds. Furthermore, the state of police housing leaves much to be desired, with many of the buildings run down and unsafe for occupancy.

Just as the Armed Forces needs a joint capability development plan that outlines how, when, and how much money will be committed to its force development, so too does PDRM.

Absent a comprehensive development plan, these endemic issues will persist and prevent PDRM from operating at optimal capacity. Police officers have needs and families like the rest of us. If these needs are not addressed adequately, then we cannot expect their morale and enthusiasm to remain high in the discharge of their duties for the public good.

In a way, addressing these issues will more directly fix the fundamental factors that are arguably causing the police and the *rakyat* so much distress. As much as the police have to be held accountable for their misconduct, we also need to consider the needs of the police service, and how to best foster an environment in which they can perform as best as they can.

The question of police abuse misconduct cannot be ignored; errant police officers acting out of impunity will no doubt cause the rift to grow further, and should be disciplined accordingly. Ideally, these wide-ranging reforms should come together in concert with more accountability so as to create a police service that is smart, community-driven, resilient, and clean.

However, a focus merely on police accountability, without any emphasis on the police's welfare, logistics, and even its impetus for existence, will be akin to putting the horse before the cart.

If we want reforms that give us the best for both our police officers and the *rakyat*, we need to rally around a bipartisan plan that both seeks to rebuild the *rakyat*'s trust in the police, while also seeing to the needs of the police.

Note: This piece was adapted, with updates and edits, from an article I co-wrote with Nik Mohamed Rashid bin Nik Zurin in *Malaysiakini* on April 3, 2021. See Chin Tong, Liew and Nik Mohamed Rashid bin Nik Zurin (2021). "Turning police from militarised force to community partner". *Malaysiakini*, 3 April. Available at: https://www.malaysiakini.com/news/569253

CHAPTER 30

Malaysia's Long Overdue Defence Reforms: Jettisoning the Age of Innocence

The age of innocence that has dominated Malaysia's attitude towards defence matters in the past three decades needs to be jettisoned. Given mounting threats in its external environment, Malaysia needs to accelerate defence reforms centred on the concept of jointness across multiple domains.

Malaysia's long overdue defence reforms can no longer be put on the backburner. For more than three decades since December 1989, when the government inked a peace treaty with the Communist Party of Malaya, Malaysians have lived in an age of innocence when it came to the question of external threats facing the country. In recent years, Malaysia's neighbourhood is looking increasingly less benign, with great power rivalry between the United States and China, and Beijing's growing assertiveness in the South China Sea.

Naïveté and nonchalance in a tough neighbourhood

On May 31, 2021, 16 People's Liberation Army Air Force (PLAAF) planes entered the airspace above Malaysia's exclusive economic zone

(EEZ) in the South China Sea. This jolted the nation to wake up to new geopolitical challenges.

For nearly a decade, the Chinese Coast Guard has maintained an almost all-year-round presence near Beting Patinggi Ali (South Luconia Shoals). Thus, in a way, the PLAAF sortie was doing in the air what their Coast Guard colleagues have been doing on the high seas for years – enforcing China's claims in the South China Sea. China claims ownership of the Luconia Shoals, which are located in Malaysia's EEZ about 80 nautical miles northwest off Borneo.[1]

In less challenging times, Malaysia did attempt to modernise its defence, including building up the Air Force and Navy for conventional warfare beginning in the 1990s. It also attempted to balance the forces between the peninsular and eastern theatres arising from the Lahad Datu incident in 2013, when a group of militants from the Philippines tried to lay claim to the state of Sabah. Following the incident, there was some talk about the need for jointness between the different arms of the Malaysian armed forces. The post-2013 conversations about jointness did not extend much beyond the previous attempt in 2004, which saw the formation of a joint force headquarters but with a limited scope of responsibilities.

In general, a nonchalant peacetime attitude of the previous establishment and the public pervaded over defence matters.

There is a need for stronger political will to advance defence reforms, otherwise old legacies will dictate the current and future path. The Malaysian Armed Forces remain single service-centric, with the largest resources and attention given to the army. While acquiring a more multifaceted outlook over the years, the Army is still moulded by the experience of jungle warfare it successfully waged against the Communists decades ago.

The Cold War legacies guided the army to fortify the Peninsula, and in the eastern theatre, concentrating on guarding the land border with Indonesia. In some instances, the Armed Forces doubled as a border patrol force to stop undocumented migrants from entering the country.

Defence White Paper

During the short stint of the Pakatan Harapan government, Defence Minister Mohamad Sabu presented Malaysia's first Defence White Paper (DWP) to Parliament on December 2, 2019, with a mission to reform the defence sector to meet the challenges of the 2020s.

The core idea of the DWP was to define Malaysia as a maritime nation with continental roots. Malaysia is surrounded by the South China Sea – arguably the world's most contentious body of water – and the Malacca Straits, the world's busiest sea lane.

A rigorous assessment of defence requirements should follow from a proper grasp of such extant realities. There needs to be an open acceptance that the jungle is unlikely to be the battleground of the future. Capabilities and capacities in multiple domains – maritime and air, urban, cyberspace, and non-conventional warfare – need to be built up rapidly.

When I was Deputy Defence Minister, I often repeated the mantra of former Chief of Armed Forces Tan Sri Zulkifli Zainal Abidin that "the army has to swim" in such a new era. Cognizant of the Army's important role, I reassured the Army that no nation could fight with just a contingent of Special Forces, the Navy and Air Force – it had to do so in tandem with the Army. Hence the role of the Army would not diminish even if defence modernisation focuses on building joint maritime capabilities.

But the other side of the coin is also true: the Army cannot fight alone. The single service-centric culture will have to give way to a genuine commitment to jointness.

There needs to be an open acceptance that the jungle is unlikely to be the battleground of the future. Capabilities and capacities in multiple domains – maritime and air, urban, cyberspace, and non-conventional warfare – need to be built up rapidly.

The Lahad Datu incident in early 2013 compelled the Armed Forces to expand its command structure in the eastern theatre. There is now a three-star general each for the Army and Navy with responsibility for East Malaysia. But serious political will is needed to achieve peninsula-eastern theatre parity in terms of troop deployment and capacities.

Serious defence reforms will need a team of capable defence civilians and a strong defence industry. The civilians in the defence ministry are currently rotated across the ministries; many of them lack expertise and specialist experience in defence. This will have to change with a cluster of senior civil servants trained in security matters as well as keeping the best civilians at the Ministry of Defence for a longer period. The defence industry will need to shed off its "sales agent" tendency and invest in innovation. Again, political will is required to transform the sector.

The DWP places heavy emphasis on building a future force with new capabilities. Currently, the Army, Navy and Air Force each have their own long-term capability plans, namely Army4nextG, 15to5 (for the Navy), and Cap55 (Capability 2055 for the Air Force). But there is currently no agreed-upon joint Armed Forces capability plan. Indeed, the Cabinet and Parliament have never officially endorsed a plan with long-term funding commitments. The five-year Malaysia Plan is not an adequate instrument for defence planning, which usually requires longer strategic horizons.

The strategic environment in the 2020s will be markedly different from the last three decades. Malaysia's comprehensive defence reforms, outlined in its first-ever DWP, need the national consensus and political will to be fast-tracked. The age of innocence needs to be replaced by an era of strategic cognizance – a cognizance of pressing realities in Malaysia's neighbourhood.

Note: This piece was adapted, with updates and edits, from an article I wrote in the journal *Fulcrum* published by the ISEAS-Yusof Ishak Institute on June 9, 2021. See Chin Tong, Liew (2021). "Malaysia's Long Overdue Defence Reforms: Jettisoning the Age of Innocence." *Fulcrum*, 9 June. Singapore: ISEAS-Yusof Ishak Institute. Available at: https://fulcrum.sg/malaysias-long-overdue-defence-reforms-jettisoning-the-age-of-innocence//

CHAPTER 31

Resetting the Security Sector in Malaysia

In recent years, there have been drastic and concurrent shifts in Malaysia's political power structure as well as its geopolitical environment. To adapt, Malaysia's security sector requires a corresponding reset.

The security apparatus, which encompasses home affairs domains, such as immigration and the management of foreign workers, as well as Malaysia's external defence, has a broad and pressing milieu of internal and external challenges to tackle.

Domestically, the police force also needs modernisation in its methods and organisational arrangements and to be made more accountable for its actions, such as custodian deaths and corruption; prison reforms and reducing overcrowding is an important agenda; immigration and the management of foreign workers and refugees require new approaches, too. All these issues will require fresh thinking among the political masters.

Externally, the great power rivalry between the US and China is at Malaysia's doorstep, especially but not restricted to the South China Sea. The crisis in Myanmar, as well as the humanitarian crisis involving the Rohingya, would continue to impact Malaysia. Rapidly worsening climate change would result in more disasters with an impact on

Malaysia. Malaysia also needs a whole-of-nation approach to deal with increasing cybersecurity threats.[1]

The larger problems

The bigger problem is that the Malaysian security establishment is decidedly focused on domestic concerns with insufficient attention paid to what is going on around the region and the world. To compound matters, the various silos in the domestic sphere rarely talk to each other.

Pre-2018, ruling party leaders were more interested in portfolios that allowed ministers to exercise personal discretion over huge contract values or funds. Given these political considerations, the Foreign Affairs portfolio was seen as a Siberia for outcasts, such as former prime minister Tun Abdullah Badawi, who spent some time in the political wilderness in the 1990s. Furthermore, strategic decisions on foreign affairs were mostly decided by the Prime Minister rather than the Foreign Minister.

During my time in the Pakatan Harapan government, I was aware that military leaders were sceptical with the Home Affairs and Foreign Affairs Ministries' approaches towards certain border and security challenges, yet there was hardly a platform at the strategic level to thrash out the differences and work out a coherent grand strategy.

Perhaps the most emblematic instance of this dissonance occurred on June 1, 2021 when the Royal Malaysian Air Force Headquarters revealed that China's military aircraft had flown above Malaysia's exclusive economic zone with a curious line that the Foreign Ministry was 'informed'. Currently, sectors of Malaysia's land borders are distributed between the Army and the General Operations Force of the

Royal Malaysian Police. The safety of the long east Sabah water frontier is placed under a convoluted Eastern Sabah Security Command (ESSCOM), which comprises members of the police, the Armed Forces and civilians.

The initial discussions during the Pakatan Harapan government era about the formation of an integrated border force, which potentially could consolidate all border management, was put on a backburner after the Sheraton Move. Under the current Unity Government, Home Minister Datuk Seri Saifuddin Nasution Ismail has renewed the discussion to establish a dedicated border force.

Cabinet clusters and lip service

The National Security Council has its origins in the management of inter-agency collaboration in the aftermath of the May 13 ethnic clashes in 1969, which explains its domestic orientation. The entity is very much driven by bureaucrats, with very little political leadership steering it from the top. Before the COVID-19 crisis, the Council usually met once a quarter.

When former Prime Minister Tan Sri Muhyiddin Yassin imposed a nationwide lockdown in March 2020, the National Security Council was chosen as the platform for inter-agency coordination, and the then Senior Minister for Security Dato' Sri Ismail Sabri was made the lead minister to update the nation daily on the security dimensions of the COVID-19 lockdown.

Muhyiddin's innovation of Cabinet clusters of security, economy, social and education, and infrastructure development, with a senior minister leading each, was an interesting arrangement. However, in practice, it was unfortunate that during the COVID-19 crisis, the Health

Ministry, under its Director-General Tan Sri Noor Hisham Abdullah, despite good intentions, guarded its turf and held a separate health update on a daily basis, rendering the cluster system moot.

The three-way clash among health, security and trade – represented by the then MITI Minister Dato' Seri Mohamed Azmin Ali – dominated the news in 2021 and significantly diminished public confidence in the government's ability to manage the crisis.

During that period, there was also very little policy coordination between the Home Affairs Ministry and other security entities. For instance, while the Foreign Affairs Ministry was campaigning to make Malaysia a member of the United Nations Human Rights Council, agencies under the Home Affairs Ministry were exceedingly harsh on refugees and undocumented migrants during the pandemic.

Hope for the security sector

In May 2023, Prime Minister Datuk Seri Anwar Ibrahim made a surprise appointment of former Ambassador to China and Foreign Ministry veteran Raja Dato' Nurshirwan Zainal Abidin as the Director-General of the National Security Council. In my congratulatory message to the very articulate Nurshirwan, I told him I could now imagine him being a sparring partner of equal intellectual heft and weight to Jake Sullivan, President Joe Biden's National Security Advisor.

I hope Nurshirwan could contribute to bringing the security sector closer. Also, in my current capacity as Deputy MITI Minister, I met Dr Wang Yun-jong, the Economic Security Advisor to President Yoon Suk Yeol of South Korea. It is time that Malaysia formulated a clearer conception of economic security with the right personnel to look into the matter.

It is time for the government to be more serious about resetting the security apparatus. Business as usual would not take Malaysia well into the future. There is a dire need for a reset in the security sectors.

Note: This piece was adapted, with updates and edits, from an article I wrote in the journal *Fulcrum* published by the ISEAS-Yusof Ishak Institute on August 30, 2021. See Chin Tong, Liew (2021). "Resetting the Security Sector in Malaysia." *Fulcrum*, 30 August. Singapore: ISEAS-Yusof Ishak Institute. Available at: https://fulcrum.sg/resetting-the-security-sector-in-malaysia/

CHAPTER 32

The Armed Forces as the Catalyst for a Rejuvenated Malaysia

The Armed Forces is one of the elements in the toolbox of Malaysia's statecraft, or, in Hans Morgenthau's words, of national power.[1]

For Malaysia, an aspiring middle power, the challenge of exercising this power will be even more difficult, as our margins of error will be much smaller compared to that of the Great Powers. Yet, if we organise ourselves strategically, and in a "whole-of-government" manner, Malaysia could punch above our weight in this changing tide of world affairs.

National resilience: a whole-of-society effort

Over the years, the Malaysian system has somehow allowed too many silos to grow across the government. Malaysia needs a sense of shared purpose and agreed common missions. We urgently need to inculcate in the collective consciousness of this nation an understanding of the idea of resilience or *ketahanan*.

Resilience is more holistic than the narrower definition of 'defence' or 'security'. Resilience is about whether we, as a nation, have what it takes to protect our society and our people from all forms of challenges and threats. Threats can come in any form. Just a while ago, very few would have seen it coming that an unseen coronavirus would simultaneously upend the way the world lives and throw many assumptions that we took for granted for decades into the dustbins of history. It is not just "whole-of-government" that we would pursue; we need to develop a "whole-of-society" consciousness, too.

The civilian leadership needs to see the strategic thinking of the Armed Forces. At the same time, the Armed Forces must always caution itself that it does not operate in a vacuum, and that it is not a distinctively separate unit but a very integral part of the government and society.

Further, the Armed Forces need to develop "jointness" – the services training to fight wars and maintain peace together – in a much deeper manner than we have ever done.

For the Armed Forces to play a catalytic role, Malaysia needs a new security mindset for the 2020s. The DWP is thus far the only government document that provides clarity on some of the following questions: What does Malaysia aspire to be, or what is the end goal? According to the White Paper, Malaysia is an aspiring middle power that has historically been a bridging linchpin between great powers in the region. Think about the critical roles played by the Melaka Sultanate and Srivijaya.

The world is now at a crossroads and we are at the geographical centre of great power competition. If we play our game well, Malaysia is well-positioned to be the linchpin between the Indian Ocean and the Pacific Ocean, what the US and her allies are now calling "Indo-Pacific". Of course, if we do not do well, we will become the proverbial mouse deer stampeded by fighting elephants (*gajah sama gajah berjuang, pelanduk mati di tengah-tengah*).

A brief history of Malaysia's security

For us to re-imagine the future, we need to know how history shapes our paths and institutions.

Before the 2018 General Election, whenever I was asked if there would be a military coup should the then Prime Minister Dato' Sri Najib Razak lose, I would answer confidently that "there would not be military coups in Malaysia as the MAF consists of professional soldiers". More importantly, the security set-up is such that the police deal with domestic politics far more than the Armed Forces.

Malaysia's security arrangement is unique in many ways when compared to our regional neighbours, as a result of historic events, particularly those of the Emergency of 1948 until 1960. The British chose to expand the police force massively with a very significant proportion of Malayan officers to deal with the Communist's challenge in 1948 while the military was constituted by battalions of the Royal Malay Regiment, the Federation Regiment, and various Commonwealth Regiments.

If you think about ASEAN and its immediate South Asian or North Asian neighbours, only Malaysia, Singapore and Brunei did not have the military as the dominant force in their societies at any point of their histories. The Malaysian police, which is centrally commanded, has always been about equal in size as the Armed Forces.[2] In the cases of Malaysia, Singapore and Brunei, the State was not constituted by the revolutionary armies after World War II. In many ways, Malaysia's security system was only fully "Malaysianised" after the end of Anglo-Malaysian Defence Agreement and the withdrawal of British Forces beyond the east of the Suez Canal in 1971. Coincidentally or perhaps as a consequence to this, the Tun Razak Hussein Government pursued a more neutral and less pro-Western non-aligned foreign policy outlook.

The Malaysian security establishment was very much pre-occupied by counter-insurgency war until the Hatyai Peace Accord in December 1989. My first Military Advisor (during my time as Deputy Defence Minister) Major General Abd Rahman Ab. Wahab shared with me many stories of the Armed Forces' gallant fights against the Communists during the Second Emergency.

One of the consequences of this experience, however, was that the focus on jungle warfare necessarily constrained the development of other branches of the Army compared to the Infantry. In a classified report by the RAND Corporation in 1964, Riley Sunderland wrote:

> *"One may surmise that the Malay battalions of 1955 were armed less elaborately because of the difficulty of training mortar crews, antitank crews, maintenance specialists, and ordnance units at a pace commensurate with the fourfold expansion of the Malay Regiment and during a campaign in which there was less need for them than for hardy riflemen and machine gunners who were at home in the jungle."*[3]

1989 was not only the end of guerrilla war by the Malayan Communist Party, but also the fall of the Berlin Wall, which signalled the beginning of the end of the Soviet bloc. The 1990s and the 2000s saw the US being the sole global hegemon. Domestically, the Malaysian Armed Forces developed the full range of conventional capabilities beyond the requirements of jungle warfare. Even so, the echoes of the infantry-centric doctrine of the Cold War remain.

The modern Malaysian Army is overwhelmingly composed of infantry battalions, with considerably less quantities of equivalent supporting formations. In terms of foreign policy, Malaysia emerged as a global voice for the Third World/the Global South and the Muslim nations during this period.

Let us be honest: Malaysia as a nation somehow slacks off in the relatively good years. As there were no threats, we sold off our urban military airport, bases and camps for property development; we grew the size of the government and the Armed Forces, but we also erected more silos. Our defence industry is acting more like agents than innovators. The list goes on.

The US and Europe were weakened by the Global Financial Crisis in 2008 while China has grown much stronger economically and militarily, and also more assertive. As China is Malaysia's near neighbour and largest trading partner, as well as competing claimants in South China Sea, we have an intricate global challenge at our doorstep. COVID-19 and the fallout from the presidency of Donald Trump have forced everyone to rethink and reset.

Crucial questions

For Malaysia to move forward to position ourselves as a maritime nation with continental roots, playing the crucial linchpin role in the geographically critical Indian Ocean and Pacific Ocean, and for the Armed Forces to play a catalytic role to rejuvenate Malaysia, we need to ask ourselves some very hard questions. For instance:

- If we are serious about the notion of a maritime nation, do we need to strengthen our Navy and Air Force?
- Within the Army, is infantry everything? Or do we need to build up engineers and other supporting arms?
- How about cybersecurity and cyber defence? How about CBRNe (Chemical, Biological, Radiological, Nuclear, and high yield

Explosives)? How about preparing for other kinds of asymmetric warfare?

- Are we committed to increasing jointness across the board beyond the Joint Force Headquarters?
- What is the role of women in the Armed Forces?
- What sort of roles do state governments have in shaping Reserve Forces?
- How do we ensure that civilians in the Ministry of Defence genuinely understand defence issues? How do we ensure that everyone who is responsible for security and defence in the Government has a shared understanding of what threats we are facing?
- How do we get everyone in the government including the Finance and Economic Ministries to understand defence procurement? How do we ensure that there is no corruption while the defence industry becomes a catalyst for scientific and technological innovations?
- And can we see the Armed Forces as having a role in addressing critical climate change issues?

Defence White Paper revisited: three pillars

Fortunately, the Defence White Paper has some ideas to offer. The strategy to reach this goal of rejuvenating Malaysia's defence has three pillars: (i) concentric deterrence; (ii) comprehensive defence; and (iii) credible partnerships. These pillars in effect are key elements of Malaysia's national power that need to be enhanced in order to meet new challenges and opportunities.

(i) Concentric deterrence

We need to think through the idea of Two Theatres, East and West, and the layers of Core, Extended, Forward. Here, we have to make considerations for Peninsular Malaysia, Sabah and Sarawak, while also keeping an eye on the Straits of Malacca, the South China Sea, and the Sulu Sea. We also need to ask some hard questions about our Force Structure. Currently, the Army has about 80,000 personnel, the Navy has about 18,000 personnel, and the Air Force has about 15,000 personnel. We may have to admit that we are tilted more towards the Army, yet our new challenges emerge from the sea, the air and the cyber space. There is an imbalance of resources against priorities and missions.

Furthermore, the Army itself needs to rethink the make-up of its divisions and brigades. We need to think about how well-supported the infantry and armour are. On this, we need to examine the ratio of combat battalions to combat support battalions.

Most of the combat support arms are grouped at division rather than brigade level. This means that any given infantry battalion will be relatively unsupported in terms of artillery, air defence, cyber, and combat engineering capabilities. And most of these capabilities are concentrated in the Peninsula, not in Medan Timur, as in the Theatre covering Sabah and Sarawak.

By comparison, in the US, a brigade combat team is required to have at least one engineering and one artillery battalion. In Russia, there can be up to three artillery battalions per brigade/regiment. Compare that to Malaysia's ratio, which can be limited to a single battalion of artillery and a squadron of engineers at division level.

Infantry and armour alone cannot win battles, especially against near peer adversaries that sport combined-arms battalions. Supporting arms are just as important as frontline arms. What used to work in the Emergencies will no longer work in our current situation.

When we go up one echelon, we see that jointness can be improved. There are currently five separate three-star echelons: the Army with its Medan Barat and Timur; the Navy with its Armada Barat and Timur; and the Air Force with its Markas Pemerintahan Operasi Udara (MPOU), divided into two Wilayah Udara.

At some point, these five different three-star echelons also need to be folded into a single command structure per Theatre. Consider a system of Joint Combatant Command, which is already in practice in the US and China. During one of my visits to Sarawak and Sabah, I was surprised to be briefed that the Army has more joint activities with its Indonesian counterpart in Kalimantan than with the Malaysian Navy and Air Force stationed in the eastern Theatre. One suggestion in this regard would be to expand the Joint Forces Headquarters from a secretariat of different, often unrelated operations to an operational command responsible for entire theatres. The nature of exercises must also change to reflect the need for coordination between different services across multiple domains.

The Joint capability plan is important to make this a success. It will become a commitment by the government to ensure consistent funding is given. The Malaysian Armed Forces must ensure that the relevant capability requirements are set based on mission priorities.

At some point, we also need to rethink how we run the reserve system. Currently, we have Wataniah and other Sukarela formations, but they are underutilised. The majority of our reserve component is composed of *Wataniah* regiments that are meant to augment active-duty frontline forces, but their training and equipment do not necessarily reflect this. Perhaps what is needed is less general duty reservists and more specialised and skilled reservists? Rejimen Pakar in Wataniah compose a very small portion of the overall total.

Reserve forces need to be seen as an equally important component, especially if we can only maintain a small professional active-duty component. In prolonged conflict, their mobilisation will be crucial to support the regular forces. In emergencies, they can be called up to fulfil immediate manpower requirements and shortages.

If the reservists are trained heavily for emergencies, perhaps the state governments can be roped in to build a mutually beneficial relationship. When there is a serious emergency, such as a major flood, the public expect the soldiers to turn up, which is a compliment to the perceived capabilities of the Armed Forces. However, too often a mobilisation of the regular forces for emergency reliefs means there is less time for the primary function of the Armed Forces: to train for war. The reservists can "reverse-augment" the regulars by giving more focus on emergency relief works. To be effective, the reservists need to be trained and equipped to near active-duty standards, like the US National Guard and US Reserve Component.

(ii) Comprehensive defence

The Malaysian Armed Forces should not be the only component in national security and defence. The Armed Forces are an integral component of government action regardless of war or peace. But the whole-of-government and society approach is still not strong.

For instance, there are three different strategic documents: the DWP; the Security and Public Order Policy by the Home Ministry; and Foreign Policy Framework of the New Malaysia by the Foreign Affairs Ministry.

Only one of them lays out a clear grand strategy and connects resources and policy to goals. The other two are less about strategy and more about a statement of responsibilities. At some point, we have to start bridging this gap and reconcile these documents.

When I was the Deputy Defence Minister, I often told my staff that not only do we need a "whole-of-government" approach, we actually need a "whole-of-MINDEF" approach and perhaps a stronger and more cohesive security cluster in the government. We need to rethink the way we run the civil service.

The general civil service we copy from India has its advantages. But with more and more specific and sophisticated problems and issues that we encounter, we cannot rely on someone who for all his life deals with palm oil policy to suddenly know how to run the Ministry of Defence competently.

In the Westminster system, the Ministers are generalists but it does not mean that the civil servants have to be generalists as well. While we may not be able to form a mini-Pentagon with Defence having its dedicated closed service defence civilians, we must at least try to build a cohort of security and defence specialists to be moved around among the security-related ministries.

I hope the Public Service Department and the government think seriously about this. We need a cohort of top civilians in government who genuinely understand defence and security issues.

(iii) Credible partnerships

Diplomacy is an essential part of Malaysia's international activism that has allowed us to punch above our weight on many regional security issues. Examples abound, including efforts to broker peace in southern Thailand and southern Philippines; the Malacca Straits Patrol with

Indonesia and Singapore; and the Trilateral Cooperative Agreement with the Philippines and Indonesia.

The Malaysian Armed Forces plays a huge role in this regard as well, being a critical element of defence diplomacy and participation in many international security operations, such as UN Peacekeeping operations in Bosnia, Sudan, Somalia, Timor Leste, and Lebanon; disaster relief missions in Indonesia; a field hospital in Cox's Bazar to assist Rohingya refugees.; and various joint exercises with other regional partners.

Managing relationships with the great powers will be important in the many years to come. The US and China are still likely to engage in a lot of friction with each other. Both sides view each other as adversaries and frame their interactions as competition. This is a risk that we have to learn to manage, as open confrontation between the two will put us at most risk (see the next chapter).

Malaysia has a role to play in helping them smooth out that friction. At some point, we need to have institutions that help to foster understanding of both the US and China for this purpose. Malaysia, particularly the Armed Forces, should aspire to do more in this respect.

In conclusion, Malaysia's elements of national power need to be applied towards a single goal. To become a middle power and a maritime nation with continental roots, we need to think carefully about how we conduct concentric deterrence, comprehensive defence, and establish credible partnerships. We live in the worst of times and the best of times. For Malaysia to be rejuvenated, the Malaysian Armed Forces with its full potential unleashed could be a catalyst.

Note: This piece was adapted, with updates and edits, from an article I wrote on my website on February 3, 2021. See Chin Tong, Liew (2021). *The Armed Forces as the Catalyst for a Rejuvenated Malaysia*. Available at: https://liewchintong.com/2021/02/03/the-armed-forces-as-the-catalyst-for-a-rejuvenated-malaysia//.

CHAPTER 33

Malaysia as an Aspiring Middle Power

For a secure and peaceful Southeast Asia, Malaysia needs to have a robust and independent foreign policy and should see itself as an aspiring middle power in the context of the great power rivalry.

In the face of the polycrisis, nations have to organise themselves at the national, regional and global levels to deal with pandemics, climate crises, the economy and geopolitics very differently from the past.

In the decades to come, the US would still remain the strongest nation on earth, yet the post-Cold War era, which saw the US being the singular dominant power, has long been a thing of the past.

The US will have to accommodate other great powers, namely China and Russia, as well as a coterie of "middle powers" such as the European states, India, Turkey, Iran, Japan, North Korea, South Korea, Indonesia and Australia.

New world order

In short, the next world order is one that will be decidedly multipolar and far more fluid, complex and perhaps more transactional than what the world had experienced since World War II. For instance, while India is a member of the Quad (Quadrilateral Security Dialogue) – a strategic security dialogue between Australia, India, Japan and the US – and aligns itself with the US when it comes to reacting to China, it unmistakably diverges from the US' approach towards the Russian invasion of Ukraine. In fact, much as China and Russia professed a "no limits" friendship, China did not endorse nor support Russia's war in Ukraine.

The danger we face in the region we live in is that China has accumulated plenty of grievances against the US, which is not new, but China now also possesses the military and economic capabilities and capacities to match that of the US in East Asia and Southeast Asia in the foreseeable future.

Some thinkers in Beijing are of the view that the US is on a permanent decline and that China would replace the US as the hegemon in the not-too-distant future. Some of them even view that wars are unavoidable when transiting from a US-led region and US-led world to one where China becomes dominant.

In response, some thinkers in Washington, D.C., are of the view that the US must preserve its pre-eminence and must not be seen sharing powers with others, namely China, as such acts would be deemed as a sign of weakness. Likewise, some in Washington think that wars are unavoidable.

When Beijing and Washington are respectively dominated by increasingly hardened views, the so-called Thucydides trap – the idea that war is inevitable when an emerging power threatens to displace an established power – may eventually become a self-fulfilling prophecy. If a war breaks out in East Asia or in the South China Sea, the region and the world will be a very dark place as any such wars could possibly lead to World War III. Therefore, we must reject this potentially disastrous zero-sum view.

Instead, in a grossly simplified manner, the world can be conceived as having three broad groups of nations: namely, the US and its closest allies constituting the first one-third; the second one-third are those that are by default anti-US; and the final one-third nations are not aligned tightly to the first or second groups.

While in East Asia the lines are more starkly drawn between those who are for and against the US, Southeast Asian states are generally, to use Professor Kuik Cheng-Chwee's word, "hedgers".

Southeast Asian states have a historic mission to ensure that the world's superpowers do not go to the brink on our doorstep. We will have to tell the US that preserving its pre-eminent position in the region and the world does not mean that there should be no power sharing with China and other middle powers. On the other hand, we will have to tell China that the middle powers and all other small nations prefer not to replace one hegemonic power with another.

We do not endorse US hegemony nor Chinese hegemony. The new multipower world order that this generation is tasked to shape should be one that has no singular dominant power, be it the US or China.

It is in this context that Malaysia must rise to the occasion to be an active actor shaping its destinies in this chaotic phase of flux when the previous world order is obviously fraying, yet the new order has yet to emerge.

Malaysia's once illustrious foreign policy

It is not new that Malaysia understood its agency in the region and the world.

As soon as Malaya became a member of the United Nations, our first Prime Minister Tunku Abdul Rahman and his government took a principled stance to become one of the vocal global voices against South Africa's Apartheid rule.

At the height of the Cold War, Tunku mostly leaned towards the United States, United Kingdom and the West in general. The Tunku was also reasonably well-connected with the Islamic world to earn him the post of secretary-general of the Organisation of Islamic Cooperation (OIC) after his departure from politics.

During the long years as Tunku's deputy, Tun Abdul Razak was quietly engaging leaders of the Non-Aligned Movement and other non-West actors, occasionally against the wishes of the pro-West Tunku. ASEAN, which is now 56 years old, was in part founded by his labour. Razak became Prime Minister in September 1970 and shifted Malaysia's foreign policy to a less pro-West stance, with a bit more independent streak, and thus opening up substantial space for Malaysia to manoeuvre.

As Richard Nixon pursued a policy of détente after assuming the US presidency in 1969, leading to a series of rapprochements with China and culminating in his visit to Beijing in 1972, Razak inked a diplomatic relationship between Malaysia and China in 1974.

Significantly, Malaysia was the first non-Communist Southeast Asian nation to recognise the People's Republic of China. Razak's visit to Beijing in 1974 and his handshake with Chairman Mao Zedong was a major election boon for him and the newly-formed BN as many ethnic Chinese voters then were still looking up to China.

Whether we like him or loathe him, Tun Dr Mahathir Mohamad put Malaysia on the world map. Before Najib's infamous 1MDB scandal, Malaysians who travelled overseas would attest that at the first mention of Malaysia, foreigners would ask about Mahathir, and possibly his erstwhile protégé and victim Datuk Seri Anwar Ibrahim. To most of the Third World, Mahathir was some kind of inspirational leader.

I do not necessarily agree with many things that Mahathir did during his 22-year tenure, but it is difficult to find fault with his foreign policy agenda, at least broadly speaking. During those years, Malaysia was a textbook case of a very engaging middle power – a state that is not a great power but influential enough to be taken notice of by the rest of the world.

Mahathir's three-pronged "activist" foreign policy included:

- The Look East Policy to cultivate the new "non-West First World" nations, especially Japan, to balance the influence of the West;
- Being the loud opinion leader of the Third World and the global South; and
- Being an active and influential Muslim nation among the Islamic world.

The breadth and ambition of Mahathir in reshaping Malaysia's foreign policy outlook was quite extraordinary back then.

However, from the late 2000s onwards, Malaysia has become increasingly insular, inward-looking, and lacking in ambition and purpose in its conduct of foreign policy and diplomacy. Under the Najib administration, the nation was bogged down by scandal after scandal, such as the 1MDB fiasco, when we could have risen to the occasion as an indispensable voice in Southeast Asia while the US and China vied for influence.

In the case of the Rohingyas, Malaysia did almost nothing obvious to influence events. Malaysia could have been more visible in leading regional opinion against the killings of civilians or exert more pressure on the Myanmar Government.

From a formidable voice of reason in the developing world, Malaysia essentially shrank in stature to a "small country" trying to extract favours from the great powers without principles or ideals.

Way forward

Malaysia should see itself as an aspiring middle power. There are multiple definitions of what constitutes a middle power and I do not intend to dwell on them. Suffice to say that Malaysia should aspire to be a middle power as envisaged by the aforementioned DWP.

The key is to be strategic and proactive in Malaysia's conduct of foreign policy and diplomacy. We must realise that Malaysia's economic fate and our people's well-being require a robust yet balanced foreign policy.

Malaysia may benefit from the US-China rivalry, which will colour the thinking and actions of global actors in the foreseeable future. For instance, Malaysia and the region have gained to a certain extent from the departures of US, European and even Chinese firms from China due to the increasingly hostile US-China relationship. These firms formed the bulk of new investments in Southeast Asian states in the past three years.

But if a war breaks out in our region, all bets are off. Therefore, we must actively shape and continuously expand our foreign policy space to ensure that Malaysia has more room to navigate in a contested world.

In the years and decades to come, the singular most important objective of Malaysian foreign policy and diplomacy is to maintain peace and to avoid wars in East Asia and Southeast Asia. To do so, it will require Malaysia to be an active middle power alongside other regional neighbours to create and expand the space in the middle or the buffer between the extremes or the hardline impulses among the thinkers and policymakers in Beijing and Washington alike.

To actively engage the world, Malaysia needs to invest a lot more in the Foreign Ministry, as well as build up a whole-of-government capability to conduct diplomacy effectively, such as through defence diplomacy or even climate diplomacy.

Knowledge, expertise and talents have to form a major part of this long-term national effort. Our universities, foreign policy think tanks and scholars must be given adequate resources and, more importantly, access to the policymakers when it comes to providing input for better policy outcomes.

It is only with a robust and independent foreign policy and readiness to build itself to be a middle power that Malaysia can ensure the peace and security in the region for the years to come.

A year since Prime Minister Datuk Seri Anwar Ibrahim took office, he has demonstrated great skills, energy, and leadership in putting Malaysia back on to the world map. It is hoped that Malaysia will engage the world more actively and strategically under Anwar's leadership and play an increasingly important role regionally and beyond whilst simultaneously working towards building a secure middle-class society at home, all in the name of Malaysia's second takeoff.

Solidarity

Thank you for reading this book. I am sure you would probably notice that I stress a lot about better jobs and better pay, and better linkages between foreign investors and domestic firms to ensure FDI benefits Malaysians. I also touch a lot upon paying attention to precarity, building good public transport, and preventing housing from becoming instruments of pure speculation.

At this juncture, I thought it would be good to share with you personal stories about people at the margins who are at the receiving end of economic policies and decisions.

My father, Liew Sooi Yong, was brought up in the cemetery area behind the old Istana Negara in Kuala Lumpur, by my widowed grandmother Lee Choy, a very tough Hakka woman, who worked as a construction worker to build graves. My grandfather passed away when my father was four years old. Some of Dad's siblings were full-time factory workers, but he worked at an automotive factory for only a year in the early 1970s because he did not fancy doing such a job. So he drove a *kereta sapu* (the original Uber/Grab, a hired car without any permits), a minibus, and later a taxi, before moving on to start a short-lived business in Chinese praying materials, and later on, multi-level marketing. My father did not finish school but read widely to educate himself.

My mother, Choo Mee Lan, was brought up in the city centre's Jalan Alor when it was a squatter's colony. Her father, my maternal grandfather, died when my mother – the eldest daughter – was 16 years old. My maternal grandmother, Chua Moi, whom I was so fond of and lived long enough to see me becoming a Member of Parliament, was an amazing woman. She was kidnapped as a nine-year old from Amoy (Xiamen), China, and worked as a child-maid until she got married during the Japanese Occupation of Malaya. She was illiterate, but when registration of citizenship took place in the 1950s, she managed to speak enough *bahasa pasar* (a pidginised form of vernacular Malay) to qualify her for Malayan citizenship, and her children all had citizenship because of her. When widowed, she contracted the laundry service for a hotel in Kuala Lumpur and sold *kuih* on the streets, with her children, my mother included, helping to make the *kuih* and wash clothes by the well.

My mother finished high school and worked as a clerk at Hotel Malaya. She later helped my father in business, and when it was the end of the road for my father's small venture, Mom started selling lottery tickets on the streets from 1989, only winding down the trade in 2019. At times, Mom sold lottery tickets for 16 to 18 hours a day, just to pay off housing loans and other debts from the earlier business venture, and to put food on the table. I sold lottery tickets, too, for two years from 1989 to 1991.

It was then that I witnessed the first economic takeoff. A restaurant in Subang Parade, Selangor very kindly allowed me to sell lottery tickets to their patrons including many Japanese, Korean and Taiwanese businessmen and engineers. I benefited from having this clientele which was previously unavailable. And, by 1991, I decided to work at a cafe in that very mall with an initial pay of RM2.50 per hour. By 1992, I benefited from a tight labour market thanks to the first economic takeoff – I was paid RM4.50 per hour. By comparison, more than three decades later, fast food chains in Malaysia today are paying less than RM10 per hour.

The beauty of Malaysia is that street kids like me from a not-well-to-do family do have social mobility. Yet, even if there was an across-the-board boom just like during the first economic takeoff, the benefits for people at the margins (like my family was in the 1990s) would be meagre and often temporary. And when troubles happen, they will be the first and the worst hit.

As most of our lottery sales were made at eateries, a week of rain would mean cash flow problems for our family because many people did not eat out. What still pains me to this day is the memory of my mother going to the pawn shop with her jewellery because a RM10,000 cheque was issued to the main lottery distributor yet we only had RM9,950 when it was due.

To be fair, we were not exactly poor. My parents owned a house paying a monthly mortgage, and we could go to school, and there was only a week in my entire childhood that we did not have money for food. But we worked very hard, and we lived precariously.

My family story of precarity is prevalent among many Malaysians regardless of ethnicity, especially after the economic scars of COVID-19. Throughout my many years in front line politics, I have met many Malaysian families who are like mine – the Grab drivers, the Foodpanda riders, the hawkers, the factory workers, the cleaners. They all work very hard in their lives yet they are constantly anxious. Each time I see the hundreds of thousands of motorcyclists queuing at the Causeway to enter Singapore at 5 am to work as low-wage labour, I tell myself, "work harder, convince more leaders that we need to do more to create better jobs and better pay for them to work in Malaysia".

I hope enough policy makers and all other economic stakeholders, from business owners to bankers and economists, in Malaysia recognise precarity as a major concern and find ways to build a secure and stable democratic society based on solidarity or in Prime Minister Datuk Seri Anwar Ibrahim's words, *madani* – sustainability, care and compassion, respect, innovation, prosperity, and trust.

The second takeoff that this book illustrates is Malaysia's second chance. I pray and hope that we can create better jobs with better pay, and many better business opportunities for Malaysian firms to rise in this once-in-a-generation upswing, and along the way, lift the lives of as many families and kids in situations like mine in the 1990s out of precarity to build a secure and prosperous Malaysian life.

Notes and References

Introduction

1 Until the early 1970s, rubber and tin were essentially the key drivers of the Malaysian economy, making up 69% of export earnings as of 1960. While there were early attempts to industrialise through the enactment of the Pioneer Industries Ordinance of 1958, rubber and tin continued to constitute over 50% of export revenue in 1970. Malaysia's early industrialisation efforts post-Ordinance were focused heavily on attracting investment for investment's sake, allowing foreign investors (often from the UK) to repatriate their profits and capital as well as offering considerable protection in the form of high tariffs. Admittedly, the manufacturing sector did grow somewhat during this period, from a low base at 8% of GDP in 1960 to 13% by 1970. However, the national import-substitution strategy, which involved replacing foreign imports of consumer goods, such as batteries and tyres, with local production, did not create enough jobs for locals, and aggravated balance of payments issues due to the substantial importation of intermediate or capital goods. For more information, see Sultan Nazrin Shah (2019). *Striving for Inclusive Development.* Selangor: Oxford University Press, and Sivalingam, G. (1994). *The economic and social impact of export processing zones: The case of Malaysia.* Geneva: International Labour Organization. Available at: https://www.ilo.org/wcmsp5/groups/public/---ed_emp/---emp_ent/---multi/documents/publication/wcms_126266.pdf

2 The Look East Policy is a creative Malaysian foreign policy innovation, resting on the novel and ambitious notion (in the 1980s) that Asian economies could be great manufacturing houses with sophisticated technologies. It came about not long after Malaysia's first foray into heavy industry, during which Japan's influence was growing rapidly. In Malaysia's quest for modernisation, the East Asian (and specifically Japanese) model of development, with its focus on economic efficiency and targeted industrial policy for sectors of strategic interest, was touted as a template for emulation. Ezra Vogel's 1979 book *Japan as Number One: Lessons for America* aptly captured the spirit of the time. See Liew, C. T. (2023) "A new era of 'Look East' would boost Japan and Malaysia". *Nikkei Asia.* Available at: https://asia.nikkei.com/Opinion/A-new-era-of-Look-East-would-boost-both-Japan-and-Malaysia

3 Introduced by Dr Mahathir in 1991, Vision 2020 envisioned that Malaysia would be fully developed by 2020 'along all the dimensions: economically, politically, socially, spiritually, psychologically and culturally'. To fulfil the vision, Dr Mahathir stressed the need for Malaysia's economy to grow at an average of 7% annually for 30 years, as well as identifying nine strategic challenges for Malaysia to overcome by 2020. One of these was the creation of a united country "with a sense of common and shared destiny" brought together by the notion of *Bangsa Malaysia* (or Malaysian nation). For the full list of strategic challenges, see https://policy.asiapacificenergy.org/sites/default/files/vision%202020.pdf

4 Bank Negara Malaysia (2023). *The Exchange Rate and the Malaysian Economy.* [online] Available at: https://www.bnm.gov.my/ar22f1

5 When I took office as the Deputy Minister of Investment, Trade and Industry in December 2022, my first task was to represent my minister, Tengku Datuk Seri Utama Zafrul Abdul Aziz, at the 10th ASEAN-EU Business Summit in Brussels. Speaking alongside His Excellency Valdis Dombrovskis, the European Commissioner for Trade, I remarked that the ASEAN states offer the European Union a buffer in a heightened geopolitical environment, marked by a significant diversion of European trade and investment from China into the region.

When it comes to building closer trade ties between EU and ASEAN states – including negotiations of free trade agreements – the environment and labour rights are often seen as stumbling blocks, but that does not have to be so. While some ASEAN states are still playing catch-up on some of these issues, the EU could view this as a capacity gap rather than an ambition gap, necessitating more investment into building such capacity, whether commercially or on a government-to-government basis. It will not be long before the ASEAN states themselves, with an increasingly educated middle class and relatively young population, find themselves having to do a lot more because their people demand it. For more information on my visit, see https://liewchintong.com/2022/12/19/the-need-for-closer-asean-eu-cooperation/

6 For an accessible explanation of what GDP really means and why it should not be the be-all and end-all of policy making, see https://refsa.org/refsa-notes-8-2022-deconstructing-economic-indicators-gross-domestic-product-gdp/

Section I

1 Department of Statistics Malaysia (2023). *Salaries & Wages Survey Report 2022.* [online] Available at: https://www.dosm.gov.my/portal-main/release-content/salaries-and-wages-survey-report-2022

2 Department of Statistics Malaysia (2023). *Quarterly Principal Statistics of Labour Force, Malaysia: Third Quarter, 2023.* [online] Available at: https://www.dosm.gov.my/portal-main/release-content/quarterly-principal-statistics-of-labour-force-malaysia-q3-2023

3 Wan Jan, W. S. (2020). *Malaysia's Student Loan Company: Tackling the PTPTN Time Bomb.* Singapore: ISEAS Publishing. Available at: https://www.iseas.edu.sg/wp-content/uploads/2020/02/TRS5_20.pdf

4 Department of Statistics Malaysia (2020). *Gig Workers in Malaysia: A Review of Definitions & Estimation.* [online] Available at: https://www.dosm.gov.my/v1/uploads/files/6_Newsletter/Newsletter%202020/DOSM_ MBLS_1-2020_Series-8.pdf

5 Zurich Malaysia (2020). *Zurich-University of Oxford Agile Workforce Study: Gig Economy Rises in Malaysia, Income Protection Lags.* [online] Available at: https://www.zurich.com.my/en/about-zurich/zurich-in-the-news/2020/2020-01-16

6 World Bank (2023). *Malaysia Economic Monitor, February 2023: Expanding Malaysia's Digital Frontier.* [online] Available at: https://documents.worldbank.org/en/publication/documents-reports/documentdetail/099063502042320186/p179681008aa910db0bca9057d2dfa76bed

7 Gallup World Poll (2018)

8 Department of Statistics Malaysia (2023). *Formal Sector Wages*. [online] Available at: https://open.dosm.gov.my/dashboard/formal-sector-wages. Note that after factoring in possible deductions and tax exemptions (including individual relief of RM9,000), an employee in Malaysia needs to earn about RM3,000-3,500 a month to qualify to pay tax.

Note further that Figure 1 only covers the formal sector or about 6.5 million employees in Malaysia. The remaining 8.5 million-odd individuals in employment, who may be in the informal sector or self-employed, are therefore excluded from the analysis. It is likely that the actual percentage of Malaysians who earn less than RM3,000 a month, and are therefore ineligible to pay income tax, is higher than 55% once all employees are taken into account.

9 Malaysia classifies households into three distinct categories based on income share: the top 20% (T20), the middle 40% (M40) and the bottom 40% (B40). The classification of the M40 is often ridiculed by those in the category because they too suffer, and suffer miserably.

According to a 2019 article by Khazanah Research Institute, the M40 is not the "middle class" that one might imagine. They essentially face the same problems as the B21-B40. They have middle-class aspirations, but they oftentimes have difficulty reaching the idealised status of the "middle class". Instead, it is more useful to think of the poorest 20% and the next 50% of households as part of a large B70 group with similar social and economic needs.

Another issue with the demarcation of households into distinct B40 and M40 categories is that the labels do not account for household size or composition, making misclassification a possibility. A household officially classified within the M40 income class but having many familial dependants shares similar financial burdens as the B40 class. Our statistics understate the financial hardships of a substantial number of ordinary Malaysians.

These labels have serious material and policy consequences, which is why we need to discuss and consider them carefully, instead of imbibing them uncritically. The government should, therefore, move away from the B40-M40 dichotomy that is now looking like a rather meaningless distinction.

For further reading, see https://www.krinstitute.org/assets/contentMS/img/template/editor/20191127_Edge_Rethinking%20Malaysian%20poverty%20and%20inequality.pdf and https://www.krinstitute.org/assets/contentMS/img/template/editor/Publication_Demarcating%20Households_Full%20Report11032020.pdf

10 Indeed, whether we act or stand idle, conditions are already changing in countries that have been supplying us with cheap, low-skilled labour. As Indonesia's economy takes off, few workers from there are willing to work in Malaysia. In Indonesia, minimum wages vary by region. Notably, Jakarta's minimum wage (at IDR5.067 million or about RM1,500 as of January 2024) is on par with Malaysia's (RM1,500 since May 2022), which means that if a worker in Sulawesi wishes to work as a migrant worker, he or she would rather head to Jakarta instead of Malaysia. As for Bangladesh, among 13 million of its people working abroad, Malaysia is not their first choice. 8 million of them are in the Middle East, and when they choose Southeast Asia, many prefer Singapore. See https://en.antaranews.com/news/299166/jakarta-sets-2024-minimum-wage-at-rp5-million and https://www.thestar.com.my/news/nation/2023/11/02/hr-ministry-reviewing-minimum-wage-order

11 Irwin-Hunt, A. (2023). "Countries setting new FDI records in 2023". *fDi Intelligence*, 18 October. Available at: https://www.fdiintelligence.com/content/data-trends/countries-setting-new-fdi-records-in-2023-83094

Part I

1 For an accessible explanation of why Malaysian consumers are legitimately concerned about cost of living increases, and by extension growing economic insecurity, even as headline inflation numbers appear stable or at least under control, see https://refsa.org/refsa-notes-7-2022-deconstructing-economic-indicatorsinflation/

2 World Bank (2023). *Educational attainment, at least completed upper secondary, population 25+, total (%) (cumulative)*. [online] Available at: https://data.worldbank.org/indicator/SE.SEC.CUAT.UP.ZS?most_recent_value_desc=true; and World Bank (2023). *Educational attainment, at least completed post-secondary, population 25+, total (%) (cumulative)*. [online] Available at: https://data.worldbank.org/indicator/SE.SEC.CUAT.PO.ZS

3 Department of Statistics Malaysia (2023). *Graduates Statistics 2022*. [online] Available at: https://www.dosm.gov.my/portal-main/release-content/graduates-statistics-2022. Note that "fresh graduates" here refers to employed graduates aged 24 and below.

4 For instance, Malaysians top the list of overstayers in Australia. See https://www.nst.com.my/news/nation/2019/11/536014/malaysians-top-list-overstayers-australia

5 Shukry, A. (2019). "Malaysians do Singapore's dirty work while foreigners do theirs". *The Jakarta Post*, 20 November. [online]. Available at: https://www.thejakartapost.com/seasia/2019/11/20/malaysians-do-singapores-dirty-work-while-foreigners-do-theirs.html

6 Murugasu, A. et al. (2019). "Are Malaysian Workers Paid Fairly?: An Assessment of Productivity and Equity". Kuala Lumpur: Bank Negara Malaysia. Available at: https://www.bnm.gov.my/documents/20124/791626/cp01_001_box.pdf

Chapter 1

1 Chun, S-H. (2018). *The Economic Development of South Korea: From Poverty to a Modern Industrial State*. London: Routledge

2 Savada, A.M. and Shaw, W. (1992). *South Korea: A Country Study*. Washington, D.C.: Federal Research Division, Library of Congress.

3 Penang Development Corporation (1990). *Penang: Looking Back, Looking Ahead: 20 Years of Progress*. Penang: Penang Development Corporation

4 Government of Malaysia (1976, p. 140). *Third Malaysia Plan, 1976-1980*. [online] Available at: https://www.pmo.gov.my/dokumenattached/RMK/RMK3.pdf

5 In 1981, out of over 20,000 workers in the semiconductor industry in Penang's FTZs, 79% were women. At that time, women were believed to be more docile and cooperative than male workers, as well as being better at handling delicate assembly activities, in addition to receiving lower pay compared to men. See Rasiah, R. (1988). "Production in Transition

within the Semiconductor Industry and its Impact on Penang", *Kajian Malaysia* (Malaysian Studies), VI(1); and Nesadurai, H. E. S. (1991). "The Free Trade Zone In Penang, Malaysia: Performance And Prospects". *Asian Journal of Social Science* [online] 19 (1-2), pp. 103-138. Available at: https://doi.org/10.1163/080382491X00069

6 Penang's high unemployment rate in the late 1960s could be attributed at least partly to the decline of Penang Port following the withdrawal of the state's free port status in 1967. Export-oriented industrialisation in the early 1970s under Tun Dr Lim Chong Eu's state government soon helped turn Penang into the factory of the nation.

7 Nesadurai, H. E. S. (1991). "The Free Trade Zone In Penang, Malaysia: Performance And Prospects". *Asian Journal of Social Science* [online], 19 (1-2), pp. 103-138. Available at: https://doi.org/10.1163/080382491X00069

8 Kocchar, R. and Sechopoulos, S. (2022). *How the American middle class has changed in the past five decades*. Washington, D. C.: Pew Research Center. Available at: https://www.pewresearch.org/short-reads/2022/04/20/how-the-american-middle-class-has-changed-in-the-past-five-decades/

9 The average salary of a McDonald's attendant in Malaysia is reported to be around RM1,600-1,700 per month (just above the minimum wage of RM1,500) according to Indeed, a job listing platform. This equates to roughly RM8-9 per hour, assuming 45 work hours per week. Employees at full-service restaurants are slightly better off, as they can expect to earn an average of RM12-13 per hour. Whatever the case may be, wages in the industry (which serve as a useful proxy for the lower end of the income distribution) have not kept up with food prices by and large. See https://malaysia.indeed.com/cmp/McDonald%27s/salaries and https://malaysia.indeed.com/career/restaurant-staff/salaries

10 Treating a McDonald's Big Mac as the average fast-food meal (in the style of *The Economist*), an à la carte Big Mac cost RM3.89 in Malaysia in 1997. Today the same burger is priced at over RM13.40. See https://www.economist.com/finance-and-economics/1997/10/30/the-big-mac-index-goes-east and https://www.mcdelivery.com.my/my/browse/menu.html?daypartId=9&catId=9

11 Government of Malaysia (2000). *Seventh Malaysia Plan*, Chapter 4: "Population, Employment and Manpower Development". [online] Available at: https://www.ekonomi.gov.my/sites/default/files/2021-05/Chapter%2004%20-%20Population%2C%20Employment%20And%20Manpower%20Development.pdf

12 Ang, J. W. et al. (2018). *Low-Skilled Foreign Workers' Distortions to the Economy*. Kuala Lumpur: Bank Negara Malaysia. Available at: https://www.bnm.gov.my/documents/20124/826852/AR+BA3+-+Low-Skilled+Foreign+Workers+Distortions+to+the+Economy.pdf

13 As I highlighted on my blog in 2012, "for every foreign worker brought into this country, someone close to the establishment makes a cut through licensing and other sorts of payment". For information on the possible acts of corruption in the hiring of foreign workers, see https://www.nst.com.my/news/crime-courts/2023/03/893331/macc-immigrants-goldmine-corrupt-law-enforcement-officials

14 World Bank (2020). *Who is Keeping Score? Estimating the Number of Foreign Workers in Malaysia*. [online] Available at: https://documents1.worldbank.org/curated/en/892721588859396364/pdf/Who-is-Keeping-Score-Estimating-the-Number-of-Foreign-Workers-in-Malaysia.pdf

15 Lee, H-A and Khor, Y. L. (2018). *Counting Migrant Workers in Malaysia: A Needlessly Persisting Conundrum*. Singapore: ISEAS-Yusof Ishak Institute. Available at: https://www.iseas.edu.sg/wp-content/uploads/pdfs/ISEAS_Perspective_2018_25@50.pdf

16 Kamis, K. and Abdul Aziz, M. (2023). "6.67mil EPF members have less than RM10,000 savings: Chief strategy officer". *New Straits Times*, 24 January. Available at: https://www.nst.com.my/business/2023/01/873081/667mil-epf-members-have-less-rm10000-savings-chief-strategy-officer

17 Ministry of Finance, Malaysia (2019). *Budget 2020, Section 1: Fiscal Policy Overview*. [online] Available at: https://www.mof.gov.my/portal/arkib/revenue/2020/section1.pdf

Chapter 2

1 The Straits Times (2023). "Brain drain: Majority of Malaysians who emigrated moved to Singapore, says human resources minister". *The Straits Times*, 8 March. Available at: https://www.straitstimes.com/asia/brain-drain-majority-of-malaysians-who-migrated-moved-to-singapore-says-hr-minister

2 Channel News Asia (c. 2023). *Clearing the Causeway*. [online] Available at: https://infographics.channelnewsasia.com/interactive/causewayjam/index.html

3 Chew, H. M. (2023). "'I'm so exhausted': Tenants face hard choices as rents surge in Singapore". *Channel News Asia*, 2 February. Available at: https://www.channelnewsasia.com/singapore/rents-increase-singapore-tenants-alternatives-3245521

4 Institute of Labour Market Information and Analysis. *A Study on Malaysians Working in Singapore* (Phase 2). [online]. Available at: https://www.ilmia.gov.my/index.php/en/component/zoo/item/a-study-on-malaysians-working-in-singapore-phase-2

5 Choy, N. Y. (2023). "Over 6,000 professionals returned to Malaysia under returning expert programme, says TalentCorp CEO". *The Edge*, 7 December. Available at: https://theedgemalaysia.com/node/693104

6 Department of Statistics Malaysia (2023). *Monthly Principal Statistics of Labour Force, Malaysia: October 2023*. [online]. Available at: https://www.dosm.gov.my/portal-main/release-content/monthly-principal-statistics-of-labour-force-dec. Note that the percentage is derived from the sum of individuals belonging to the first three categories under Malaysia's Standard Classification of Operations – managers, professionals and technicians and associate professionals – as a share of the total number of employed persons as of 2022.

Chapter 3

1 Department of Statistics Malaysia (2023). *Monthly Principal Statistics of Labour Force, Malaysia: October 2023.* [online]. Available at: https://www.dosm.gov.my/portal-main/release-content/monthly-principal-statistics-of-labour-force-dec.

2 The 2008 wage was converted into 2023 terms using DOSM's CPI calculator. The RM1,900 salary offered to Penang garbage collectors in 2008 through to the early 2010s was more than double the minimum wage of RM900 that came into effect in Malaysia in May 2012. For the calculator, see https://www.dosm.gov.my/cpi_calc/index.php

3 Marshall, A. (1890). *Principles of Economics*. London: Macmillan.

4 Wolfers, J. and Zilinsky, J. (2015). *Higher Wages for Low-Income Workers Lead to Higher Productivity*. Washington, D.C.: Peterson Institute for International Economics. Available at: https://www.piie.com/blogs/realtime-economic-issues-watch/higher-wages-low-income-workers-lead-higher-productivity

5 Modern Slavery and Human Rights Policy and Evidence Centre (2021). *Forced labour in the Malaysian medical gloves supply chain during the Covid-19 pandemic.* [online] Available at: https://modernslaverypec.org/assets/downloads/Malaysia-research-summary.pdf

6 On a side note, the debate on minimum wage is sometimes not very helpful. Organisations representing businesses protest militantly on each hike of minimum wage when the minimum wage is just setting the base.

7 For further reading, see Section 2 of NIMP 2030 at https://www.nimp2030.gov.my/nimp2030/modules_resources/bookshelf/NIMP_20303/index.html. In addition, to illustrate by way of an index, the Economic Complexity Index indicates that Malaysia performs fairly well in trade, coming in 24th globally in measures of the diversity and sophistication of exports, though it continues to lag behind the East Asian economies and parts of Western Europe. However, when it comes to innovation (captured by patent applications in technology) and research (captured by scientific output), Malaysia drops to 38th and 62nd respectively. See https://oec.world/en/rankings/eci/hs6/hs96?tab=ranking

8 Murugasu, A. et al. (2019). *Are Malaysian Workers Paid Fairly?: An Assessment of Productivity and Equity*. Kuala Lumpur: Bank Negara Malaysia. Available at: https://www.bnm.gov.my/documents/20124/791626/cp01_001_box.pdf

Part II

1 Mazzucato, M. (2021). *Mission Economy: A Moonshot Guide to Changing Capitalism*. London: Allen Lane. For further reading on mission-oriented policy making in context, see the following microsite prepared by staff at REFSA: https://refsa.org/missions/

2 Research for Social Advancement (REFSA) (2021). *REFSA Fact Sheet #1/2021: Mission Oriented Strategies*. [online] Available at: https://refsa.org/refsa-fact-sheet-1-2021-mission-oriented-strategies/

Chapter 4

1 Department of Statistics Malaysia (2023). *Salaries & Wages Survey Report 2022.* [online] Available at: https://www.dosm.gov.my/portal-main/release-content/salaries-and-wages-survey-report-2022

Chapter 5

1 For more information on the Madani Economy, see https://www.pmo.gov.my/membangun-malaysia-madani/ekonomi-madani-memperkasa-rakyat/

2 As mentioned by the Prime Minister, Malaysia's economic growth on a usual day can easily reach 4% or 4.5% because of the endowment that we have, including a strong industrial scene, an educated workforce, and a strategic geographic location. In fact, a similar growth rate has been achieved in the past 25 years.

We have the potential and the capability to grow at a more rapid rate. If we work hard enough and introduce new measures and reforms, we can now grow at 5.5%. If we are even more ambitious, a 6% growth rate is within reach. Growing at 6% per annum is important because we can double the size of GDP within a decade whereas growing at 5% means we would need 15 years to achieve the same target.

3 World Bank (2023). GDP (current US$) [online]. Available at: https://data.worldbank.org/indicator/NY.GDP.MKTP.CD?most_recent_value_desc=true&year_high_desc=true and International Monetary Fund (2023). *World Economic Outlook Database* [online]. Available at: https://www.imf.org/en/Publications/WEO/weo-database/2023/October/weo-report?a=1&c=001,998,&s=NGDPD,PPPGDP,PPPPC,PPPSH,&sy=2021&ey=2028&ssm=0&scsm=1&scc=0&ssd=1&ssc=0&sic=0&sort=country&ds=.&br=1. Note that PPP (i.e. purchasing power parity) accounts for differences in exchange rate and cost of living, but nominal GDP (official national data converted into USD) is the most common measure of economic size for international comparisons.

4 Ministry of Finance Malaysia (2023). *Budget 2024: Section 1, Fiscal Policy Overview.* [online] Available at: https://belanjawan.mof.gov.my/pdf/belanjawan2024/revenue/section1.pdf

5 Department of Statistics Malaysia (2023). *Quarterly Principal Statistics of Labour Force, Malaysia: Third Quarter, 2023.* [online] Available at: https://www.dosm.gov.my/portal-main/release-content/quarterly-principal-statistics-of-labour-force-malaysia-q3-2023

6 United Nations Development Programme (2022). *Human Development Report 2021/2022.* [online] Available at: https://hdr.undp.org/system/files/documents/global-report-document/hdr2021-22pdf_1.pdf

7 The draft had 85 national-level action plans and 165 sector-level action plans, the latter of which included sectors whose links to industry were weak at best, such as tourism services, making the initial document bloated and unfocused.

8 As expressed on the government's NIMP 2030 website: "To advance economic complexity, it will require the industry to innovate and produce more sophisticated products, which

can be supported by Mission 2, through the adoption of advanced technology. By embracing technology, it can also assist the industries in reducing carbon emissions, which supports Mission 3. Additionally, as part of Mission 3, the aim is to enter new green growth areas, which can contribute to advanced economic complexity. Lastly, Mission 4 aims to create an enabling environment that fosters entrepreneurship, supports SMEs, and promotes equitable participation in economic activities. This is key in supporting the other 3 Missions." See https://www.nimp2030.gov.my/index.php/pages/view/60?mid=456

9 For the full list of indicators, their 2030 targets and the baseline performance in 2021, see https://www.nimp2030.gov.my/index.php/pages/view/401?mid=487

Chapter 6

1 Mishel, L. (2018). "Yes, manufacturing still provides a pay advantage, but staffing firm outsourcing is eroding it". *Economic Policy Institute*, 12 March. Available at: https://www.epi.org/publication/manufacturing-still-provides-a-pay-advantage-but-outsourcing-is-eroding-it/ and Press Trust of India (2018). "Pay in manufacturing 5.2% higher than India's median salary". *Press Trust of India*, 24 September. Available at: https://www.livemint.com/Companies/kaYPQwJErSDPvX3gzEqAAL/Pay-in-manufacturing-52-higher-than-Indias-median-salary.html

2 Tengku Mohamed Asyraf et al. (2019). "Is Malaysia Experiencing Premature Deindustrialisation?" Kuala Lumpur: Bank Negara Malaysia. Available at: https://www.bnm.gov.my/documents/20124/766189/p3ba.pdf

3 McKinsey Global Institute (2012). *Manufacturing the future: The next era of global growth and innovation*. New York: McKinsey & Company. Available at: https://www.mckinsey.com/~/media/McKinsey/Business%20Functions/Operations/Our%20Insights/The%20future%20of%20manufacturing/MGI_Manufacturing%20the%20future_Executive%20summary_Nov%202012.pdf

Chapter 7

1 International Labour Organization (2021). *Statistics on labour productivity*. [online] Available at: https://ilostat.ilo.org/topics/labour-productivity/

2 A quick look at the OECD's data for total hours worked per employee is enough to dispel this belief: out of over 40 countries, Germans have the shortest average hours worked at 1,341 hours a year per employee (an average of less than 5.5 hours spent actually working in a day) while Colombians have the longest working hours at 2,405 hours (at least 9.5 hours daily). Yet nobody doubts that Germany is among the most productive economies in the world while Colombia is far behind, both in terms of GDP per hour worked and even in absolute terms. See https://data.oecd.org/emp/hours-worked.htm and https://ourworldindata.org/grapher/labor-productivity-per-hour-pennworld table?tab=table&time=latest&country=DEU~COL

3 European Commission (n.d.). *Total factor productivity in agriculture*. [online] Available at: https://agridata.ec.europa.eu/Qlik_Downloads/InfoSheetSectorial/infoC27.html

4 The process started with a Readiness Assessment (RA) – coordinated by the Malaysian Productivity Corporation (MPC), a MITI agency, and conducted by assessing bodies including SIRIM – which assessed firms' preparedness to adopt IR4.0 processes. SMEs that had completed the RA exercise were then entitled to apply for a grant of up to RM500,000 from MIDA under the Industry4WRD Intervention Fund, to put in place IR4.0 solutions.

The process was not seamless and unified. Applicants had to separately walk through the MPC processes, which usually took four months, and then the MIDA processes, which took another six weeks. There also often existed a mismatch between the expectations of SMEs and the RA outcome.

From the time Industry4WRD was launched in 2018 until the end of the Intervention Programme in late 2023, MPC received 2,409 applications, of which 1,375 were approved for the RA. Out of these 1,375 firms, 545 went on to apply to MIDA for intervention funds. Subsequently, only 345 of these 545 grant applications were approved, with just 99 firms receiving full disbursement of the grant.

5 The RA process also needs to be recalibrated to make it a powerful tool. To improve its effectiveness, a working committee with representatives from the government, government agencies, financial institutions and industry players will formulate the method to integrate financial parameters and ESG-related capacity building into the assessment criteria. This initiative will not only facilitate the financing journey for SMEs by exploring alternative financing solutions other than government grants but will also provide financial institutions with a reference point for evaluating potential clients, preparing these local SMEs for emerging business opportunities.

The enhanced RA process should not exclude other important stakeholders, such as technology solution providers alongside assessing bodies and financial institutions in order to reach a credible consensus on the use of RA for capital mobilisation and utilisation.

6 World Economic Forum (2020). *The Future of Jobs Report 2020.* [online] Available at: http://www3.weforum.org/docs/WEF_Future_of_Jobs_2020.pdf

Chapter 8

1 MATRADE (2023). *MATRADE Promotes Malaysia as a Global Leader in E&E.* [online] Available at: https://www.semiconsea.org/sites/semiconsea.org/files/2023-06/MATRADE%20Promotes%20Malaysia%20as%20a%20Global%20%28Final%29.pdf

2 Ibid.

3 InvestPenang (c. 2022). *Penang: The Silicon Valley of the East.* [online] Available at: https://www.semi.org/en/sea-newsletter-penang-the-silicon-valley-of-the-east

4 Thadani, A. and Allen, G. C. (2023). *Mapping the Semiconductor Supply Chain: The Critical Role of the Indo-Pacific Region.* Washington, D. C.: Centre for Strategic & International Studies. Available at: https://www.csis.org/analysis/mapping-semiconductor-supply-chain-critical-role-indo-pacific-region

5 Liew, J. T. (2020). "Cover story: Where are Malaysian players in the semiconductor value chain?" *The Edge Malaysia*, 15 October. Available at: https://theedgemalaysia.com/article/cover-story-where-are-malaysian-players-semiconductor-value-chain

6 *BERNAMA* (2023). "Govt, semiconductor industry players should work closely to ensure continuity of future talents, says Rafizi". *BERNAMA*, 27 August. Available at: https://www.mida.gov.my/mida-news/govt-semiconductor-industry-players-should-work-closely-to-ensure-continuity-of-future-talents-says-rafizi/

7 Reuters (2021). "Intel to invest $7 billion in new plant in Malaysia, creating 9,000 jobs". Reuters, 15 December. Available at: https://www.cnbc.com/2021/12/16/intel-to-invest-7-billion-in-new-malaysia-plant-creating-9000-jobs.html; Cantrill, A. (2023). "Infineon to Invest Up to €5 Billion in Malaysia Site Expansion". Bloomberg, 3 August. Available at: https://www.bloomberg.com/news/articles/2023-08-03/infineon-to-invest-up-to-5-billion-in-malaysia-site-expansion; and *New Straits Times* (2023). "MIDA: Texas Instruments to invest up to RM14.6 billion and create 1,800 more jobs in Malaysia". *New Straits Times*, 13 June. Available at: https://www.nst.com.my/business/2023/06/919496/mida-texas-instruments-invest-rm146-billion-and-create-1800-more-jobs

8 Thurow, L. C. (1994). "Microchips, Not Potato Chips". *Foreign Affairs* 73(4): 189-192.

9 For more information on the success stories in Malaysia's precision engineering industry, see https://www.mida.gov.my/wp-content/uploads/2020/07/Machinery-SIB-2022-2023.pdf

10 Ministry of Investment, Trade and Industry, Malaysia (c. 2023). *Overview of Electrical & Electronics Sector*. [online] Available at: https://www.miti.gov.my/NIA/electrical-electronics.html

11 There are at least 10 companies in Penang involved in various stages of precision engineering, including die casting, plastic moulding, the assembly of printed circuit boards and modules for industrial machinery. See https://investpenang.gov.my/precision-equipment-engineering/

12 Penang Automation Cluster (c. 2023). *About PAC*. [online] Available at: https://pa-cluster.com/about/

13 Miller, C. (2022). *Chip War: The Fight for the World's Most Critical Technology*. New York: Scribner, page 54.

14 Board of Engineers Malaysia (2022). *Laporan Mengenai Isu Gaji Permulaan Jurutera Rendah* ['Report on the Issue of Low Starting Pay among Engineers']. [online] Available at: http://bem.org.my/documents/20181/221308/Laporan+LJM+-+Isu+Gaji+Permulaan+Jurutera+Rendah+%2826.8.2022%29.pdf/7214a727-9d1e-4e58-b463-324f20d2de8a. According to the report, some of the possible reasons for low starting pay among engineers include a mismatch in skills (i.e. inadequate creation of high-skilled jobs in line with qualifications); a perceived oversupply of engineering graduates; a lower pay scale in the civil service for engineering services compared to healthcare and financial services, which is reflected in the private sector; and high training costs relative to output at the entry level.

15 Chong, E. and Adam Khong, F. (2018). *The Living Wage: Beyond Making Ends Meet* [online]. Kuala Lumpur: Bank Negara Malaysia. Available at: https://www.bnm.gov.my/documents/20124/826852/AR+BA4+-+The+Living+Wage+Beyond+Making+Ends+Meet.pdf

16 Tee, K. (2023). "Tech minister: Healthy STEM talent pool key to Malaysia becoming high-tech nation by 2030, but challenges remain". *Malay Mail*, 29 March. Available at: https://www.malaymail.com/news/malaysia/2023/03/29/tech-minister-healthy-stem-talent-pool-key-to-malaysia-becoming-high-tech-nation-by-2030-but-challenges-remain/62031

17 Talent.com (c. 2023). *Engineer average salary in Singapore, 2023*. [online] Available at: https://sg.talent.com/salary?job=engineer; and Indeed.com (c. 2023); Indeed, *Entry level engineer salary in Singapore*. [online] Available at: https://sg.indeed.com/career/entry-level-engineer/salaries

18 Department of Statistics Malaysia (2023). *Salaries and Wages Survey Report 2022*. [online] Available at: https://www.dosm.gov.my/portal-main/release-content/salaries-and-wages-survey-report-2022

19 *New Straits Times* (2023). "Malaysia's semiconductors lustre & importance of retaining it". *New Straits Times*, 20 February. Available at: https://www.nst.com.my/business/2023/02/881588/malaysias-semiconductors-lustre-importance-retaining-it

20 It is interesting that the expert in question comes from the ministry in charge of foreign affairs, not industrial development, trade or the economy, which just goes to show the growing importance of semiconductors in considerations of national security.

21 *BERNAMA* (2022). "US, Malaysia ink Memorandum of Cooperation to strengthen semiconductor supply chain resilience". *BERNAMA*, 12 May. Available at: https://www.mida.gov.my/mida-news/us-malaysia-ink-memorandum-of-cooperation-to-strengthen-semiconductor-supply-chain-resilience/. While the memorandum stops short of explicit monetary commitments, it sets the stage for greater engagement between Malaysia and the US in semiconductors. For example, the signing of the memorandum has been accompanied by roundtables involving the US Department of Commerce, Malaysia's MITI and domestic industry experts on available opportunities in the semiconductor sector amid ongoing geopolitical trends. The memorandum also serves as a useful starting point or frame of reference for ongoing negotiations under the US-led Indo-Pacific Economic Framework for Prosperity (IPEF), which calls for strengthened cooperation in supply chain resilience across member countries, including Malaysia.

Chapter 9

1 *Bangkok Post* (2023). "EV target within sight". *Bangkok Post*, 30 October. Available at: https://www.bangkokpost.com/opinion/opinion/2674264/ev-target-within-sight; and Land Transport Authority, Singapore (n.d.). *Our EV vision*. [online] Available at: https://www.lta.gov.sg/content/ltagov/en/industry_innovations/technologies/electric_vehicles/our_ev_vision.html

2 Davenport, C. and Boudette, N. E. (2023). "Biden Plans an Electric Vehicle Revolution. Now, the Hard Part". *New York Times*, 13 April. Available at: https://www.nytimes.com/2023/04/13/climate/electric-vehicles-biden-epa.html

3 There are 22 agencies involved in regulating charging facilities, and each seems to want to issue a licence. Rather than reinforcing the longstanding 'silo' mentality, the authorities should align themselves 'behind the window', acting as the "developmental state" in ensuring and facilitating the fast development and delivery of charging stations. The goal is for charging point operators – businesses that install and maintain EV charging stations and serve customers – to face just a single window.

4 An exception to this is to facilitate the building of AC charging stations in high-rise buildings that do not have the same access to AC home charging as those who reside in landed property.

Chapter 10

1 Ministry of Investment, Trade and Industry, Malaysia (2023). *Media Statement on the Malaysia Steel Council (MSC) Meeting on the 13th of July 2023* [online]. Available at: https://www.miti.gov.my/miti/resources/Media%20Release/MEDIA_STATEMENT_MEDIA_STATEMENT_ON_THE_MALAYSIA_STEEL_COUNCIL_(MSC)_MEETING_ON_THE_13TH_OF_JULY_2023.pdf

2 South East Asia Iron and Steel Institute (2023). *Malaysian government plans to tackle regional overcapacity*. [online] Available at: https://www.seaisi.org/details/23751?-type=news-rooms

3 South East Asia Iron and Steel Institute (2023). *The Challenges of Overcapacity & Decarbonisation in the ASEAN Steel Industry*. Personal communication.

4 For more information on the steel value chain, see https://theedgemalaysia.com/article/flat-steel-companies-spotlight

5 Ministry of Natural Resources and Environment, Malaysia (2022). *Fourth Biennial Update Report Under the United Nations Framework Convention on Climate Change*. [online] Available at: https://unfccc.int/sites/default/files/resource/MY%20BUR4_2022.pdf

Chapter 11

1 The Chief Secretary's Circular had previously required civil servants to wear a suit and tie to official events every day except Thursdays (as the designated 'batik day'). This was inconsistent with Prime Minister Anwar's preferred style of dress at public appearances – his "no tie" fashion statement in Parliament and many official functions. Of course, I hope the Circular will be further amended to accommodate short-sleeved batik and encourage the everyday wearing of short-sleeved corporate outfits, all with the aim of saving energy.

2 We can go even further. Imagine if the government committed to turning all its buildings into energy efficient buildings in the next few years, supported by policies such as Net Energy Metering and Energy Performance Contracting. The environment wins, and a new

sector is created in which many contractors will have work to do and can borrow from the banks. With the state as the driving force for change, the government could promote similar initiatives across the private sector by, for example, giving incentives to hotels, malls and factories that conduct energy and water audits and carry out retrofitting to make their buildings energy efficient. The government can also come in to set standards and ensure workers are certified, such as requiring all contractors to hire Malaysian workers with certificates as green job technicians, paying them at least RM3,500 in the process. Such a massive green exercise would help us build back better and could create 100,000 jobs or more.

3 Bank Negara Malaysia (2023). *Annual Report 2022*. [online] Available at: https://www.bnm.gov.my/documents/20124/10150308/ar2022_en_book.pdf

4 ARUP and Oxford Economics (2023). *The Global Green Economy: capturing the opportunity*. [online] Available at: https://www.arup.com/-/media/arup/files/publications/g/the-global-green-economy-report.pdf

5 Energy Commission of Sabah (2023). *Sabah Energy Roadmap and Master Plan 2040*. [online] Available at: https://ecos.gov.my/sites/default/files/uploads/downloads/2023-09/SABAH%20ENERGY%20ROADMAP%20AND%20MASTER%20PLAN%202040%20%28SE-RAMP%202040%29.pdf. What is needed now is massive investment into renewable energy to fulfil households' energy needs and carefully planned industrial usage. To this end, at the time of writing, MIDA and I have been working with Sabah's Finance Minister Datuk Seri Masidi Manjun and State Industrial Development and Entrepreneurship Minister Phoong Jin Zhe to put forward a "leapfrog" plan for the state. Lagging states and regions are usually told to "catch up", but leapfrogging carries a different connotation that at some point the latecomer can jump ahead. In this regard, if the aforementioned investments into renewable energy could be mobilised, Sabah will leapfrog.

Chapter 12

1 Ministry of Finance, Malaysia (2023). "Federal govt debt could be fully settled in 2053". *BERNAMA*. [online] 30 March. Available at: https://www.mof.gov.my/portal/en/news/press-citations/federal-govt-debt-could-be-fully-settled-in-2053-mof

2 As of the first half of 2023, the household debt-to-GDP ratio stood at 81.9%, lower than its peak of 93.3% in late 2020 but still about 10% points above the trend in the late 2000s, according to BNM's biannual Financial Stability Reviews. This suggests that households, especially lower-income households, continue to commit a high share of their income to servicing debt rather than for savings, investment or other living costs.

Chapter 13

1 Ministry of Natural Resources, Environment and Climate Change, Malaysia (2022). *Fourth Biennial Update Report Under the United Nations Framework Convention on Climate Change*. [online] Available at: https://unfccc.int/sites/default/files/resource/MY%20BUR4_2022.pdf

2 Ministry of Finance, Malaysia (2023). *Section 3: Federal Government Expenditure*. [online] Available at: https://belanjawan.mof.gov.my/pdf/belanjawan2024/revenue/section3.pdf. Note

that different sources cite different figures where the size of the fuel subsidies is concerned. In February 2023, Deputy Finance Minister Ahmad Maslan stated in Parliament that the government had spent RM50.8 billion on fuel subsidies in 2022 (https://www.channelnewsasia.com/asia/malaysia-ahmad-maslan-fuel-subsidies-targeted-rich-t20-3314286). In October 2023, according to the Auditor General's Report, expenditure on fuel subsidies had come up to RM45.2 billion the year before (https://lkan.audit.gov.my/laporan/manage/1784). However, in November 2023, the Ministry of Finance released its customary slew of documents for the 2024 Federal Budget, one of which covers expenditure, which is the latest and most authoritative source on federal spending. The RM52 billion figure referred to in the text comes from this document.

3 Ministry of Finance, Malaysia (2023). *Anggaran Perbelanjaan Persekutuan 2023 ['Estimated Federal Expenditure 2023']*. [online] Available at: https://belanjawan.mof.gov.my/pdf/belanjawan2023/perbelanjaan/Anggaran-Perbelanjaan-Persekutuan-2023.pdf

4 CEIC. *Saudi Arabia Fuel Prices: Retail: Gasoline 95*. [online] Available at: https://www.ceicdata.com/en/saudi-arabia/fuel-prices/fuel-prices-retail-gasoline-95. As of January 2024, RON 95 costs about 2.33 SAR per litre in Saudi Arabia (or about RM2.90) while it is RM2.05 per litre in Malaysia.

5 Jabatan Audit Negara (2023). *Bahagian II: Analisis Kewangan Kerajaan Persekutuan ['Part II: Analysis of the Federal Government's Finances]*. [online] Available at: https://lkan.audit.gov.my/laporan/manage/1784. As the Ministry of Finance's budget-related expenditure analysis does not provide a breakdown of federal spending on fuel subsidies, the percentage in the text comes from the Auditor's General Report instead, which states that the government spent RM23.1 billion on petrol (RON 95), RM18.7 billion on diesel and RM3.4 billion on LPG subsidies in 2022.

6 Ministry of Finance, Malaysia (2023). *Anggaran Perbelanjaan Persekutuan 2023 ['Estimated Federal Expenditure 2023']*. [online] Available at: https://belanjawan.mof.gov.my/pdf/belanjawan2023/perbelanjaan/Anggaran-Perbelanjaan-Persekutuan-2023.pdf

7 In Prime Minister and Finance Minister Anwar's speech before the Dewan Rakyat at the tabling of Budget 2024 on October 13, 2023, he pointed to the huge discrepancy between the 40% increase in the sale of subsidised diesel since 2019 and the meagre 3% rise in the number of diesel-powered vehicles over the same period as being highly suggestive of smuggling activity. From March to August 2023 alone, the Ministry of Domestic Trade and Cost of Living recorded 459 cases of diesel smuggling, totalling over 4 million litres of diesel valued at RM9 million. See https://www.malaymail.com/news/malaysia/2023/08/24/domestic-trade-and-cost-of-living-ministry-extends-anti-diesel-smuggling-operation-until-december-31/87004

8 Ahmat, N. et. al. (2012). Perubahan Harga Petrol dan Risiko Keselamatan Jalan Raya ('Petrol Price Changes and Risks to Road Safety'). *Prosiding Perkem VII* [online], 2, pp. 1435-1444. Available at: https://www.ukm.my/fep/perkem/pdf/perkemVII/PKEM2012_5C2.pdf

9 Many have talked about targeted subsidies at the pump. First, such talk assumes that only the "B40" would need help. Second, whoever thought of targeted subsidies has

underestimated the ingenuity of Malaysians. Whatever system put in place would be gamed within months if not weeks. Such a programme heavily hinges on the use of extensive data technology to police who would receive fuel subsidies.

Some other economists are talking about cash transfers. Cash transfers are easy to start but very hard to taper off. Cash transfers without a timeframe to sunset will add strains on the fiscal condition.

10 Carsome (2023). *Are Electric Motorcycles Here to Stay? Here's All You Need to Know about the Top E-bikes in Malaysia.* [online] Available at: https://www.carsome.my/news/item/electric-bikes-malaysia

11 Ministry of Finance, Malaysia (2023). *Appendix II: Tax Measures Budget 2024.* [online] Available at: https://belanjawan.mof.gov.my/pdf/belanjawan2024/ucapan/tax-measure.pdf

12 Carput (c. 2023) *How Much Does EV Charger Installation Cost in Malaysia?* [online] Available at: https://carput.my/how-much-does-ev-charger-installation-cost-in-malaysia/

13 The "Mobilising Investments for Clean Energy in Malaysia" report by Khazanah and the World Economic Forum, which I launched on September 12, 2023, cites a case study in India in which the lowering of fuel subsidies was accompanied by a gradual increase of subsidies for renewables. More impressively, poor rural families were given a solar battery pack, five LED lights, and a DC power plug among others. Malaysia's per capita income is about four times that of India; if India can do it, Malaysia certainly can, provided there is political will.

In addition, the report recommends that Malaysia consider tapping into multilateral development banks (MDBs), such as the World Bank and Asian Development Bank, for climate financing and expertise. MDBs have built up extensive global knowledge and experiences concerning a wide range of issues, especially the green transition, which Malaysia can utilise. Conventional financial institutions would feel more reassured by risk sharing through concepts like "blended financing", which would include the expertise and participation of MDBs.

For more information, see https://www3.weforum.org/docs/WEF_Mobilizing_Investments_for_Clean_Energy_ in_Malaysia_2023.pdf and https://theedgemalaysia.com/node/682896

Chapter 14

1 This would only be the case if GST were implemented well, which is a big 'if'. In April 2015, when GST first came into effect, I visited shops in Kluang, Johor, which complained of hostile inspections and harassment by Customs enforcement officers with an intention to find fault.

2 Yong, P.K. (2022). *Harmonising Malaysia's Sales and Services Taxes – The Better Alternative to Re-introducing the GST.* MIER Industry Perspective Series, Vol. 1. Kuala Lumpur: Malaysian Institute of Economic Research. Available at: https://www.mier.org.my/post/webinar-on-harmonising-sales-and-services-taxes-the-better-alternative-to-reintroducing-gst

3 Lembaga Hasil Dalam Negeri Malaysia (2023). *Tax Rate*. [online] Available at: https://www.hasil.gov.my/en/individual/individual-life-cycle/how-to-declare-income/tax-rate/

Chapter 15

1 Ministry of Investment, Trade and Industry, Malaysia (2023). *iESG*. [online] Available at: https://www.miti.gov.my/index.php/pages/view/9849

2 According to Prime Minister Anwar in his speech at the Global Halal Summit in September 2023, Malaysia's high standards of halal certification have received praise from both global leaders and Muslim consumers around the world. Being shaped by 'maqasid syariah' (higher purpose), the halal sector goes beyond food and must be linked to a robust industrial development programme. For more information, see https://liewchintong.com/2023/09/16/%f0%9d%97%aa%f0%9d%97%b5%f0%9d%97%ae%f0%9d%98%81-%f0%9d%97%9c-%f0%9d%98%82%f0%9d%97%bb%f0%9d%97%b1%f0%9d%97%b2%f0%9d%97%bf%f0%9d%98%80%f0%9d%98%81%f0%9d%97%ae%f0%9d%97%bb%f0%9d%97%b1-%f0%9d%97%ae/

Chapter 16

1 "Controlling stake" here, as the Putrajaya Committee on GLC High Performance defines it, is the government's ability to appoint board members and senior management as well as to make major decisions, including contract awards, strategy, restructuring and financing, acquisitions and/or divestments, whether directly or otherwise.

2 Government of Malaysia (n.d.). *FAQs – Putrajaya Committee on GLC High Performance*. Available at: https://pcg.gov.my/faqs/

3 *The Star* (2023). "GLCs/GLICs role in making Malaysia a developed nation". *The Star*, 13 March. Available at: https://www.thestar.com.my/news/nation/2022/03/13/glcglics-role-in-making-malaysia-a-developed-nation

4 For ease of reference, the rest of this chapter uses the catch-all term "GLCs" to refer to "GLCs and/or GLICs", unless an explicit reference to the latter is needed.

5 Elliott, L. (2020). "Spend what you can to fight Covid-19, IMF tells member states". *The Guardian*, 15 April. Available at: https://www.theguardian.com/business/2020/apr/15/spend-what-you-can-to-fight-covid-19-imf-tells-member-states

6 Ministry of Health Malaysia (2020). *Human Resources for Health Country Profile 2015-2018 Malaysia*. [online] Available at: https://www.moh.gov.my/moh/resources/Penerbitan/HRH/Human_Resources_For_Health_Country_Profile_2015-2018.pdf

7 Yap, L. K. (2023). "Improving timber certification on ESG". *The Star*, 6 March. Available at: https://www.thestar.com.my/business/business-news/2023/03/06/improving-timber-certification-on-esg

Part VI

1 Department of Statistics Malaysia (2022). *Key Findings of Population and Housing Census of Malaysia 2020: Urban and Rural*. [online] Available at: https://v1.dosm.gov.my/v1/index.php?r=column/ctheme&menu_id=L0pheU43NWJwRWVSZklWdzQ4TlhUUT09&bul_id=ZFRzTG9ubTkveFR4YUY2OXdNNk1GZz09

2 Rasiah R., Salih. K., and Cheong, K. C. (2022). *Malaysia's Leap into the Future: The Building Blocks Towards Balanced Development*. Singapore: Springer, p. 81.

Chapter 17

1 Wellington Webb, the former mayor of the American city of Denver, is said to have first uttered this timeless quote at a mayoral summit in April 2000. See https://web.archive.org/web/20131102060013/http://usmayors.org/uscm/us_mayor_newspaper/documents/04_17_00/lyon_front_pg.htm

2 Interestingly, calls for the urban rejuvenation of Kuala Lumpur are not new. As early as 1966, an article in The Straits Times of Singapore highlighted the city's growing pains and the need to redevelop the inner city where people worked and played: "There are two Kuala Lumpurs. There is the Kuala Lumpur *represented by Parliament House and the National Monument, the Merdeka Stadium and Stadium Negara, the National Museum and the attractive complex of Moorish buildings on the river bank, recently enhanced by the magnificent National Mosque. This Kuala Lumpur is proudly metropolitan and can stand with dignity among the cities of the world. Then there is the other side of Kuala Lumpur where most people work and shop, a Kuala Lumpur harking back to frontier days, grubby with age, wasteful in its use of valuable land, as constricting and unsightly as a suit of clothes long outgrown.*" See https://eresources.nlb.gov.sg/newspapers/digitised/article/straitstimes19660621-1.2.43.2

Chapter 18

1 Department of Statistics Malaysia (2023). *Household Expenditure Survey Report 2022 (Malaysia & States)*. [online] Available at: https://www.dosm.gov.my/portal-main/release-content/household-expenditure-survey-report--malaysia--states-. Note that 'housing' here refers to rent or maintenance fees, water, electricity, gas and other fuels.

2 Jane Jacobs' *The Death and Life of Great American Cities* was describing exactly the demise of cities due to the combined effect of automobiles and "suburbanisation" that happened over the following decades in Malaysia.

3 Urban sprawl further eats up resources through the laying of water pipes, electricity grid cables, telecommunication infrastructure, roads and so on.

4 Bank Negara Malaysia (2023). *Banking System: Loan/Financing Applied by Purpose*. [online] Available at: https://www.bnm.gov.my/documents/20124/12049798/1.10.xlsx. Note that car loan here refers to the "purchase of passenger cars" while housing loan refers to the "purchase of residential property" through loan/financing.

5 Bank Negara Malaysia (2021). *Spotlight: Housing (Un)affordability*, [online]. Available at: https://www.bnm.gov.my/documents/20124/6459002/fsr21h2_en_housing.pdf

6 Ismail, S. et al. (2015). "The Malaysian Housing Market", in Ismail, S. et al. *Making Housing Affordable*. Kuala Lumpur: Khazanah Research Institute, pp. 5-10.

7 In 2019, I had an interesting chat with a tycoon. To my utter surprise, he, of all people, suggested to me that the government should start thinking about providing free housing for the needy. I probed him further, and it turns out that his point is this – all governments will have to think ahead to prevent economic revolts of the type that have happened on the streets of Santiago, Chile; in other South American cities; and in Hong Kong.

He reasoned that the economic system must either pay workers more or it must reduce the costs of housing and transport. To him, it is better for the government to pay for housing through taxes, than for businesses to try to raise salaries fast enough to contain discontentment and despair. Of course, at some point, the tycoon should pay a bit more tax, which he acknowledges, to keep the economy away from systemic failure.

This is especially the case now that the era of competitive tax cuts is over. Even low-tax economies like Hong Kong and Singapore, which benefit from not having to shoulder the cost of sustaining hinterlands, will refrain from tax cuts even if they have yet to contemplate a tax hike, due to an ageing population.

8 *The Economist* (2020). "Home ownership is the West's biggest economic-policy mistake". *The Economist*, 16 January. Available at: https://www.economist.com/weeklyedition/2020-01-18

9 Tan, R. (2023). "Offices galore, enough to fill 10 'Merdeka 118' towers". *Free Malaysia Today*, 22 May. Available at: https://www.freemalaysiatoday.com/category/nation/2023/05/22/office-galore-enough-to-fill-10-merdeka-118-towers/

10 For example, old buildings in inner cities can be re-populated with minor adjustments, giving our buildings a new lease of life. I am a supporter of heritage conservation, but through re-purposing usage, not turning all heritage buildings into museums, cafés and hotels. In any case, the rejuvenation of inner cities and the redevelopment of public spaces cannot happen without the involvement of architects, as I pointed out in my speech at the Malaysian Institute of Architects Awards Dinner in June 2019. See https://liewchintong.com/2019/06/30/changing-thinking-habits-to-make-our-cities-resilient/

11 Rajasurian, V. (2022). "The impact of car parks on residential property prices". *Free Malaysia Today*, 12 April. Available at: https://www.freemalaysiatoday.com/category/leisure/property/2022/04/12/impact-of-car-parks-on-residential-property-prices/

Chapter 19

1 Our World in Data (2017). *Registered vehicles per 1,000 people, 2017*. [online] Available at: https://ourworldindata.org/grapher/registered-vehicles-per-1000-people?tab=table. Note that the most recent data available for this international comparison is from 2016-17.

2 ASEAN Secretariat (2022). *ASEAN Key Figures 2022.* [online] Available at: https://asean. org/wp-content/uploads/2022/12/AKF_2022_423.pdf. This figure includes inactive vehicles. While the actual number of active vehicles on the road is likely to be lower, the fact remains that private vehicle ownership in Malaysia is unusually high given the level of income.

3 Ibid.

4 Nielsen (2014). *Rising Middle Class Will Drive Global Automotive Demand in the Coming Two Years.* [online] Available at: https://www.nielsen.com/news-center/2014/rising-middle-class-will-drive-global-automotive-demand/

5 Semana (2010). "Una ciudad avanzada no es en la que los pobres pueden moverse en carro, sino una en la que incluso los ricos utilizan el transporte público." *Semana*, 13 December. Available at: https://www.semana.com/nacion/articulo/una-ciudad-avanzada-no-pobres-pueden-moverse-carro-sino-incluso-ricos-utilizan-transporte-publico/125258-3/

6 Employees' Provident Fund and Universiti Malaya's Social Wellbeing Research Centre (2023). *Belanjawanku: Expenditure Guide for Malaysian Individuals & Families* [online]. Available at: https://web.archive.org/web/20230809202649/https://www.kwsp.gov.my/documents/20126/142907/Belanjawanku+2022-2023+-+EN.pdf/670c9c4e-40a6-f4c6-ada2-f74fd09c58e6?t=1686619560631. According to their estimates, a single public transport user in the Klang Valley has an average monthly expenditure of RM1,930 compared to a car owner whose average monthly spending is estimated to be RM2,600.

7 Congestion has harmed quality of life for Malaysians in a big way while causing huge economic and productivity losses. According to the World Bank's Malaysia Economic Monitor in 2015, congestion imposed a high economic and personal toll. It is estimated that commuters in Greater Kuala Lumpur (GKL) travel 29km/h slower on average during morning peak hours compared to off-peak hours due to congestion, translating into income losses of RM10.8-19.6 billion annually for the city, or 1.0-1.8% of Malaysia's GDP from delay costs alone. Including the costs of fuel wasted and the economic cost of CO2 and other emissions, the total cost of congestion in GKL is estimated conservatively at 1.1–2.2% of GDP in 2014. See https://documents.worldbank.org/curated/en/2015/06/24646735/malaysia-economic-monitor-transforming-urban-transport

8 Ministry of Transport, Malaysia (2023). *Road Accidents and Fatalities in Malaysia.* [online] Available at: https://www.mot.gov.my/en/land/safety/road-accident-and-facilities; and Ministry of Transport, Malaysia (2023). *Malaysia Road Fatalities Index.* [online] Available at: https://www.mot.gov.my/en/land/safety/malaysia-road-fatalities-index

9 Atlas Magazine (2021). Car accidents injuries: death rate per country. [online] Available at: https://www.atlas-mag.net/en/article/road-safety-in-2017

10 Bank Negara Malaysia (2023). *Financial Stability Review First Half 2023.* [online] Available at: https://www.bnm.gov.my/documents/20124/11980735/fsr23h1_en_book.pdf

Chapter 20

1 Ravindran, S. (2022). "Mayor: Public transport ridership rising in KL". The Star, [online] 16 December. Available at: https://www.thestar.com.my/metro/metro-news/2022/12/16/mayor-public-transport-ridership-rising-in-kl

2 Prasarana Malaysia (2023). *My50 Unlimited Travel Pass*. [online] Available at: https://myrapid.com.my/our-products/my50/

3 *Free Malaysia Today* (2022). "MP calls for more details on govt's approval of 3 highways". *Free Malaysia Today*, 30 May. Available at: https://www.freemalaysiatoday.com/category/nation/2022/05/30/mp-calls-for-more-details-on-govts-approval-of-3-highways/

4 *New Straits Times* (2023). "Selangor govt cancels PJD Link elevated highway project". *New Straits Times*, 31 July. Available at: https://www.nst.com.my/news/nation/2023/07/936954/selangor-govt-cancels-pjd-link-elevated-highway-project

5 Allianz (2023). *Allianz Global Wealth Report 2023: The next chapter*. [online] Available at: https://www.allianz.com/content/dam/onemarketing/azcom/Allianz_com/economic-research/publications/allianz-global-wealth-report/2023/2023-09-26-GlobalWealthReport.pdf

6 *Malay Mail* (2023). "Anthony Loke says bus services in Klang Valley to be integrated". *Malay Mail*, 12 September. Available at: https://www.malaymail.com/news/malaysia/2023/09/12/anthony-loke-says-bus-services-in-klang-valley-to-be-integrated/90421

7 I first did the math almost a decade ago in a statement I issued in 2014: *"A very good European bus costs around RM600,000. The annual operating cost of a bus is generally not more than RM200,000, staff and fuel costs included. So, RM 2 million will buy you a bus with 7 years of operating costs. On the back of the envelope, RM 2 billion will give you a thousand units of buses"* (see https://dapmalaysia.org/en/38526/how-to-delay-gst-implementation-government-pays-people-to-take-buses/)

To update the calculations for today (in line with inflation and prioritising electric buses over diesel buses), an electric bus would cost around RM2 million. A UNESCAP study in India estimated the average operational cost of an electric bus to be 61 rupees (or about RM3.40) per km. Assuming a city bus travels 300km per day every day, this would imply an annual operational cost of RM370,000 per bus. An electric bus has a lifespan of up to 15 years, and the battery can last about 7 years without replacement. So RM4.59 million will buy you an electric bus lasting 7 years. Adding 3,276 fully electric buses (at current prices) to bring the total fleet size to 4,000 for efficient operations will cost about RM15 billion (for 7 years), a fraction of the annual fuel subsidy bill. For the sources of the assumptions, see https://www.thestar.com.my/aseanplus/aseanplus-news/2023/04/17/is-less-pollution-worth-the-costs, https://www.unescap.org/sites/default/files/10.%20Financing%20Election%20Buses_Resource%20Person.pdf and https://blogs.worldbank.org/transport/are-hybrid-and-electric-buses-viable-just-yet

8 Prasarana Malaysia (2023). *Prasarana's Ridership.* [online] Available at: https://myrapid.com.my/bus-train/ridership/

Chapter 21

1 United Nations Economic and Social Commission for Asia and the Pacific (1986). *Country Monograph Series No. 13: Population of Malaysia.* New York: United Nations. Available at: https://repository.unescap.org/bitstream/handle/20.500.12870/4375/ESCAP-1986-RP-Population-Malaysia.pdf?sequence=1&isAllowed=y

2 Lai, C. K. (2007). *Building Merdeka: Independence Architecture in Kuala Lumpur 1957-1966* Kuala Lumpur: Petronas.

Chapter 22

1 *BERNAMA* (2022). "Losses due to floods estimated at up to RM6.5 billion". *BERNAMA*, 17 January. Available at: https://www.bernama.com/en/general/news_disaster.php?id=2044085

2 Ng, E. (2023). "Malaysia records $187.8m in losses to floods in 2022; Terengganu, Kelantan worst hit". *The Straits Times*, 23 February. Available at: https://www.straitstimes.com/asia/se-asia/malaysia-records-187m-losses-to-floods-in-2022-terengganu-kelantan-worst-hit

3 Channel News Asia (2023). "Johor records highest rainfall in four days since 1991 as Malaysia flood situation worsens". *Channel News Asia*, 5 March. Available at: https://www.channelnewsasia.com/asia/malaysia-flood-johor-highest-rainfall-1991-evacuate-deaths-3326076

Chapter 23

1 The Federal Government's revenue projection is taken from Budget 2023 while the total revenue figure for the state governments comes from the various state government budget documents for the year 2023. Here is the breakdown of revenue by state: Sarawak (RM11bn), Sabah (RM5.3bn), Selangor (RM2bn), Terengganu (RM1.8bn), Johor (RM1.7bn), Perak (RM1.2bn), Pahang (RM1.1bn), Kelantan (RM0.98bn), Kedah (RM0.74bn), Penang (RM0.52bn), Malacca (RM0.46bn), Negeri Sembilan (RM0.45bn) and Perlis (RM0.11bn).

2 Even though the Malaysian Islamic Party (PAS) has been running Kelantan since 1990 and several states have been in the hands of the then opposition Pakatan Rakyat/Harapan since 2008, the UMNO of yesteryear could still exert control through having the Prime Minister dictate to UMNO chief ministers his wishes, and through using federal-appointed civil servants to run affairs in opposition-held states.

3 Mahmood, J. (2021) *12th Malaysia Plan & National Budget.* [presentation] Available at: https://www.globalfuturecities.org/sites/default/files/2022-08/211214%20Ministry%20of%20Finance%20Presentation.pdf

4 Leung G.H. et al (2022). *Enabling Decentralisation and Improving Federal State-Relations in the Federation of Malaysia.* Penang: Penang Institute. Available at: https://penanginstitute.org/wp-content/uploads/2022/06/web_version_final.pdf

5 Ministry of Finance, Malaysia (2023). *Budget 2024, Section 3: Federal Government Expenditure.* [online] Available at: https://belanjawan.mof.gov.my/pdf/belanjawan2024/revenue/section3.pdf

6 Ragu, D. (2022). "Johor gets more federal funds than Selangor, says economist". *Free Malaysia Today*, 20 June. Available at: https://www.freemalaysiatoday.com/category/nation/2022/06/20/johor-gets-more-federal-funds-than-selangor-says-economist/

Chapter 24

1 Dharma Negara, S. and Hutchinson, F. E. (2021). "The Impact of Indonesia's Decentralization Reforms Two Decades On". [online] *Journal of Southeast Asian Economies*, 38(3), pp. 289-95. Available at: https://www.jstor.org/stable/27096079

2 Majlis Bandaraya Petaling Jaya (2021). *Ucapan Bajet* 2022 ['Budget 2022 Speech'] [online]. Available at: https://www.mbpj.gov.my/sites/default/files/ucapan_bajet_2022_-_final.pdf; Buletin Mutiara (2022). *Lima fokus utama Bajet 2023 MBPP sejajar SDG, Visi Penang2030* ('Five Focus Areas of MBPP's Budget 2023 Aligned with SDGs and Penang2030 Vision']. [online]. Available at: https://www.buletinmutiara.com/lima-fokus-utama-bajet-2023-mbpp-sejajar-sdg-visi-penang2030/; *The Star* (2022). "Perlis table RM293.36mil budget for 2023". *The Star*, 20 December. Available at: https://www.thestar.com.my/news/nation/2022/12/20/perlis-table-rm29336mil-budget-for-2023; and Jabatan Kewangan dan Perbendaharaan Negeri Melaka (2023). *Bajet 2023 Negeri Melaka* ['Malacca State's 2023 Budget']. [online] Available at: https://jkpnm.melaka.gov.my/xs/dl.php?filename=77c8f490dc1772f5f3016287a23250d0.pdf

Chapter 25

1 Two of which are the Ministry of Defence and MITI (the third being the Ministry of Works), the very two ministries that I have served in. I like to joke that I still have not set foot in Putrajaya.

2 Wahab, F. (2023). "DBKL announces RM2.6bil budget for 2023". *The Star*, 4 January. Available at: https://www.thestar.com.my/metro/metro-news/2023/01/04/dbkl-announces-rm26bil-budget-for-2023; Office of the Premier of Sarawak (2022). *Ucapan Belanjawan Tahun 2023* ('2023 Budget Speech']. [online] Available at: https://premier.sarawak.gov.my/web/attachment/show/?docid=bTg2VXJCbVNNbHBnVGNXempTZ01NUT09Ojo4qUvH5zCtUUdUUDf_Zp4q; Selangor State Government (2022). *Anggaran Belanjawan Selangor 2023* ('Selangor 2023 Budget Estimates'). [online] Available at: https://www.selangor.gov.my/index.php/dl/554756755a3356746457316862693942626d646e59584a68626c39435a577868626d7068643246755a323979587a49774d6a4d756347526d

Chapter 26

1 Md Tah, I. et al. (2022). Keperluan Mewujudkan Semula Akta Perkhidmatan Parlimen di Malaysia ('The Need to Re-enact the Parliamentary Service Act in Malaysia'). *Journal of the Malaysian Parliament*, 2, pp. 97-127. https://doi.org/10.54313/journalmp.v2i.60

Chapter 27

1 Soo, W. J. (2023). "Parliamentary Special Select Committees can now discuss matters without referring to ministers, says Dewan Rakyat Speaker". *Malay Mail*, 6 June. Available at: https://www.malaymail.com/news/malaysia/2023/06/06/parliamentary-special-select-committees-can-now-discuss-matters-without-referring-to-ministers-says-dewan-rakyat-speaker/72878

2 Parliament of Malaysia (2023). *Penyata Jawatankuasa Peraturan-Peraturan Mesyuarat Majlis Mesyuarat Dewan Rakyat (DR9/2023)* https://www.parlimen.gov.my/ipms/eps/2023-10-10/DR.9.2023%20-%20DR9.2023.pdf

3 For the second session of the 15th Parliament in 2023, the committee stage of the budget began on November 6 and ended on November 27, a total of 12 sitting days to clear the ministerial budget for 26 ministries. Each ministry usually gets about 3-4 hours of scrutiny, except for larger ministries, which might get an entire day.

Imagine if we had around 7-8 actual policy committees consisting of 10-15 MPs from both sides, with each committee tasked to look into about 3 or 4 ministries, and each ministry received 4-5 committee days of scrutiny. The committees could call up civil servants to get a detailed understanding of how ministerial budgets are devised and some of those who sit on the committees will eventually develop expertise in their particular area of focus.

4 I have previously referred to this loss of parliamentary autonomy as the 'cannibalisation' of the Parliament's administration. To understand the context, we have to first go back three decades. As I have mentioned, the Parliamentary Services Act 1963 was repealed in November 1992, which was during the speakership of Tun Mohamed Zahir Ismail. The abolition of the Act was said to have been precipitated by internal issues and disputes between the speaker and the parliamentary staff.

The downward spiral brought about by the repeal came to a crescendo in 2005, during Nazri Aziz's tenure as the Minister of Parliamentary Affairs. Nazri had almost been dropped from Tun Abdullah Badawi's Cabinet after the General Election a year earlier. His name was only "pencilled" into the list at the last minute before Abdullah's audience with the King at the appeal by the then Deputy Prime Minister Dato' Sri Najib Razak.

Nazri had no portfolio in the first week, and the parliamentary affairs role was an afterthought. He had no *ketua setiausaha* (chief secretary of a ministry) or other bureaucrats to serve him, and was even ignored by the then secretary of the Dewan Rakyat. To exert his presence and impose his will on Parliament, he managed to persuade the Cabinet to take away the powers of the secretaries of the Dewan Rakyat and Dewan Negara and restrict them to the affairs of the Chambers only.

While Nazri is a jovial and friendly character whose presence MPs from both sides of the aisles enjoy a conversation with, and was able to promote some international causes via Parliament, he did very little to reform the actual workings of Parliament.

See https://doi.org/10.54313/journalmp.v2i.60 and https://liewchintong.com/2021/09/03/there-is-no-better-time-than-now-for-parliamentary-reform/

Chapter 28

1 *Malay Mail* (2017). "A look at some high-profile RCIs in Malaysia". *Malay Mail*, 1 July. Available at: https://www.malaymail.com/news/malaysia/2017/07/01/a-look-at-some-high-profile-rcis-in-malaysia/1411439

2 One of the strategic thrusts of the Tun Dzaiddin report is the tabling of an Independent Police Complaints and Misconduct Commission (IPCMC) bill, which as an Act of Parliament would provide a mechanism for holding police officers accountable for all manner of misconduct, from corruption to abuse of power and wrongful deaths during custody. A Parliamentary Special Select Committee chaired by Ramkarpal Singh was originally scheduled to have it tabled in late 2019. It was due for its first reading in Parliament in August 2020, but it was later retracted and modified by the PN government to become the IPCC bill, which had far fewer powers and required the commission to report to the Home Minister rather than the Law Minister. The IPCC bill passed in July 2022, and at the time of writing, the government is in the process of selecting the members of the newly minted commission.

3 Ministry of Defence, Malaysia (2020). *Defence White Paper*. [online] Available at: https://www.mod.gov.my/images/mindef/article/kpp/DWP-3rd-Edition-02112020.pdf

4 In developed countries, such open discourse about defence plans is common. Australia, for example, has both an Integrated Investment Program and Defence Industrial Capability Plan. See https://www.defence.gov.au/about/strategic-planning/defence-white-paper and https://www.defence.gov.au/business-industry/industry-capability-programs/defence-industrial-capability-plan

Chapter 29

1 Ali, K. (2019). *Taklimat Berkaitan Aspek Perkhidmatan / Perjawatan Kepada Special Select Committee Berkaitan Pelaksanaan IPCMC* [*'Briefing on PDRM's Service / Staffing Aspects to the Special Select Committee on the Implementation of IPCMC'*]. [presentation] Available at: https://www.parlimen.gov.my/images/webuser/IPCMC/Memorandum/No.%2010%20-%20Kertas%20Taklimat%20oleh%20Jabatan%20Pengurusan%20PDRM%20oleh%20DCP%20Kasuahdi%20bin%20Haji%20Ali%20-%20Timb.%20Pengarah%20Pengurusan.pdf

2 *Harian Metro* (2017). "Tambah IO polis percepat kes di mahkamah ['Increase number of police investigative officers to speed up court cases']. *Harian Metro*, 14 January. Available at: https://www.hmetro.com.my/mutakhir/2017/01/197140/tambah-io-polis-percepat-kes-di-mahkamah

3 Kong, W. (2013). "4,000 new police officers needed every year". *The Borneo Post*, 2 August. Available at: www.theborneopost.com/2013/08/02/4000-new-police-officers-needed-every-year/

4 Adam, A. (2021). "Citing prison overcrowding, group urges reform to rehabilitate minor drug users". *Malay Mail*, 13 February. Available at: https://www.malaymail.com/news/malaysia/2021/02/13/citing-prison-overcrowding-group-urges-reform-to-rehabilitate-minor-drug-us/1949398

Chapter 30

1 National University of Singapore (n.d.). *Luconia Breakers (South Luconia Shoals)*. [online] Available at: https://cil.nus.edu.sg/wp-content/uploads/2017/08/South-Luconia-Shoals-Luconia-Breakers-Final.pdf

Chapter 31

1 Section 6 of the National Security Council Act of 2016 (Act 776) stipulates that its members consist of the following officeholders: the Prime Minister as Chairman; the Deputy Prime Minister as Deputy Chairman; the Minister charged with the responsibility for Defence; the Minister charged with the responsibility for Home Affairs; the Minister charged with the responsibility for Communications and Multimedia; the Chief Secretary to the Government; the Chief of Defence Forces; and the Inspector-General of Police. Most observers on security matters around the world would immediately notice the absence of a Foreign Minister in the structure.

Chapter 32

1 In 1948, German-born American political scientist Hans Morgenthau identified eight elements of national power, namely: (i) geography, (ii) natural resources, (iii) industrial capacity, (iv) military preparedness, (v) population, (vi) national character, (vii) national morale, and (viii) the quality of diplomacy. See Morgenthau, H. J. (1948). *Politics Among Nations*. New York: Alfred A. Knopf, pp. 80-108.

2 MAF has about 113,000 active personnel while the Royal Malaysia Police has over 130,000 police officers and civil servants. See International Institute for Strategic Studies (2023). *The Military Balance 2023*. London: Taylor & Francis, p. 270. and Royal Malaysia Police (n.d.). *Mengenai Polis Diraja Malaysia ('About Royal Malaysia Police')*. [online] Available at: https://www.rmp.gov.my/infor-korporate/polis-diraja-malaysia

3 Sunderland, R. (1964). *Army Operations in Malaya, 1947-1960 (U)*. Santa Monica: The RAND Corporation. [online] Available at: https://apps.dtic.mil/sti/tr/pdf/AD0354142.pdf

Index